SANTO DOMINGO
and
BEYOND

SANTO DOMINGO
and
BEYOND

Documents and Commentaries
from the Fourth General Conference
of Latin American Bishops

Edited by
Alfred T. Hennelly, S.J.

ORBIS BOOKS

Maryknoll, New York 10545

The Catholic Foreign Mission Society of America (Maryknoll) recruits and trains people for overseas missionary service. Through Orbis Books, Maryknoll aims to foster the international dialogue that is essential to mission. The books published, however, reflect the opinions of their authors and are not meant to represent the official position of the society.

Copyright © 1993 by Orbis Books

Text of the Final Document of the Fourth General Conference of Latin American Bishops © 1993 by CELAM. English translation of the Final Document © 1993 by the United States Catholic Conference, Inc., Washington, D.C. All rights reserved. Translation of the "Opening Address of the Holy Father" copyright © 1993 by Catholic News Service (CNS), Washington, D.C., used with permission.

Published by Orbis Books, Maryknoll, NY 10545

Library of Congress Cataloging-in-Publication Data

Conferencia General del Episcopado Latinoamericano (4th : 1993 : Santo
  Domingo, Dominican Republic)
    Santo Domingo and beyond : documents and commentaries from the
  Fourth General Conference of Latin American Bishops / edited by
  Alfred T. Hennelly.
      p.   cm.
    Includes bibliographical references and index.
    ISBN 0-88344-920-X (pbk.)
    1. Catholic Church — Latin America — Congresses.   2. Catholic
  Church — Caribbean Area — Congresses.   3. Church and social problems —
  Latin America — Congresses.   4. Church and social problems —
  Caribbean Area — Congresses.   5. Church and social problems —
  Catholic Church — Congresses.   6. America — Discovery and
  exploration — Religious aspects — Catholic Church — Congresses.
  7. Latin America — Church history — Congresses.   I. Hennelly, Alfred
  T.   II.   Title.
  BX1425.A1C64   1993
  282'.8 — dc20
                                              93-36862
                                                 CIP

Contents

PART III
BEYOND SANTO DOMINGO: COMMENTARIES AND REFLECTIONS

Preface

As an observer of the Santo Domingo conference of Latin American bishops in October, 1992, I have voiced my own experience and reflections on that meeting in the second article of this volume. Quite a few months have passed since that was written, and in this preface I wish to present a more expansive perspective or panorama, ranging further than the final document or even the articles in this book.

Part of such a perspective has been provided by the Jesuit theologian, Karl Rahner, in what is perhaps the most widely-cited essay in the entire corpus of his reflections, "Towards a Fundamental Theological Interpretation of Vatican II."[1] The most famous thesis in this essay — repeated so frequently as to become almost a theological cliché over the past decade — is Rahner's assertion that Vatican II constituted the Roman Catholic church's first official "self-actualization" precisely as a *world church*.[2] He asserts further that under "the appearance of an obvious and gradual development something like a qualitative leap took place here, even though this world church's new essence is marked to a considerable extent not only potentially but actually by characteristics of the old Western world."[3] Rahner's vision, moreover, was not confined to the inner life of the church, but emphasized that the church "as a totality becomes conscious of its *responsibility for the dawning history of humanity*."[4]

But what is even more important, in my opinion, is Rahner's theology of Christian history, which he somewhat audaciously divided into only *two* preeminent transformations: 1) the transition from the period of Jewish Christianity to what became the Christianity of Europe; and 2) in Vatican II, the transition from a European church and its satellites to what is now in the process of becoming a world church.[5]

I choose the word "becoming" here with its full meaning; the church is *not yet* a world church, as Rahner himself acknowledged. And here I wish to move beyond Rahner and state the obvious, that the "self-actualization" of the world church has thus far received its greatest impetus and leadership from the church of Latin America.[6] The evidence for this is contained in part in the reflections of the four "mini-councils" of the Latin American bishops at Rio de Janeiro, Brazil (1955), Medellín, Colombia (1968), Puebla, Mexico (1979), and recently at Santo Domingo, the Dominican Republic (1992), which also marked the quincentenary of the original "evangelization" of the Americas. But even more, Latin America has made a spectacular contribution to the creation of world *theology* through the articulation of a theology of liberation, whose reverberations have been felt throughout the world.[7]

The Santo Domingo conference marks the latest milestone and Latin America's most recent contribution toward the world church of the future. While it is an important event, however, this conference is only one more piece in a much vaster picture, one that we Christians understand in terms of the same fire of the Holy Spirit as on the day of Pentecost, and the same Reign of God that Jesus preached in the hills and valleys of Galilee. The Santo Domingo conference has contributed its own pieces to the great mosaic of the Reign, some segments lustrous and resplendent, others seemingly dull and uninspired, but still serviceable. It remains for the vast continent of Latin American and the Caribbean, as well as the entire world church, to ponder the Santo Domingo documents and, more importantly, to transform the theory into well planned and implemented practice, so as to advance the coming Reign of God. And the never-ending focus of that practice must always center on the legions of poor and oppressed women and men who struggle to survive throughout the globe.

At this point, I would like say a few words about the essays included in this volume. The first two articles were situated before the text of the Santo Domingo document, as a background for the reader and especially for those not familiar with this context. Thus, Edward L. Cleary, O.P., a professor of Latin American studies at Providence College, has provided a fine overall survey of the events and trends from the time of the last bishops' conference in Puebla (1979) up to the time of the recent meeting. My own contribution surveys the events and the documents that immediately preceded and continued throughout the conference, and offers my own reflections and evaluations, as an observer at the conference.

The essays that follow the final conference document itself have been solicited to reflect a broad spectrum of backgrounds and perspectives. Thus, Jon Sobrino, the well-known Jesuit theologian from El Salvador, has produced a brilliant theological study of the conference from the perspective of liberation theology. Following this, Guillermo Cook, an astute scholar and associate of the Latin American Mission, provides a very candid Protestant viewpoint, which reflects his broad experience both in Latin America and the United States. Virgilio Elizondo, rector of San Fernando Cathedral and founder of the Mexican American Cultural Center, both located in San Antonio, Texas, reflects on the documents in the light of his pastoral work among Hispanic Americans. María Pilar Aquino, who teaches theology in the University of San Diego, provides a penetrating and critical assessment from the viewpoint of Latin American women. Finally, Stephen P. Judd, a Maryknoll missioner with a doctorate in the sociology of religion, and over fifteen years of experience among the Aymara and Quechua peoples of the Andes, examines the document in light of the theology being created now by indigenous peoples. This is of great importance, given the theme of the Santo Domingo conference, which relates directly to the original evangelization of indigenous peoples in the Americas five hundred years ago.

I would like to express my gratitude to all the authors who so generously contributed their time and expertise to the creation of this volume. I also wish to thank Robert Ellsberg, Catherine Costello, and all those at Orbis Books who have contributed so much to this book. Thanks are due as well to the United States Catholic Conference, for their cooperation in this publication of the Santo Domingo documents. My gratitude is also due to my compañero and driver in Santo Domingo, Rev. Robert Pelton, C.S.C., of Notre Dame University, who provided me with many valuable insights, spiced with good humor. Finally, we both will always be in immense debt to José Rafael Pacheco and his wife Rafaela Pacheco of Santo Domingo for their marvelous hospitality and for welcoming us into their home and into their hearts.

Alfred T. Hennelly, S.J.
New York City

NOTES

1. *Theological Studies* 40 (December, 1979), 716-727. Another version of this essay may be found in "The Abiding Significance of the Second Vatican Council," in *Theological Investigations XX: Concern for the Church* (New York: Crossroad, 1981), 90-102.

2. Ibid., 717.

3. Ibid., 719. Rahner also notes perceptively "that at the Council a [world] Church appeared and became active that was no longer the Church of the West with its American spheres of influence and its export to Asia and Africa."

4. Ibid. Emphasis added.

5. Ibid., 721.

6. An excellent buttress to this statement may be found in the article by Archbishop Rembert Weakland, "How Medellín and Puebla Influenced North America," *Origins* 18 (April 13, 1989), 757-60. He notes with regard to the question of method: "Theologizing out of lived experience corresponds in a most profound way to the North American psyche and to our educational tradition. One could say without doubt that this way of proceeding, that was so evident in Medellín and at Puebla, corresponds in an incredible way to the makeup of the American people" (p. 758). And in his final paragraph he asserts that what "is important for North America now is to intensify its option for the poor in concrete ways. What is important for both Latin American and North America is not to lose heart in the renewal—the liberating renewal—that Vatican II brought about and of which we have all been the beneficiaries" (p. 760).

7. I have documented these achievements in Alfred T. Hennelly, S.J., ed., *Liberation Theology: A Documentary History* (Maryknoll, N.Y.: Orbis Books, 1990).

Abbreviations

AA   *Apostolicam Actuositatem,* Vatican Council II, *Decree on the Apostolate of the Laity*

AG   *Ad Gentes,* Vatican Council II, *Decree on the Missionary Activity of the Church*

CA   *Centesimus Annus,* John Paul II, encyclical letter *On the Hundredth Anniversary of Rerum Novarum* (1991)

CD   *Christus Dominus,* Vatican Council II, *Decree on the Bishops' Pastoral Office in the Church*

CELAM   Consejo Episcopal Latinoamericano—Latin American Bishops Conference

CIC   *Codex Iuris Canonici, Code of Canon Law* (Revised 1983)

CT   *Catechesi Tradendae,* John Paul II, apostolic exhortation, *On Catechesis in Our Time* (1979)

CL   *Christifideles Laici,* John Paul II, post-synodal apostolic exhortation *On the Vocation and the Mission of the Lay Faithful in the Church and in the World* (1988)

EN   *Evangelii Nuntiandi,* Paul VI, apostolic exhortation *On Evangelization in the Modern World* (1975)

FC   *Familiaris Consortio,* John Paul II, apostolic exhortation *On the Family* (1981)

GS   *Gaudium et Spes,* Vatican II, *Pastoral Constitution on the Church in the Modern World*

LE   *Laborem Exercens,* John Paul II, encyclical *On Human Work* (1981)

LG   *Lumen Gentium,* Vatican II, *Dogmatic Constitution on the Church*

MD   *Mulieris Dignitatem,* John Paul II apostolic letter *On the Dignity and Vocation of Women* (1988)

OA   John Paul II, *Opening Address,* to bishops in Santo Domingo, October 12, 1992.

OT   *Optatam Totius,* Vatican II, *Decree on Priestly Formation*

PC   *Perfectae Caritatis,* Vatican II, *Decree on the Appropriate Renewal of the Religious Life*

PDV   *Pastores Dabo Vobis,* John Paul II, post-synodal apostolic exhortation *I Will Give You Shepherds* (1992)

PP   *Populorum Progressio,* Paul VI, encyclical *On the Development of Peoples* (1967)

RM   *Redemptoris Missio,* John Paul II encyclical letter *On the Permanent Validity of the Church's Missionary Mandate* (1990)

SC   *Sacrosanctum Concilium,* Vatican II, *Constitution on the Sacred Liturgy*

SRS   *Sollicitudo Rei Socialis,* John Paul II encyclical letter *On Social Concern* (1987)

UR   *Unitatis Redintegratio,* Vatican II, *Decree on Ecumenism*

Part I

TOWARD SANTO DOMINGO:

PERILS AND PROMISE

The Journey to Santo Domingo

Edward L. Cleary, O.P.

The historic Second General Conference of the Latin American church in 1968 represented an unusual confluence of events (massive social changes) and talented actors (liberation theologians). The Latin American bishops and theologians meeting in Medellín, Colombia, used the modern plans for renewal, the documents of Vatican Council II, and fitted the main themes and objectives of the council to the Latin American situation. This effort was uncommon for several reasons. No other church had systematically applied the conclusions of Vatican II to their region. What is more, the Latin American bishops did not merely apply the teachings of the Council; they offered a bold new interpretation that represented a significant development in Catholic social teaching themselves. Out of Medellín there emerged a new Christian vocabulary: option for the poor, liberation, structural sin. This bold language was astounding to those who remembered the Latin Americans' relative silence during the council.

The Medellín Conference did not affect the world church directly. The documents of the conference did not initially have wide circulation outside Latin America and the United States, and even press coverage was minimal. Only through later meetings in Europe did the Latin American innovations gradually become known throughout the world. The Latin American influence became especially evident at what many commentators consider a defining moment in modern church history, the synod of bishops in Rome in 1971. The world of the poor made itself heard there and Latin America led the way through discussions of world development and also liberation. Central to the universal church in its twentieth century change from an other-worldly to this-worldly spirituality was this phrase of the synod, repeated in hundreds of languages: "Action on behalf of justice and participation in the transformation of the world fully appear to us as a constitutive dimension of the preaching of the Gospel, or, in other words, of the Church's mission for the redemption of the human race and its liberation from every oppressive situation" (*Justice in the World*, Introduction).

Because of the eventual impact of Medellín, considerable attention was focused on the Third General Conference of Latin American Bishops convened at Puebla, Mexico, in 1979. By then, given the growing theological prominence of the Latin American church and of its publicized conflicts with military governments in eight of the ten South American countries, more than thirty-two hundred journalists and observers flocked to the Puebla conference. The Latin American church was achieving heroic status in the world of daily journalism. It was becoming the "voice of the voiceless," defender of human rights in oppressive situations.

The Puebla Conference confirmed advances, affirmed for the hestitant no turning back, and made a strong step forward. However, enough ambiguities persisted that conservatives would find justification for cautionary interpretations which they increasingly thrust into debate. Four trends, then only partially observed, would become predominant in the period emphasized here, the fourteen years (1979–1992) leading up to the Fourth General Conference of Latin American Bishops at Santo Domingo. These are: democratization, dreadful turns in socioeconomic trends, religious vitality and competition, and the imprint of a strong and conservative papacy.

DEMOCRATIZATION

In 1979, military rule had a strong grip on the majority of Latin American countries, but even then the disposing causes for the military's retreat from the presidential palaces were at work. The military stepped aside first in Ecuador (1979), then Peru (1980), Bolivia and Honduras (1982), Argentina (1983), Brazil and Uruguay (1985), and finally Chile (1990), when General Augusto Pinochet vacated Casa La Moneda. The toll on the populace of guerrilla and state-induced terror was fearsome. Abductions, torture, disappearances, and death had helped to produce a deep sense of insecurity, generalized fear, confusion, and denial.[1] By and large, the church had stood firm as the single structured voice of opposition.

The gradual advance of democracy in Latin America in the 1980s matched to a considerable degree the process occurring in Spain, Portugal, and Central Europe, a process characterized by Samuel Huntington as a "second wave" of democracy. Primary in Huntington's analysis of the causes of democratization are the socioeconomic gains of the 1960s and 70s (including those under authoritarian governments).[2] But key also for him is religion, especially Catholicism, in this second wave of democratization in the modern world. The church, which had once been seen as antithetical to democracy,[3] was now credited with helping to establish democracy in Poland, the Iberian peninsula, the Philippines, and most of Latin America.

In the years following the Medellín conference the church throughout Latin America (with the exception of a lengthy period in Argentina) firmly opposed authoritarian regimes. As the single social institution with a measure of freedom in society, the Catholic church formed the only solid opposition to military dictatorships, denied legitimacy to the regimes, protected human rights, and fostered an ideology of freedom from captivity and of liberation from oppression.

At the level of the world church, Catholic leaders affirmed individual rights and the need of governments to serve the best interests of their people. The principles of Vatican II and the social encyclicals of Pope John XXIII and Paul VI helped advance the discussion of human rights and democracy. As an innovation of his leadership, John Paul II made trips to Latin American countries at crucial points in their histories to reinforce the local churches' commitment to freedom, which, as he often said in one form or other, is the condition and the basis for the human person's true dignity. Particularly striking were his words to General Pinochet and his fellow Chileans: "To the Gospel message, of course, belong all the problems of human rights; and, if democracy means human rights, it also belongs to the message of the church."[4]

The stands taken by the popes and the bishops would have been largely ineffectual appeals without grassroots support and without coordination between elite members and grassroots organizations. Bishops and other church leaders fostered protection and support, and gave some resources for opposition movements. The church also offered resources in terms of organizations (sports clubs, cultural groups) and buildings in which opposition leaders found protection necessary to discuss political options and to generate strategies for a democratic future. Young priests, sisters, and lay leaders encouraged and took part in nonviolent social movements serving the interests of the poor masses. The base Christian communities became the focal point of much of the reporting about opposition movements.

The church's support for democracy in Latin America was crucial in a number of countries. In a recent expression of the evolution in the church's position on democracy, Pope John Paul expressed an underlying evaluation: "The Church values the democratic system inasmuch as it ensures the participation of citizens in making political choices, guarantees to the governed the possibility both of electing and holding accountable those who govern them, and of replacing them through peaceful means when appropriate."[5] The Latin American church helped establish a basis for democracy by fostering dialogue and respect for the human person. Further, the social teaching of the church supported such central ideas to the working of democracy as participation in government and the rule of law.

The Latin American bishops have been realistic in their appraisal of the functioning of democracy, characterized at Santo Domingo as *más formal que real* (more form than reality).[6] Democracy was barely getting a start in most Latin American countries, while in two older democracies, Colombia and Venezuela, corruption and the bending and shaping of public resources and programs to suit the interests of a few were becoming increasingly scrutinized and challenged. By the time of the Santo Domingo meeting, reformist elements of the military were threatening the foundations of the thirty-year democracy of Venezuela.

The present era is another in the waves of "democracy" periodically occurring in Latin America. What offers greater hope than ever that democracy will last is not only the support and initial tutelage by the institutional

church, but more importantly the new social movements and nongovern-
mental organizations functioning at the grassroots in which the church has
a major hand and which offer subsoil (organizations and skilled actors) for
the functioning of democracy.

Perhaps nowhere is this clearer than in the case of Brazil. Base Christian
community members strongly fostered the growth of the industrial worker
unions and the later formation of the Brazilian Workers' Party headed by
Luís Inácio da Silva (Lula) who was narrowly defeated for the presidency
of Brazil in 1989 and may yet win it in 1994. Brazilian workers found a
national voice, in part through the church. In 1992 came the impeachment
of President Fernando Collor de Mello, a first for Brazil (and Latin America). The swing in Brazil and elsewhere[7] away from tolerance for corruption
is attributed to a mix of many factors, including the ethics of justice and
equitable participation fomented by church-inspired grassroots organizations.

However much the church contributed to a change to democratic
regimes, the assessment of some observers is that the church in Latin America has been uncertain about its role in a democracy.[8] In Peru the church
acted hastily and imprudently during the 1990 presidential elections. In
Brazil and Argentina it took up limited moral issues and missed larger
issues. In the initial transition to democracy, the church was like a war hero
unsure of what to do in peace but with great accomplishments remembered
and hoped for. What is the voice of the voiceless to do after others recover
their right to speak and appear in public debate?

But the church is learning new roles to play in public life in Guatemala,
Bolivia, and Venezuela. The bishops of Bolivia and Guatemala are almost
all uniformly in the line of the reforms of Vatican II. In the 1990s they may
supplant the Brazilian hierarchy as leaders of the progressive church in
Latin America. But what of the Venezuelan bishops, virtually unknown
outside their country? How did they merit the appraisal as an institution
of great credibility? As Senator Pedro Pablo Aguilar said: "Among Venezuelan institutions it is the church which has gained the greatest respect-
ability, the greatest confidence. Of the church we can say that in the
[current] conflict it is the partner of good faith."[9] The Venezuelan church
arrived at this point in a largely secular society by relocating itself. Whereas
it had taken the part of the modernizing elite members (many of whom it
educated), now it chooses to stand clearly on the side of the poor.

Thus the first requisite for a church in a democracy that hopes to function effectively as a moral influence in democracy in Latin America may
be *ubicación* (placement) clearly on the side of the poor where it can speak
effectively about participation of the masses in society. Further, the poorest
millions who receive almost none of society's resources or protections have
no doubt that the voice of the voiceless is still needed for them. Catholicism
which existed before, say 1968, was a religion embedded in the status quo.
This cultural Catholicism was unable to leaven the social structures of Latin

America that the Medellín conference characterized as a situation of social sin.[10] Reformed Catholicism, taking the side of the poor, has the opportunity of supporting structures that reduce class and racial barriers, of infusing considerations of justice into public debate, and of making government accountable for its expenditures.

SOCIOECONOMIC DREAD

The set of socioeconomic data that hang heavily on the minds of most analysts dealing with Latin America has been the downward economic trends that have produced social havoc in many parts of Latin America. Travelers and residents alike who remember gracious living in tropical or temperate climates are faced with homeless children, crime, and other signs of breakdown.

The depth of economic decline has produced scenes to exceed those pictured by Dickens: millions crowding on what was recently barren land; families who have never known regular employment, and masses of children living on the streets. Until twenty years ago in Latin America most orphans were cared for by religious groups or typically, as had been the case for centuries, by relatives or neighbors. The category of homeless child was virtually unknown in Latin America. Now, in Brazil alone, some seven million homeless children in a population of 150 million roam the streets; one million are said to live in the Rio area.

By contrast, visitors to Providencia and other middle- and upper-class sections of Santiago find stylishly dressed shoppers in well-stocked stores and malls, and enough cars and vans to make driving annoying. Even the subways are well maintained and not overcrowded. The bifurcation of classes in Latin America became more evident from 1980 on.[11] In Chile five of the thirteen million citizens live very well. "There always were two Chiles; only now the extremes seem even farther apart," said Gerald Whelan, a Holy Cross priest and naturalized citizen of Chile.

The causes of the economic decline of the masses and the affluence of a select group are well documented by the United Nations and many other organizations. The U.N. called the 1980s the "lost decade" in Latin America. Some of the causes seem remote. But, among the global causes, one stands out: the public debt. Since the Puebla conference, Latin American bishops have shown great interest in the problem.[12] At first they attempted to wrestle with the problem as a moral issue. Mexican bishops talked about errors on both sides and about moral failures.[13] Later, lenders and borrowers began making practical adjustments. A breakthrough in the spiral of inflation occurred first in one of the most unlikely places: Bolivia.

Inflation in Bolivia ran to five or six figures. The country was regarded as a basket case, the Latin American equivalent of Bangladesh. James Malloy, a longtime observer of Bolivia, recalls going with friends to a restaurant in La Paz at this time. They were asked if they wished to pay before or after the meal; such were the swings of the inflation curves. Bolivia bargained with its creditors, imposed the harsh measures of the International Monetary Fund at moderately great social cost, and brought its inflation rates to an admirable level. Other nations took notice and tried to follow Bolivia's example. One after the other, Latin American countries elected telegenic young men who promised to control inflation and corruption, to cut government payrolls (usually excluding the military from reductions), and to shape the country along the lines of neoliberal capitalism.

The world had changed. With the demise of the Soviet Union, there were no longer any economic options aside from the one world system with its market economy, or neoliberalism, as Latin Americans tended to call it. No alternatives presented themselves. The left was in disarray, discredited in countries like Chile, and articulating nothing that compelled interest. Latin America had to fit in with the new world order.

It was not an attractive model to Latin Americans for at least two reasons. First, the earlier capitalism that many Latin Americans knew was predatory capitalism, which tended to function without free competition, or modern *hybrid* capitalism with many constraints and extensive state ownership.[14] The bishops at Medellín had described it in 1968 as fostering internal domination and external dependence, part of the situation of social sin in the region. Second, Latin Americans perceived themselves as being on the margin of the new world order. Early in the 1990s Latin American writers repeatedly worried about the new isolation of Latin America. In fact, the exclusion of the region was an old theme and constant complaint of Latin Americans.[15]

No wonder then that the Catholic church should see integration of the region as one of the answers to the new world order. At least Latin Americans would have one another to trade and deal with, and a united force with which to bargain with countries at the center of the new world order.[16] Latin Americans had essential things in common: one faith, one culture, and Portuguese and Spanish similar enough to allow for ease of communication. But did Latin Americans really have one religion, one culture? Ethnic and racial minorities increasingly came forward in recent years to claim a measure of autonomy while religious competitors in some countries were achieving a certain parity with the Catholic church.

VITALITY AND COMPETITION IN THE RELIGIOUS SCENE

The enormous changes in social and economic conditions in Latin America and the Caribbean have facilitated corresponding religious change.[17] Many economists and social scientists have documented these changes beginning in the 1950s and intensifying in the 1980s and 90s.[18] Alejandro Portes, Daniel Levine, and others point to the larger social processes taking place in Latin America. They note agrarian concentration (farming in much larger units), vast migrations and formation of megacities (Mexico City and

São Paulo are among the world's largest), improved transport, expanded literacy, and access to radio, television, and other media. Crucial to understanding the changes, social and religious, which have been taking place in Latin America is the view of these grand social forces combining to undermine the long-standing ties between elites and masses. In a word, people came loose from ties that bound them to family and church and, being both social and religious persons, they sought new expressions for religion. Millions joined Pentecostalism or base Christian communities in Catholicism, both of which offered solidarity, challenge, status.

The appearance of David Stoll's *Is Latin America Turning Protestant?* and David Martin's *Tongues of Fire: The Explosion of Protestantism in Latin America*[19] called the general reader's attention to a phenomenon previously known to a handful of scholars. Many Latin American Catholics and even members of mainline Protestant churches call these groups *sectas*. Travelers to Latin America see them everywhere with lively worship on Sundays and weekday evenings in thousands of small or large structures.

Much discussion of sects or evangelical and fundamentalist growth in Latin America has been misleading for several reasons. First, Protestant gain does not mean decline in the number of persons attending Catholic or, for that matter, spiritist religious services. Second, Catholicism is enjoying an extensive awakening. Third, considerable growth is occurring in Afroamerican religion.[20] Fourth, a notable blurring of lines between religions has occurred. To say, for example, that one is Catholic does not preclude his or her practicing Candomblé religion, as well.[21] Fifth, *sectas*, used by John Paul at Santo Domingo, repeating the Latin American bishops, is a global term inadequate to the reality and hurtful to some of the groups so labeled. Sixth, the greatest growth among evangelicals occurs among Pentecostal groups, many of whom are indigenous to the countries where they operate; that is, they are Latin American groups and have been integrated in Brazilian or some other Latin American culture for a long time. Seventh, of the large amounts of money raised for non-Catholic activities in Latin America, the vast majority of the money stays in the United States or is spent in Latin America by groups who are not enjoying the greatest growth in Latin America.

To visualize the religious scene, one would first view Latin America and the Caribbean with the vast majority having a belief in God and having a deeply religious sense. Studies of this phenomenon are rare in many countries and one relies for the most part on anecdotal accounts. But important religious research has been carried on in Brazil. This is fortunate because Brazil, with the ninth or tenth largest economy in the world, includes modernizing as well as traditional sectors, a microcosm, to an extent, of Latin America. Summarizing evidence in Brazil, Jesús Hortal says: "It is practically impossible, outside of very restricted intellectual circles, to find in Brazil someone who proclaims himself atheist. And, more, society as a whole, rejects that kind of declaration, as evident in a recent electoral dispute in the prefecture of São Paulo."

At the same time, however, a view of the region shows millions of cultural Catholics. Only a small percentage regularly attend church. The figure customarily cited for the region, recognizing considerable variation, say, between Guadalajara (high attendance) and Chihuahua (low attendance) or between Colombia and Venezuela, is ten to fifteen percent.[22] Fernando Montes, S.J., editor of *Mensaje*, does not believe that regular church attendance is a good indicator of religion in Latin America, but he agrees that millions of Latin Americans tend to be Catholics who, for sociocultural reasons, not religious conviction, are baptized, married, and buried in a Catholic church. They are, as the church-growth advocates describe them, *campos blancos*, empty fields waiting for a religious planting and harvest. Thus, the argument that Protestants and others are somehow "stealing" somebody else's sheep does not have great merit when "sheep" are virtually unattended.

Among Catholics a notable religious ferment has been occurring. Sunday worshipers fill churches in many Latin American countries.[23] The emergence of impressive leaders—lay, priests, and bishops—became evident from the mid-1960s on.[24] The clearest manifestation of this renewal is an increase of vocations to the priesthood, a prominent indicator of vitality or decline in a church highly dependent on professional clergy. In the years 1972–1990 the numbers of major seminarians (students studying philosophy [typically two years] or theology [four years]) increased from 300 to 700 percent in all but three countries.[25] The church has built new seminary buildings all over Latin America.

The quality of seminarian also changed, reflecting the church's emphasis on service to the poor. After interviews over ten years with students and administrators of schools of theology in Mexico City, Guatemala (Guatemala City and Sololá), Cochabamba, Asunción, and Santiago (Chile), I would characterize a large number of seminarians as having work experience, coming from lower-class families which have been active for a generation or two in lay movements, desirous of working with the poor, and favoring a social-justice orientation in their future ministry.[26]

But the major hope for the transformation of the Catholic church in Latin America and for Latin America itself is the quality of Catholics informally educated in lay movements, especially in small groups. They have had an education in reading the Bible directly, have gained leadership experience in directing groups, and acquired a communal sense of being church.

The movements for the renovation of lay persons in the Catholic church are so numerous that bishops are hard pressed to remember all their names. In a place like Guatemala City thousands of lay persons have participated in Cursillos de Cristiandad (fifty thousand participants in this movement alone), Camino Mejor, Legion of Mary, Cursillos de Capacitación, small

Christian groups, Marriage Encounter, or the Catholic Charismatic Renewal, and have assumed responsibility for roles in the parish or projects in the neighborhood. The general shift has been from passivity to active participation among many of the 40 to 45 million practicing Catholics in Latin America. *Pastoral de conjunto*, shared responsibility, has become the major achievement of the last half-century.[27]

But tending to active Catholics, often in neighborhoods of six thousand or more persons or in vast rural areas with poor roads, takes virtually all the time of the fifty-three thousand priests and slightly more than over one thousand bishops in Latin America.[28] The church thereby tends to ignore inactive Catholics, the approximately 250 to 300 million who appear in church only for a feast day or their weddings or funerals. Further, the more contact priests had with persons in lay movements, the more they realized the profound ignorance on the part of even active Catholics about essentials of faith, especially about the person of Jesus Christ. For centuries ignorance about the Bible had been extensive, if not universal. And popular religious devotions had taken a deep hold in families who had almost no contact with clergy for ages. Practitioners of these devotions frequently concentrated on secondary aspects of religion and knew little of the Catholicism of biblical scholars or theologians. Many lay Catholics, measuring themselves against the reforms of Vatican II or against the biblical awareness of some of their evangelical neighbors, acutely felt this void and sought further renewal in evening Bible classes, weekend retreats, and personal study.

Awareness of ignorance in cultural as well as practicing Catholics is the great engine driving priests and lay Catholics toward a "new evangelization." This phrase, virtually unknown in Catholic circles until recent years, came to the fore in Latin America as the 500th anniversary of Columbus's arrival in the Americas approached. Pope John Paul used the opportunity of a trip to the Dominican Republic in 1983 to suggest a nine-year process of preparation for 1992 as a vast evangelization program in Latin America. The "new" contrasted with the "old" evangelization program of the first missionaries, which was heroic but inadequate.

Growth or Decline among Non-Catholics

Reliable numbers of the practitioners of religion are difficult to obtain. But it may be that for every practicing Catholic in Latin America and the Caribbean, there is an equal number of persons practicing non-Catholic or native religion. For social scientists or church people studying the religious scene numbers are less important than the social processes facilitating the changes or the motives for either conversion to other religions or stronger commitment within religious groups, such as that occuring among small Christian communities. Nevertheless, such figures as are available tell some of the story. Perhaps the most reliable figures are provided by Patrick

Johnstone.[29] His figures are also the basis of Stoll's statistics in *Is Latin America Turning Protestant?*[30]

Viewed thus, Latin America has six countries with impressive numbers of Protestants and fifteen with lesser percentages (see Table 1).

Early studies by pioneer social scientists concentrated on Protestant Pentecostals in Brazil and Chile. Church-growth advocates showcased Guatemala. Marlise Simons provided a ground-breaking article on Central American evangelical growth in the *New York Times Magazine*.[31] But the greatest success story of Protestants has been largely overlooked, although closer at hand, and provides implications for Hispanics in other parts of

Table 1
Protestants and Evangelicals in Latin America
Percentage of Total Population

	% Protestants	% Evangelicals
Puerto Rico	27.2	20.8
Chile	22.5	21.6
Guatemala	20.4	19.0
Brazil	17.4	16.0
Haiti	17.2	12.3
El Salvador	14.0	12.8
Panama	11.8	9.8
Honduras	9.9	8.8
Nicaragua	9.3	6.3
Costa Rica	7.7	6.5
Dominican Republic	6.4	4.7
Bolivia	7.6	6.5
Argentina	5.5	4.7
Mexico	4.0	3.1
Paraguay	4.0	2.5
Peru	3.6	3.0
Ecuador	3.4	3.2
Colombia	3.1	2.4
Uruguay	3.1	1.9
Venezuela	2.6	2.1
Cuba	2.4	2.1

(Estimates for 17 of the 21 countries above: about 75% Pentecostal Christian)
Source: Patrick Johnstone, *Operation World* (Wayneboro, Ga.: STL, 1986).

the United States: Puerto Rico has about a million Protestants in a population of three and a half million.[32]

Who are these Protestants of Latin America? For the most part they are not the older groups, the Lutherans, Presbyterians, Baptists, or Methodists. These mainline groups have respectable numbers, include prominent members of society, and intellectuals who have made important contributions to Latin American theology. But the stars of evangelical growth are the Pentecostals. Many of their churches have long and deep roots in Latin America. In the beginning many Pentecostals joined from the lowest sectors in Latin America society, so these churches were sometimes called "havens of the masses." But within their numbers were many shopowners, teachers, and small-business managers.[33] They anchored growth, which occurred especially in the difficult founding years of the first half of this century. Now in the last half-century Protestants are found in all social classes and professions.

The achievement of social acceptance of Protestants in Latin American society has a long and painful history and is far from completed. The argument has been made by some Latin American Catholics, as well as John Paul II, that Protestantism represents an alien culture, one antithetical to Latin American cultural unity. But Protestants have proven themselves Latin American with status and prestige earned among their neighboring Catholics. They have neither destroyed nor weakened Latin American unity, but have made notable individual and collective contributions to Latin American societies through hard work, sobriety, and enterprise.

From what religious background come the converts to Pentecostalism? No surprise that most are from Catholic backgrounds, but large numbers are former members of other Protestant churches. Whole congregations of historical Protestants joined Pentecostal churches in Guatemala and elsewhere.[34] Nor are all the former Catholics from the "cultural Catholic" group. What evidence we have thus far also points to several other types: (1) Catholics from the charismatic renewal who found little sympathetic treatment in a local church; (2) former Catholics who continued to seek a mystical form of religion, missing for them in post–Vatican II Catholicism and attracting them to some form of Pentecostal religion; (3) a significant group of upper- and middle-class Catholics who resisted the pressure put on them for more equitable land distribution and other measures attributed to the social teaching of the church, and who joined groups that until recently have been apolitical; (4) many Catholics in Central America who identified themselves as *evangélico* to avoid the blanket killing that fell upon active Catholics, like catechists and Catholic Action members who taught the social implications of the Bible. They preferred for a time to be evangelical and "safe," returning to Catholic worship and affiliation.

The Sects, New Religious Movements, New Age

Whence comes the depiction of the *sectas*? The word covers a great variety of religious groups. Since the 1970s Catholics and Protestants alike have been bewildered by the presence in their countries of advocates for new religious movements. Hundreds of new religious groups have gone through formal processes in foreign ministries to register their organizations; other groups have informally entered Bolivia, Argentina, Brazil, and other countries, and set about establishing their enterprises. Many Latin Americans initially received these groups with courtesy and toleration. A few of the groups repaid this openness poorly. Groups similar to Jim Jones's cult in San Francisco and Guyana began similar operations in Latin American countries. Soon the same sort of reports of "brainwashing" heard some years ago in the United States became more common in Latin America.

The newest element in the mix of the sects appeared in the 1980s and 90s. New Age books moved quickly through Spanish and Portuguese translations, while radio stations throughout the continent further spread the New Age message and "sound." Old-line Catholic apologists attempting to track this new line of attack on their religion are baffled, and tend to see the devil and the United States behind the invasion. But the group that probably provokes the most reaction has been on the scene for some years, has had modest success, and tends to be marked by aggressive and offensive proselytism. The Jehovah's Witnesses never seem to tire of knocking on doors, trading upon Latin American courtesy, while openly challenging Catholic beliefs.

Reactions by Catholics to non-Catholic growth in Latin America has been percolating for years. The First General Conference of Latin American Bishops in 1955 made statements about the danger of a Protestant presence in Latin America. But Protestants were then only a tiny percentage of the population and the bishops appeared to be crying wolf. But in 1992, when John Paul II spoke of the sects as "rapacious wolves" devouring Latin American Catholics and "causing division and discord in our communities,"[35] he was reflecting the serious concerns many Catholic bishops felt and expressed in documents leading up to Santo Domingo.[36] He was referring to groups aggressively attacking the Catholic church, calling it a dead institution and the Whore of Babylon, and gaining many formerly Catholic adherents.

But wolf and sect characterizations do not express well the complex non-Catholic religious world of Latin America nor the full thought of the Catholic church about the Pentecostal phenomenon: the term "sects" is often used in a way that loosely mixes together all non-Catholic groups in Latin America, including cults and New Age philosophies with Pentecostal and evangelical Protestantism. This use of the term perpetuates typical Latin American Catholic stereotypes and prejudices about non-Catholics and so is avoided by careful observers.[37] The attack on "sects" also ignores the lengthy and serious dialogue that has been taking place between Catholics and "classic" Pentecostals sponsored by the Pontifical Council for Promoting Christian Unity.[38]

Most Catholics, including bishops, have grown up with only distant association with Protestants. As Melinda Roper, former president of the Maryknoll Sisters and now working in Panama says: "Nothing in the background of the bishops helps them understand having non-Catholics around them in abundant numbers. Aggressive proselytism, to them, is out of place and divisive in a culture where religious affiliation is not to be publicly challenged."[39]

WITHIN THE CHURCH: CONSERVATISM, CONFLICTS, REACTIONS

Pope John Paul II, who was elected Pope in 1978, made his first papal journey to Mexico and the Puebla Conference in 1979. Although early statements made en route to the conference suggested that he would take a hard line on liberation theology, his subsequent address to the assembled bishops and at other appearances in Mexico forced a more nuanced interpretation of his overall message.

His addresses to Indians at Oaxaca, to students at Guadalajara, and to workers at Monterrey carried messages of support for social justice that were eagerly received by progressives and moderates in the Latin American church. Millions of Mexicans responded to the gregarious visitor, everywhere lining the streets and highways. In those few days John Paul forged a bond with Latin America as no global leader had ever done. With the passage of time this bonding became increasingly complex, as the pope's visits to the region became almost commonplace. But, by the time of the Santo Domingo meeting, it was noted that most Latin Americans had seen the pope on their own soil, a fairly extraordinary fact.

Scholars will be assessing John Paul's effect on the Latin American church for years to come. It is the opinion of many observers that his influence on the Latin American church has not been a thoroughly positive one. In the years before John Paul II, the Latin American church had attained a new level of vitality and creativity. Young bishops with bright ideas were appointed, foreign clergy and sisters, most of them with modern plans for renewal, were sent to Latin America at the Vatican's request, and creative experiments were encouraged. Latin America became an experimental ground that produced the theology of liberation, small Christian communities, and lay movements of an incredible variety, all of this drawing the attention of the global church.

John Paul and the Vatican leadership have reversed many of these trends. Many more conservatives were appointed bishops; progressive experiments were questioned, controlled, or quashed; conservative leaders were imposed or encouraged at CELAM headquarters and at many key posts, as in seminaries and adult training institutes. Within a growing climate of control, many bishops and other church leaders occupying the center ground found self-censorship or inactivity preferable to outspoken prophecy. As Luis Ugalde, S.J., president of Andrés Bello University in Caracas, has said: "There has been a climate of distrust and internal disqualification that drains the vigor of a church facing the urgent tasks of the continent."[40]

Conservative Catholics, always present in Latin America, found encouragement for greater activity and more effective organizing in this climate. Opus Dei counted six of its members among the forty bishops of Peru, enough to swing the weight of the episcopacy and to dampen its activist stands.[41] Father Marcial Maciel who created in Mexico the Legionnaires of Christ, considered more conservative than Opus Dei, points to two thousand seminarians worldwide.[42] Evangelization and educational efforts that took apolitical or conservative stances increasingly drew favor. Father Alfonso Navarro, another Mexican conservative innovator, began SINE, an evangelization program that gained followers in Texas and Central America as well as throughout Mexico. Ambitious television programing by Evangelization 2000 and other groups captured wide audiences in Brazil and elsewhere.[43]

Liberation theologians, key intellectual guides of the Medellín conference, were systematically excluded from the roster of experts and advisers for the Puebla Conference. Beginning in 1983 a direct and prolonged attack on key Latin American theologians began: Gustavo Gutiérrez, Peruvian priest and widely-recognized proponent of liberation theology, faced a list of criticisms of his work. The next year a major agency, the Congregation for the Doctrine of the Faith, headed by Cardinal Joseph Ratzinger, accused Leonardo Boff, the Brazilian theologian, of serious theological deviations, called him to Rome, silenced him for almost a year, and removed him from teaching and editorial posts.

Worldwide reaction by bishops and theologians brought a large measure of vindication for liberation theology, especially in the second of two Instructions from the Congregation for the Doctrine of the Faith (1986).[44] And John Paul II's letter to the Brazilian bishops, calling liberation theology "useful and necessary," helped immensely to keep the theology of liberation as part of the language many Latin American bishops used to express the church's role in Latin America.[45]

Nevertheless, the attacks and many subsequent and insistent inquiries and questioning from Rome to bishops, theologians, and schools in Latin America had a chilling effect on Latin Americans hoping to renovate the church from within.[46] The chill was strongly felt especially in key progressive churches of Brazil and Peru.[47]

The flourishing schools of theology in Latin America, many with half their students aspiring lay teachers, increasingly found themselves constrained in the choice of professors, knowing that new appointments of liberationists would not be approved by Rome. In a survey of the main theology schools of Bolivia, Paraguay, and Chile in 1989, I found no professor known to be teaching liberation theology. Students nonetheless said that they learned of liberation viewpoints through forums sponsored by one or another group associated with Catholic universities in those countries, through contact with activist priests, or through reading widely available books and journals. Further, religious orders (which tend to be more progressive than diocesan clergy) increasingly joined together in many countries to form schools of theology apart from schools and institutes under episcopal control.

Base Christian communities have been a barometer of the Latin American church. Their importance as a single indicator is debatable, since there are many ways to express one's religion and sense of community. Their political significance has sometimes been overblown, but they have clearly been a centerpiece of the reforms of the Latin American church. Recently, however, there have been signs of diminishing numbers, as bishops have begun withdrawing support for the communities, shifting their attention to other pastoral strategies. In general, this has signaled a spiritualizing, centralizing tendency. Like most voluntary associations, the communities tend to die or diminish without the support of institutional leadership.

The spine of the church giving it shape and character at the top has been the national conferences of bishops. The theology of Vatican II greatly strengthened these conferences, and within the national conferences bishops learned how to lead their churches at a national level. Regularly recurrent meetings, often twice a year, and special purpose meetings more often, afforded the bishops the opportunity to view the whole country and not just their diocese.

After the awakening that occurred at Vatican II, the Latin American bishops came of age on their home soil. A look at their pastoral letters since Puebla often — although not universally — shows vision and courage in taking public positions.[48] The conferences also display the tensions in the church and the effect of conservative influences. In a word, the national conferences are good indicators of the directions of the Latin American church, better indicators than CELAM. The national conferences allow conflict, afford an arena of discussion, and follow Latin American rules of the game (one person, one vote, no outsiders).

The dynamism of the conferences derives in part from the methodology typically employed: see, judge, act (or, description of a situation, biblical and theological reflection, proposals for action). "When one describes the human situation of our countries and reflects on these conditions in the light of Isaiah, Amos, Jeremiah and asks what their meaning is today in Latin America, the texts become dynamite documents," said Stephen Judd, M.M., of the Maryknoll General Council.[49] In contrast to church statements in other regions, the Latin American method tends to carry its users, willy-nilly, into realistic discussions of national and church problems.

PREPARATIONS FOR SANTO DOMINGO

A central issue for the Santo Domingo meeting thus became: Would the Latin American instrument of see-judge-act be the method used in the assembly for addressing contemporary issues? Without this direct approach, the collective mind of the Latin American bishops would be much less likely to be expressed.

Moreover the fear expressed among progressive church leaders was that the Vatican would effectively change the structure of the meeting into that of a synod wherein the pope and the Vatican would select the themes to be discussed, impose control of discussion, and do away with or deemphasize final conference documents. This fear increased when on December 12, 1990, the pope announced that three themes would be used to guide discussion at the conference: evangelization, human promotion, and Christian culture.[50] While the first two clearly reflected Latin American concerns, "culture" had more ambiguity, having been used by church leaders on the right to counter the concerns of liberationists.

The *Documento de Consulta* (Consultative Document) was issued by CELAM headquarters as the first step in constructing a document to be used as the basis of the Santo Domingo meeting. The document was so vague and generalized and unreflective of acutely experienced Latin American misery that even traditional episcopal conferences, such as Argentina, complained strongly. Under the new leadership of Brazilian Bishop Raymundo Damasceno Assis, secretary general, CELAM composed another document, the *Secunda Relatio*, incorporating numerous suggestions of the national bishops conferences. CELAM sent this to Rome; some modifications were made, and the document was issued as *Documento de Trabajo* (Working Document). Pablo Richard has argued that theologians can best view the collective mind of the Latin American bishops in the *Secunda Relatio* and the "Working Document."[51]

CONCLUSION: SIGNS OF THE TIMES

The sociopolitical situation shows a turn toward democracy and dreadful living conditions for increased numbers of Latin Americans. Faced with this situation the church thinking of itself as serving the world needed to read the signs of the times.

At the time of the Puebla Conference a great debate in and out of Latin America was about the role of religion in fostering revolutionary change. In the immediate background of the conference was the victorious insurrection of the revolutionary Sandinistas against the dictator, Anastasio Somoza. Now, three years after the electoral defeat of the Sandinistas, there is little attention paid to revolutionary politics, if one is to judge from the documents of the bishops leading up to Santo Domingo. The collective mind of the Latin American bishops can be viewed in the *Secunda Relatio* and the *Documento de Trabajo*, documents collected from consultations in Latin America. No alternative political or economic system is considered. As its primary focus the church has chosen to emphasize the option for the poor within incipient democracies. The central question then is how to make societies more responsive to the needs of the groups pushed to the edge of society, groups without many of the educational or health benefits associated with modern human existence.

Ethnicity and women's concerns have replaced revolution as current issues of the Latin American church. The economically poor and youth remain the constant concern of the church, but bishops have expanded their vision of the marginal and excluded to focus on Indians and women. In the case of Indians this has occurred for several reasons: First, indigenous groups are finding their own voice after centuries of virtual silence.[52] This way was dramatically highlighted in 1992 with the award of the Nobel Prize for Peace to a Guatemalan Indian woman, Rigoberta Menchú, which occurred in the first week of the Latin American Bishops' Conference. Second, decades of careful work *with* Indian groups by anthropologists and pastoral leaders nurturing Indian leadership have paid off. Third, the magnitude of scholarship and commentary surrounding the Fifth Centenary of Columbus's arrival brought empathy to a previously forgotten cause.

A notable evolution in treatment of the subject of women in the church and in society took place between Puebla and Santo Domingo.[53] Whereas Puebla takes up the injustices inflicted on women and passively borne, the *Documento de Trabajo* describes the rise of women looking for appropriate channels of expression.[54] "A new style of being woman is being born in Latin America" for "women who assume social responsibilities at the same level of men in all aspects of life." Further, "women are discriminated against at upper leadership levels both in society and in the church and their capabilities are not sufficiently recognized."[55] Thus a greater awareness of the state of women and their aspirations has taken place in Latin America, and without the grinding aggravations that occurred in the proposals for a pastoral letter on women in the United States.

Indigenous groups for centuries have been silent witnesses to the abuse of the environment and have helped to focus attention of other Latin Americans on this issue. Ecology, mentioned as a secondary consideration at Puebla, was pushed forward as a major issue for the churches, as part of their holistic concern for threats to life.

Thus, within democracies as they imperfectly function in Latin America, the church sought signs of the times, challenges the church selected for its agenda into the next century. Besides the turn toward democracy and the new world economic order, these signs include: human rights broadly conceived, solidarity with the poor and struggling, land, work, ecology, migration, and Latin American integration. The church thus marked off for itself issues for which it would act as advocate and conscience in Latin America. The search for the church's roles in democracy was coming to focus. Specific issues were highlighted and a solid basis established in the social teaching of the church and in a Latin American theology.

In this theology the voices of women and Indians are increasingly heard.

NOTES

1. See Juan Corradi et al., eds., *Fear at the Edge: State Terror and Resistance in Latin America* (Berkeley: University of California Press, 1992); and Lawrence Weschler, *A Miracle, A Universe: Settling Accounts with Torturers* (New York: Pantheon, 1990). Tina Rosenberg's *Children of Cain: Violence and the Violent in Latin America* (New York: Penguin, 1991) presents case histories of persons who inflicted violence.

2. Huntington, *The Third Wave: Democratization in the Late Twentieth Century* (Norman: University of Oklahoma Press, 1991).

3. Seymour Martin Lipset, Kyoung-Ryung Seong, and John Charles Torres, "Social Requisites of Democracy," *World Development Report 1984* (New York: Oxford University Press, 1984), p. 29.

4. Quoted in Huntington, "Religion and the Third Wave," *The National Interest* 24 (Summer 1991), p. 34.

5. *Centesimus Annus*, 46.

6. Final Document, CELAM IV, no. 191.

7. *New York Times*, Dec. 30, 1992, noted a growing intolerance in Latin America for politicians who enrich themselves in office, and cited examples: "Heads of state in Venezuela, Argentina, Peru, Bolivia, and Paraguay have all faced public outcries over charges of corruption."

8. Edward L. Cleary and Hannah Stewart-Gambino, eds., *Conflict and Competition: The Latin American Church in a Changing Environment* (Boulder: Lynne Rienner, 1992).

9. Arturo Sosa A., "Iglesia y profundización de la democracia," *SIC* 55, 546 (July 1992), 252.

10. See Puebla Conference final document, nos. 28, 435, 1300, and Juan Hernández Pico, "Martyrdom Today in Latin America: Stumbling-block, Folly, and Power of God," in Johannes-Baptist Metz and Edward Schillebeeckx, eds., *Martyrdom Today* (New York: Seabury, 1983), p. 37.

11. The somewhat improved situation of poverty in Chile is considered by Jaime Ruiz-Tagle P. in *Mensaje*, no. 415 (Dec. 1992), 580–83.

12. See Edward L. Cleary, ed., *Path from Puebla: Significant Documents of the Latin American Bishops since 1979* (Washington: National Conference of Catholic Bishops, 1988).

13. Mexican Bishops Conference, "At the Service of the Human Community: An Ethical Consideration of the International Debt" (1987), in Cleary, ibid., pp. 339–48.

14. See Thomas E. Skidmore and Peter H. Smith's depiction of hybrid capitalism in *Modern Latin America*, third edition (New York: Oxford University Press, 1992), pp. 401–3.

15. See, for example, Leopoldo Zea, *The Role of the Americas in History* (Savage, Md.: Rowman and Littlefield, 1992), pp. 201–3.

16. See, for example, Carol Barton, "MERCOSUR: The Unmagical Market," *Christian Century*, Jan. 4, 1993, 428–32.

17. For a discussion of the theoretical underpinnings, see Cleary, "Evangelicals and Competition in Guatemala," in Cleary and Stewart-Gambino, eds., *Conflict and Competition,* pp. 168–69; also Cleary, "Conclusion: Politics and Religion," same volume, pp. 197–200.

18. The dating of these massive changes may be earlier. Emilio Willems notes: "after 1930, when the rate of social change picked up momentum and the traditional culture began to crack under the strain of the great depression, industrialization, and population increase" (*Followers of the New Faith*, pp. 64–65). See also the prediction that industrialization would be a catalyst of Pentecostal growth in Brazil in C.W. Gates, *Industrialization: Brazil's Catalyst for Church Growth* (South Pasadena, Calif.: William Carey Library, 1972).

19. Stoll (Berkeley: University of California Press, 1990); Martin (Oxford: Blackwell, 1990).

20. Jesús Hortal, "Panorama e estatísticas do fenómeno religioso no Brasil," *Perspectiva Teológica* 24 (1992), 74–76.

21. Hortal, "Panorama," p. 68.

22. See, for example, Thomas C. Bruneau, *The Catholic Church in Brazil: The Politics of Religion* (Austin: University of Texas Press, 1982), 28. Brian Smith estimates between 5 and 20 percent throughout Latin America in *The Church and Politics in Chile: Challenges to Modern Catholicism* (Princeton: Princeton University Press, 1982), p. 44. Older estimates can be found in William J. Coleman, *Latin American Catholicism: A Self Evaluation* (Maryknoll, N.Y.: Maryknoll Publications, 1958), pp. 23–33; see esp. discussion of Mass attendance as an indicator, pp. 32–33; Ivan LaBelle and Adriana Estrada, *Latin America in Maps, Charts, Tables. No. 2: Socio-religious Data (Catholicism)* (Mexico City: Center for Intercultural Formation, 1964) pp. 255–57. [N.B. "Religious Practice on Sundays" is not defined quantitatively.]

23. See, for example, the description of the religious situation by the Guatemala City newspaper *La Hora*, July 18, 1990.

24. Cleary, chapters 1 and 2, *Crisis and Change: The Church in Latin America Today* (Maryknoll, N.Y.: Orbis Books, 1985).

25. Sources for statistics are *Statistical Yearbook of the Church* (Vatican City: Polyglottis Vaticanis) and *Catholic Almanac* (Huntington, Ind.: Our Sunday Visitor).

26. Those interviewed also expressed reservations about some candidates. See Cleary, "Flocking to Seminaries," *National Catholic Reporter*, Nov. 10, 1989, p. 15.

27. This achievement is tempered by a relative absence of committed lay Christians in secular structures of society. See Marcos McGrath, "The Medellín and Puebla Conferences and Their Impact on the Latin American Church," pp. 83, 89, 92; and Luis Ugalde, "The Present Crises of Society and the Church: An Eye to the Future," pp. 131–32, both in Cleary, ed., *Born of the Poor: The Latin American Church since Medellín* (Notre Dame, Ind.: University of Notre Dame Press, 1990).

28. *Statistical Yearbook of the Church 1990* (Vatican City: Typis Polyglottis Vaticanis, 1992).

29. Patrick Johnstone, *Operation World* (Portland, Ore.: Multnomah Press, 1986).

30. See esp. note on sources in Appendix 1, p. 334.

31. *New York Times Magazine* (Nov. 7, 1982), 44–47.

32. Interview with Luis Fidel Mercado, president of Seminario Evangélico de Puerto Rico, May 18, 1992, about extensive study being conducted on Protestantism in Puerto Rico.

33. Everett A. Wilson, "Identity, Community, and Status: The Legacy of the Central American Pentecostal Pioneers," in Joel A. Carpenter and Wilbert R.

Shenk, eds., *Earthen Vessels: American Evangelicals and Foreign Missions, 1880–1980* (Grand Rapids, Mich.: Eerdmans, 1990), p. 148.

34. For Guatemala, see Virgina Gerrard Burnett, "A History of Protestantism in Guatemala," Ph.D. dissertation, Tulane University, 1986, pp. 190–91.

35. Address to CELAM IV Conference, see n. 52.

36. See, for example, *Documento de Trabajo*, IV Conferencia General (Bogotá: Consejo Episcopal Latinoamericano, 1992), nos. 294–95.

37. See Edward L. Cleary, "Report from Santo Domingo," *Commonweal* (Nov. 20, 1992), 7–8; and Carlos Martínez García, "Secta: Un concepto inadecuado para explicar el protestantismo mexicano," *Boletín Teológico* (March 1991).

38. A brief history is given by John A. Radano, "The Pentecostal–Roman Catholic International Dialogue, 1972–1991," *Mid-Stream* 31,1 (Jan. 1992), 26–31. See also Peter Hocken, "Dialogue Extraordinary," *One in Christ* 24,3 (1988), 202–13, and Jerry L. Sandidge, *Roman Catholic/Pentecostal Dialogue (1977–1982): A Study in Developing Ecumenism*, two volumes (Frankfurt: Verlag Peter Lang, 1987). Bishop Ricardo Ramirez's argument for ecumenism among Spanish-speaking Christians in the United States is published in *Origins* 22, 3 (May 28, 1992), 40–44.

39. Interview, Santo Domingo, Oct. 12, 1992.

40. Ugalde, "Present Crises," in Cleary, *Born of the Poor*, p. 133.

41. Jeffrey Klaiber, S.J., "The Church in Peru: Between Terrorism and Conservative Restraints," in Cleary and Stewart-Gambino, p. 88.

42. Rev. Marcial Maciel founded the Legionnaires in Mexico in 1941 and in the United States in 1965. See, for example, "Legion Thrives," *National Catholic Register*, April 16, 1989.

43. See Ralph Della Cava, "The Ten-Year Crusade toward the Third Christian Millennium: An Account of Evangelization 2000 and Lumen 2000," in Douglas A. Chalmers et al., eds., *The Right and Democracy in Latin America* (Westport, Conn.: Praeger, 1992), pp. 202–22.

44. Congregation for the Doctrine of the Faith, "Instruction on Certain Aspects of the 'Theology of Liberation'" (August 6, 1984) and "Instruction on Christian Freedom and Liberation" (March 22, 1986) in Alfred Hennelly, ed., *Liberation Theology: A Documentary History* (Maryknoll, N.Y.: Orbis Books, 1990), pp. 393–414 and 461–97.

45. "Letter to Brazilian Episcopal Conference" (April 9, 1986) in Hennelly, ibid., pp. 448–506.

46. See, for example, Jean-Yves Calvez, "Medellín and Puebla in the Perspective of the World Church," in Cleary, ed., *Born of the Poor*, pp. 191–94.

47. See Thomas C. Bruneau and W.E. Hewitt, "Catholicism and Political Action in Brazil: Limitations and Prospects," in Cleary and Stewart-Gambino, *Conflict and Competition,* pp. 45–62 and 87–103.

48. See Cleary, *Path from Puebla*, for a survey of bishops conferences from 1979 to 1988.

49. Interview, July 10, 1992.

50. *CELAM*, no. 238 (Jan.-Feb. 1991), 1, 3, and 4.

51. "La Iglesia Católica después de Santo Domingo," *Pastoral Popular*, nos. 224–25 (Nov.-Dec. 1992), 14–22.

52. See Xavier Albó, "Del Dios de Dolar al Dios de la vida," *SIC* 55, 546 (July 1992), 288–94.

53. Theological perspectives by women were also developing. Overviews with

bibliographical references: María Clara Bingemer, "Women in the Future of the Theology of Liberation," in Marc Ellis and Otto Maduro, eds., *Expanding the View: Gustavo Gutiérrez and the Future of Liberation Theology* (Maryknoll, N.Y.: Orbis, 1990), pp. 173–93, and María Pilar Aquino, "Doing Theology from the Perspective of Latin American Women," in Roberto S. Goizueta, ed., *We Are a People: Initiatives in Hispanic American Theology* (Minneapolis: Augsburg Fortress, 1992), pp. 79–105. For a view of Hispanic women, see Ada María Isasi-Díaz and Yolanda Tarango, *Hispanic Women: Prophetic Voice in the Church* (Minneapolis: Augsburg Fortress, 1993).

54. Puebla, passim, esp. nos. 834–40.

55. Consejo Episcopal Latinomericano, *Documento de Trabajo* (Bogotá: CELAM, 1992), nos. 272–76.

A Report from the Conference

Alfred T. Hennelly, S.J.

After the completion of the Latin American bishops' conference at Puebla, Mexico, in 1979, the Salvadoran theologian Jon Sobrino published a comparison of the meeting with the preceding conference at Medellín, Colombia, in 1968. "With good reason," he asserted, "some have said that Medellín was a leap forward and that Puebla was a dainty step forward."[1] If I may extend this comparison to the most recent bishops' conference held at Santo Domingo, Dominican Republic (Oct. 12–28, 1993), I would maintain that this meeting was certainly not a leap forward nor an elegant step forward. Rather, it could only be called a *shaky step* into the future. It was a step that many thought might not even be taken because of serious differences among the participants right up to the end of the seventeen-day conference.

Even though the bishops approved the *Final Document* unanimously (with five abstentions), differences remain with regard to christology, ecclesiology, theological method, and other important areas. I would add here, however, that the meeting did provide an excellent opportunity for the bishops to become acquainted and exchange views after the thirteen years that had elapsed since Puebla. Furthermore, I believe the Final Document was led by the Spirit of God to employ the biblical parable of the wheat and the weeds, with both fruitful and worthless results, which may not be definitively discerned until the final judgment.

INTRODUCTION TO THE CONFERENCE

A fine survey of events that have occurred in Latin America since the Puebla meeting has already been provided by Edward Cleary in the first chapter of this book.[2] My task will be to focus on the preparations that were undertaken for the conference and how these have affected (or *not* affected) the *Final Document*. Also, I will refer to the major outlines of the Santo Domingo document, but will leave the overall analysis and evaluation of it to other authors in chapters following the text of the *Final Document*.

For a beginning, it may be helpful to provide a brief description of the venue of the conference and its manner of proceeding. The heart of the entire meeting was located in Santo Domingo in a large auditorium in the

24

Seminary of San Pablo, which appeared to have a freshly constructed wall around the property and a meticulous cleanup within the walls. The other central location was the Hotel Dominican Fiesta, about a mile away, where press releases and press conferences were provided, along with an excellent array of telecommunications (the fax machines, it is said, were used by interested theologians in place of voyaging to Santo Domingo). The bishops, finally, were scattered in various hotels and religious houses throughout the city, and were usually bussed to the above sites. This dispersion throughout the city probably impeded communication and a lack of central leadership on the part of the Latin American bishops.

It is important to note that no journalists (and of course nobody else) were allowed into the San Pablo auditorium, except for the inaugural speech of the pope, which the journalists had already read. Thus, for the full seventeen days of the meeting, all the journalists and observers were enveloped in a kind of intellectual miasma, consisting of table gossip, brief snatches of conversation with bishops, a veritable plethora of rumors, and even the eager purchase of U.S. and local papers to find out what was going on! The bishops' press conferences were of little help regarding hard facts, until the journalists revolted and were then provided with more candid speakers, such as Cardinal Arns from São Paulo, Brazil. Some of the journalists had attended a pan-European theological conference earlier in the year, and said they were allowed to hear the debates; their requests for the same procedure at Santo Domingo were categorically denied. Thus, the only "hard" sources were the Latin bishops and the Vatican officials, and they generally presented a positive face, ignoring controversies. Thus far, I have not been able to find bishops and officials who have published analyses in depth of the conference (with one exception, to be treated later).

THE ROAD TO SANTO DOMINGO

In 1983 at a talk to Latin American bishops in Haiti, Pope John Paul announced for the first time that the topic for the CELAM IV (Latin American Bishops' Conference) would be "New Evangelization."[3] He also proclaimed that the conference would begin in the Dominican Republic on October 12, 1992, the anniversary of the landing of Columbus and the beginning of the first evangelization five hundred years ago. These were the Pope's words to the bishops:

The commemoration of the half-millennium of evangelization will gain its full meaning if it is a commitment on your part as bishops, together with your priests and faithful: a commitment not to reevangelization but to a new evangelization, new in ardor, methods, and expression. Permit me in this regard to sum up in a few words and dwell with you on those aspects which seem to me to be fundamental for the new evangelization.[4]

During the intervening nine years between the Haiti speech and the CELAM IV conference, an enormous amount of time and energy was devoted throughout Latin America to meetings, study, and research, discussions with laity, and working drafts (which soon became good-sized books) in preparation for the meeting. There seems to be general agreement that *three* of these draft documents assumed the greatest importance for the conference.

The first of these was entitled *Consultative Document (Documento de Consulta): New Evangelization, Human Development, and Christian Culture,*[5] and was published in 1991. The Latin bishops, however, were dissatisfied with this version, partly because it did not incorporate the studies and ideas of the national bishops' conferences. Ironically, therefore, it appears that the *consultative* document was rejected, because it had not *consulted* the bishops and also because it did not follow in the path of Medellín and Puebla. Consequently, another draft document, called the *Secunda Relatio,*[6] or *Second Report*, was drawn up. It provided an excellent synthesis of the ideas of all the national conferences. In my opinion, this was the most important and substantive document of the conference, precisely because it represented the carefully considered theological and pastoral views of the bishops throughout the entire continent, who rather obviously were in the best position to speak on behalf of their very diverse flocks, and who had spent a great deal of time over nine years preparing documents with the help of the whole church. However, the *Second Report*, for whatever reasons, was not acceptable to Vatican officials and to conservative Latin bishops.

Finally, with a great deal of hard work by the secretary general of CELAM, Bishop Raymundo Damasceno Assis, and his assistants, the *Second Report* was incorporated into the previous consultative document, leading to a new and final document, called the *Working Document* or *Documento de Trabajo.*[7] This final document was sent to Rome in April 1992, but was not finally approved until some months later. Obviously, this interfered with the widespread distribution and discussion of the materials before the conference. Thus the clergy, laity, and base communities had little time to read, discuss, and provide feedback to the bishops. The *Working Document* was considered to be a useful tool for discussion at the conference, although many thought it lacked the substance, inspiration, and prophetic bite of the *Second Report*.

Furthermore, a few months before the meeting, the Latin Americans were astonished and stunned to hear that Rome had added a *second* general secretary to the conference, in addition to Bishop Assis. The co-secretary general was none other than Bishop Jorge Medina Estévez[8] of Chile, a lifelong friend and supporter of the former Chilean dictator, General Augusto Pinochet. Medina, a hardshell conservative, was not elected by the Chilean bishops' conference, which strongly opposed his appointment to the conference and to such an influential position.

At any rate, reliable sources report that on the very first day of the conference, Bishop Medina announced that the *Working Document (Documento de Trabajo)* was to be discarded, thus sabotaging years of work by the Latin American bishops. Instead of discussing that document in plenary sessions, the bishops were subjected for several days to long, primarily conservative and useless lectures, that were already familiar to the audience. Finally, they were allowed to break up into smaller working groups or committees, thirty in all, that discussed specific issues and problems. Obviously, this division into committees, while useful and perhaps necessary, divided the bishops and further impeded strong leadership among the Latin bishops.

The reports of the small groups, moreover, were not open to plenary sessions, but were sent to the drafting committee, which synthesized the results and presented them for discussion and voting in the plenary sessions. Both individual bishops and episcopal conferences were also able to present to the drafters petitions for changes or additions to the drafts. I have heard estimates varying from five thousand to over ten thousand of these interventions, which obviously further stalled the progress of the Final Document.

Up to the last few days of the conference, then, there were serious forebodings that the seventeen-day meeting would come to naught, no document at all, which in my view would have been interpreted as a tragic farce by Latin Americans and the world, and perhaps also the beginning of the end for the bishops' conference. At any rate, under the leadership of Archbishop Luciano Mendes de Almeida of Brazil, working with his staff through long nights and a frantic final weekend (known in American universities as "all-nighters"), a document was finally produced.

The above account should show at least why the Final Document shows signs of haste, poor organization, and few signs of prophetic fervor or ardor, the last being the attitude stressed for success of the new evangelization by the bishops. But at least there was a document — a document that I believe has a fair amount of both wheat and weeds, as we shall see. Also, as a result of the above brief history, bishops' conferences around the world will continue to ponder whether in the future they will have to struggle with Rome to inculturate the gospel of Jesus of Nazareth in their own native countries — and not merely import the static theologies of Roman religious culture. This reflection might well be the most important result of the conference for the universal church.

With the demise of the *Working Document (Documento de Trabajo)*, the Latin bishops were faced squarely with the selection of some other working paper as a framework for the final document of the conference. This problem was soon resolved in perhaps the only way possible — that is, by adopting the framework and many of the ideas of Pope John Paul's lengthy "Opening Address to Fourth General Conference of Latin American Episcopate" on October 12, 1992.[9] This document is included in the papal messages at the beginning of the volume; it is generally agreed that it did not open new paths, but also did not close any doors. The pope's outline emphasized (1) a "new evangelization," (2) "human development," and (3) "Christian culture," which comprise the three main chapters of the final text: *Santo Domingo: Conclusiones.*[10] I will refer to this final text later on.

AN EXPERT WITNESS

I referred earlier to the fact that only the bishops and Vatican officials were eyewitnesses of what went on in the Santo Domingo conference, and that to my knowledge they did not publish detailed analyses of the meeting. The exception that I mentioned is the Vatican secretary of state, Cardinal Angelo Sodano, who was appointed by the pope to chair the conference. The cardinal gave an astonishingly candid account of his own achievements during an interview in the periodical *30 Days* soon after the conclusion of the conference.[11]

Sodano begins with the statement: "The whole event can clearly be summed up positively because of the evident and increasingly mature sense of joint responsibility on the part of the bishops," clearly referring to the Latin American bishops.[12] One wonders if this "joint responsibility" is true. Bishop José María Pires of Paraibo, Brazil, complained that the lectures "were a waste of time. . . . It would have been much better instead to discuss the working document."[13] Archbishop Marcos McGrath also pointed out these procedural snags and protested that they "caused us to reach the final week without a document having been developed."[14]

Cardinal Sodano in his second paragraph then stated that Christ was the source of truly ecclesial reflection (as everyone would agree), and continued boldly:

In following this perspective, therefore, the traditional formulation of Latin American ecclesial texts, the method the Latin American episcopate has been using for so many years, *was abandoned*: the method of "seeing, judging, acting"; this, even though the Latin American reality was certainly "seen" with all its grave contradictions.[15]

In other words, the cardinal continues, "there was a transition from the dominion of sociological analysis of the reality and its problems to focus on the primacy of Christ's annunciation," and "by shedding light on the essential starting point, the [Latin American] Church may be free and creative in all its various pastoral efforts."[16]

A great deal could be said on these texts, but I will be brief. In the first one, the method that the Latin American bishops had "been using for so many years, was abandoned." Abandoned by whom? Certainly not by the Latin American bishops! That is crystal clear in the *Second Report (Secunda Relatio)*, where the see-judge-act method is explicitly adopted, actually provides the three major parts of the *Second Report*, and intends it for the conference. Thus, the method *was abandoned* by Cardinal Sodano and CAL (the Commission on Latin America), who I would say thereby insulted all the Latin American bishops at the conference.

The second text is a patent ideology, as even a superficial hermeneutic suspicion reveals. The Latin Americans *all* acknowledge Christ's primacy, and *at the same time* recognize the urgent need of "sociological analysis" and the use of other social sciences in order to bring human reason to bear on the crushing problems of the poor, problems which are constantly increasing their misery and ending their lives prematurely. This urgency is not evident in the cardinal's interview. He even changes the "option" for the poor (emphasized as central at both Medellín and Puebla) into one of many "pastoral guidelines." Sadly, too, Jesus is used as an ideology: "In view of this, Santo Domingo made the option for Christ the only one."[17] Are we then to choose Jesus Christ *instead* of the poor?

OTHER VOICES FROM BELOW

In July 1991, a group of theologians, social scientists, Indians and Afroamericans, and various other groups formed a movement called *Amerindia* (the Latin American indigenous peoples). Its goals at the conference were to advise interested bishops, to prepare documents and interventions, to maintain permanent contacts with a bishops' commission, to handle public relations, and to keep a low profile throughout the meeting. As far as I can see, their efforts were quite successful.[18] Here I will discuss some of their evaluations and conclusions.

In an article on the interpretation of the final document, *Amerindia* stresses that the tensions between CAL and the Latin bishops, as well as their two opposed theologies, have left their imprint on the document from beginning to end. Thus, in order to understand it, the Final Document must be read

> with reference to this fundamental contradiction that the entire conference wrestled with from the beginning to the very end ... We can affirm that the theology of Latin America is in the chapter [2] on Human Development, in the priorities for pastoral objectives, and in the unity and pluralism of cultures in the chapter [3] on Christian culture. The theology of CAL is found in the profession of faith, in the chapter [1] on the New Evangelization, and on Christian Culture.[19]

Readers of the final document, therefore, should be prepared to find by and large the CAL or Roman theology in chapter 1, nos. 1–156, pp. 35–116, in the authorized Spanish text. (A major exception may be found in the well-balanced comments on feminism in nos. 104–10, pp. 97–100.) The Latin American theology, then, is totally dominant in chapter 2, nos. 157–

227, pp. 117–42. The rather brief chapter 3 includes nos. 228–303, pp. 143–72. It contains elements of both theologies mentioned above, with many haphazard and contrasting ideas; I will leave it to the other authors in this volume and to its readers to anticipate the eschaton and discern the wheat and the weeds. *Amerindia* also suggests criteria for reading the text—that is, by first reading chapter 2 on human development and using that as a central axis for interpreting the rest of the document.[20]

In the same article, there is an interesting description of the two theologies. The CAL/Roman approach is described as:

> One that reflects a disincarnate and fundamentalistic attitude. This is expressed on a number of levels: an ecclesiology centered on the church as a kind of new Christendom; a pneumatology that is identified with the hierarchical church; an absence of the kingdom and of evangelization as seen in *Evangelii Nuntiandi*; and a silence with regard to the path followed by the Latin American church, e.g., basic ecclesial communities, liberation theology, the insertion of religious life, and CLAR [the Conference of Latin American Religious].[21]

The Latin American theology is described somewhat briefly as a true reflection of the reality and the life of the Latin American church, which "is expressed mainly in the themes concerning the poor, the indigenous cultures, the afroamericans, etc."[22]

Another occurrence highlighted by *Amerindia* has been dubbed after the fact as the "crisis of October 22." More precisely, it took place in the second session of that afternoon and "was the most decisive moment of the entire conference. It was then that the significance of the remaining days and the fate of the final document was entirely decided."[23] Briefly, it was suggested and approved by vote of the bishops that the final text be shortened, but *no criteria* were provided with regard to *which* themes were to be amputated from the document. As a result:

> The majority of the members of the drafting committee and the experts and theologians brought by the Vatican were to be put in charge of the reductions. They had been waiting for this moment, and the [Latin American] bishops graciously and gratuitously gave them their chance to make substantial changes in the first complete draft of the work of the committees.[24]

Obviously, the cuts that were made were primarily in the areas where the Latin American theology was preeminent, and this helps to explain the sketchy and superficial writings in chapter 2 on human development, although the nine topics chosen in that chapter were excellent. A good deal of material was excised also from the work of the thirty commissions. Some have suggested that the original first complete draft must be consulted to understand the evolution of the conference.

THE LATIN AMERICAN DOCUMENT

In the last frenetic days of the Santo Domingo conference, when many had given up hope of a final document, some observers from Europe moved about the Dominican Fiesta Hotel, talking animatedly to bishops, journalists, and other observers. Their urgent proposal was that the bishops (who appeared in disarray) could solve their problems and disagreements by adopting *in toto* the *Second Report* (*Secunda Relatio*) as the official final document. When asked for their reasons, the European groups emphasized that they had spent a great deal of time — singly and in groups — in analyzing and evaluating the report. They had all concluded that it was a worthy successor to the Medellín and Puebla meetings, and had broken new ground in many ways for the future of the church in Latin America.

Although I predicted to the Europeans that their suggestion would be impossible at that late date (it was not even considered), I recognized that they were absolutely correct about their reasoning. It became clear, also, that the *Second Report* should not be swept into the dustbin of history, but should be published throughout Latin America as a companion volume to the actual final document. This would allow the entire church to read and evaluate the two documents.

At this point, also, I am here referring to the *Second Report* as the "Latin American Document," for a number of reasons. A primary reason is that its *contents* were purely derived from Latin Americans — that is, the bishops, their national conferences, and their dialogues with the whole church, from theologians to campesinos. These contents then were carefully sifted by Latin American experts and crafted into a coherent, inspiring, and prophetic *framework*. I agree, then, with my European *confrères* that the *Second Report* comprises the best existing expression of the quintessence, the very soul, of the Latin American church.

SOME PERTINENT EXAMPLES

It is not probable that the *Second Report* will be translated into English; thus it may be helpful to provide some examples of its approach for the benefit of the English-speaking audience. After a brief introduction, the report moves into the first of three major parts, entitled "A Pastoral View of the Reality."[25] This title represents the "see" of the "see-judge-act" method. Its first chapter regarding a *historical* view of evangelization in Latin America runs to almost twenty large pages.[26] One of many striking statements is the following:

> It is necessary to recognize with humility the errors of the past, where they are found, and to seek pardon for the offenses perpetrated

against the Gospel that was being preached. In this way we will grow in Christian maturity, and we will be faithful to the truth, which is Jesus Christ.[27]

By contrast, the *Final Document* allots two and a half small pages to five centuries of evangelization, which are basically triumphalistic, with the exception of two quotes of Pope John Paul, stressing the need to ask pardon for the crimes against the indigenous peoples and the Afroamerican slaves.[28]

Chapter 2 continues with "a view of the *social* reality of Latin America." One paragraph must suffice to show the very different language and tone in the report:

> The perspective of "seeing from the standpoint of the poor" becomes present when they call attention to the fact that it is not only a question of those problems that come "from outside" but also "from inside," since in our church the majority is poor. The poor are not an OBJECT to be studied, but they are the SUBJECT itself of the problem and agents of its solution, while they suffer in their own flesh the sinful situations which are seen especially in the fact that the few have much and the many have little.[29]

Chapter 3 is concerned with "a view of the reality of the church in Latin America." Although the base ecclesial communities are mentioned with faint praise in the *Final Document*, they are lauded in numerous parts of the *Second Report*. Speaking of the lack of experience of a vital community in the cities, the text continues:

> To transform these numerous groups into living communities, the church of Latin America has the precious experience of BASE ECCLESIAL COMMUNITIES. These small communities which flourish on the outskirts of the cities and in the countryside, with permanent religious services and presided over by duly trained and authorized laity, constitute the most powerful evangelizing structures for the present and for the future.[30]

The text also asserts that the parish structure should be a community of base communities, and that "the CEBs [*comunidades eclesiales de base*] are not a movement in the church, but rather a model of the church."[31]

Although it is one of the major accomplishments of the Latin American church, praised, renowned, and criticized by the whole world, *liberation theology* is not mentioned in the final document. But the report mentions it often, at times cautiously, as seen in this text: "Together with the social teaching of the church, we have also to take seriously the theology of liberation, in order to understand it in its authentic sense, and to recognize its positive contribution in bringing pastoral agents into contact with social reality, and in its commitment to the evangelization of the people."[32]

The second part of the report is dedicated to the "judge" element in the see-judge-act triad. It is entitled "theological and pastoral illumination"—that is, judging what has been seen through theological lenses. One of the most common critiques of the *Final Document* is that its christology, although strongly emphasized, is abstract and lacking the human features seen in the Latin American christologies, such as that of Jon Sobrino. Once again, the report begins with two and a half pages regarding the real, not abstract, Jesus. This is merely a sample:

> Jesus evangelizes and liberates with his life, with his message, and with his historical and liberating praxis . . . One of the aspects that most stands out in his life is the prophetic element, both in announcing the kingdom of God (in the parables of the kingdom) and in denouncing the sin of human beings (Mt 23:13–36). This clear and definitive approach brought conflict and persecution upon him, even for eating with sinners, to whom he was sent by the Father. But Jesus remained faithful to the Father and to the cause of the oppressed.[33]

As regards ecclesiology, the *Second Report* reaches poetic as well as theological heights when it points out what the Latin American church is trying to be and continues to be. This is impossible to summarize, but it is an inspiring vision for all Christian churches:

> It is a *poor* church, in the process of conversion, which gives first place to the poor; in solidarity and communion with the impoverished masses of the continent. In situations of injustice and poverty, it brings its message to those who suffer the most. It is a church that renews its vision from the viewpoint of the poor.[34]

This and many other insights on the church today make this one of the high points in the report. Such a vision is not found in the *Final Document.*

Another area where the report has much to contribute lies in the ecumenical sphere, especially with regard to relations with the pentecostal and evangelical communities (I refuse to call them "fundamentalist sects," as is often the usage in Latin America). Aside from the use of the term "sects," this appears to me to be a well-balanced and thoughtful approach:

> The "sects" confront the church with a challenge: they demonstrate the necessity of promoting a renewed model of the church based on a life in community. The best way to face the sects is to promote the CEBs; the sects oblige us to search for a greater insertion among the people, to accelerate the process of inculturation, to diversify ministries in the church and to find new ways of establishing dialogue.[35]

In general, this was not the approach in the *Final Document*, nor in the introductory speech of Pope John Paul.

I will end this too long litany with what is perhaps the most gaping lacuna in the *Final Document.* In the last three decades, Latin America has experienced the martyrdom of literally thousands of men and women in the Christian churches. It has created admiration, inspiration, but also horror and pity throughout the entire world. Can its own bishops really be that blind to the fact that they are living in a "church of the martyrs," as surely as any other century in the past two millennia?

At any rate, near its end, the *Second Report* presents a poignant tribute to all those who have shed their blood for Christ in Latin America. This is only a brief selection:

> The martyrs are a gift of God to the church. The church is grateful for the gift God has made of the testimony and martyrdom of so many sisters and brothers, bishops, priests, and laity, who have arrived at the ultimate consequences of their path of fidelity to God, to the church, and to their sisters and brothers.[36]

A PROPHETIC MESSAGE

Before the final document of Santo Domingo begins, there is a message from the Latin American bishops to the peoples of Latin America and the Caribbean. Messages like this can be hastily skipped over to arrive at the main text, but I would encourage readers to pause and reflect carefully on this message. This letter was written by the Latin bishops themselves and not by others at the conference and, like the *Second Report*, it incontestably manifests the true theology of the Latin American church. Not only that, but it encapsulates the profound depths of the soul, heart, and mind of the peoples of Latin America and the Caribbean. It was written by the true inheritors of the noble legacy of Medellín and Puebla.

NOTES

1. John Eagleson and Phillip Scharper, eds., *Puebla and Beyond* (Maryknoll: Orbis Books, 1979), 302.

2. For more in-depth study of recent Latin American history, see Edward L. Cleary and Hannah Stewart-Gambino, eds., *Conflict and Competition: The Latin American Church in a Changing Environment* (Lynne Riener: Boulder/London, 1992); Daniel Levine, *Popular Voices in Latin American Catholicism* (Princeton: Princeton University Press, 1992); Susan Epstein, ed., *Power and Popular Protest: Latin American Social Movements* (Berkeley: University of California Press, 1989); Scott Mainwaring and Alexander Wilde, eds., *The Progressive Church in Latin America* (Notre Dame: University of Notre Dame Press, 1989); and M. Bruneau et al., eds., *The Catholic Church and Religions in Latin America* (Montreal: McGill University Press, 1984).

3. "Pope John Paul II to CELAM: The Task of the Latin American Bishop," *Origins* 12 (March 24, 1983).

4. Ibid., 661.

5. *Documento de Consulta: Nueva Evangelización, Promoción Humana, Cultura Cristiana* (Santo Domingo: IV Conferencia General del Episcopado Latinoamericano, 1991).

6. *Secunda Relatio: Síntesis de Aportes al Documento de Consulta* (Consejo Episcopal Latinoamericano: Santafé de Bogotá, 1992). The first part of the title is not Spanish, but Latin. According to the *Oxford Latin Dictionary* (New York: Oxford University Press, 1982), 1604, *relatio* has seven meanings. The one that seemed to fit the present context is "the relating of (events, etc.) in words, narration, recital." Thus, I have translated *relatio* by the English word "report."

7. *Documento de Trabajo: Nueva Evangelización, Promoción Humana y Cultura Cristiana* (Consejo Episcopal Latinoamericano: Santafé de Bogotá, 1992).

8. See Leslie Wirpsa, "Curia Ignites Angry Protest at CELAM IV," *National Catholic Reporter* (November 6, 1992), and Gary MacEoin, ibid. (November 13, 1992); also Peter Steinfels, "CELAM & the Vatican: A Preferential Option for Dickering," *Commonweal* (November 20, 1992), 5–6.

9. See *Mensajes del Santo Padre Juan Pablo II* (Santo Domingo: Ediciones MSC, 1992), 39–62. The English translation of the inaugural discourse may be found in *Origins* 22 (October 22, 1992), 321–32.

10. *Santo Domingo Conclusiones: IV Conferencia General del Episcopado Latinoamericano (Octubre 12–28 de 1992)* (Colombia: Ediciones Paulinas, 1992).

11. *30 Days* (November 11, 1992).

12. Ibid., 24.

13. Peter Steinfels, *Commonweal* (November 20, 1992), 6.

14. Ibid.

15. *30 Days*, 25.

16. Ibid.

17. Ibid., 25–26.

18. "Informe de AMERINDIA sobre la IV Conferencia del Episcopado de A.L. y del Caribe en Santo Domingo," 1–2. All these documents were Xerox copies.

19. "Documento no. 3: Interpretación del Documento Final en el Contexto Amplio de Santo Domingo," 2.

20. "Documento no. 4: Criterios para leer el Documento de Santo Domingo," 2.

21. Ibid.

22. Ibid.

23. "Documento no. 1: Cronología de la IV Conferencia de Santo Domingo," 9–10.

24. Ibid., 10.

25. *Second Report*, 18.

26. Ibid., 18–36.

27. Ibid., 19.

28. *Santo Domingo Conclusiones*, 60–62.

29. *Second Report*, 37.

30. Ibid., 62.

31. Ibid.

32. Ibid., 150. See also p. 115: "It is necessary to affirm that the theology of

liberation continues to be a source of reflection that brings life and hope to many people in Latin America. There can be no New Evangelization if there is no authentic and integral liberation."

33. Ibid., 92.
34. Ibid., 100.
35. Ibid., 147.
36. Ibid., 167.

Part II

SANTO DOMINGO:

DOCUMENTS

Translated by Phillip Berryman

Letter of Pope John Paul II to the Bishops of Latin America

To the Diocesan Bishops of Latin America

On the occasion of the Fifth Centenary of the Evangelization of America, I convoked the Fourth General Conference of the Latin American Episcopate, whose goal was to study, in the light of Christ, "the same yesterday, today, and forever" (Heb 13:8), the great themes of the new evangelization, human development, and Christian culture.

Divine Providence gave me the consolation of being able personally to inaugurate this assembly in Santo Domingo on 12 October. On the 28th of that same month the Conference's work was finished, and the presidents sent me the conclusions that the bishops present had drafted.

I was greatly pleased to see the profound pastoral concern with which my brothers in the Episcopate examined the topics that I had proposed, in order to contribute to the development of the life of the Church in Latin America in view of the present and the future.

The final texts of this Conference, whose publication I have authorized, can now give direction to the pastoral work of each diocesan bishop in Latin America. Each diocesan pastor, together with his priests, "his co-workers" (cf. *Lumen Gentium*, 28), and the other members of the particular Church that has been entrusted to him, will make the discernment necessary to see what is most useful and urgent in the particular situation of his diocese.

A broad consensus among the bishops of the particular Churches in a given country could also lead to joint pastoral formulas or plans, always with respect for the identity of each diocese and the pastoral authority of the bishop, who is the visible center of unity and, at the same time, its hierarchical bond with the Successor of Peter and the universal Church (cf. *Lumen Gentium*, 23).

As is obvious, the Conclusions of the Santo Domingo Conference must be analyzed in the light of the magisterium of the universal Church and should be implemented in fidelity to existing canonical discipline.

For my part, I trust that the pastoral solicitude of the bishops of Latin America will give all the particular Churches of the continent a renewed commitment to the new evangelization, human development, and the Christian culture.

May Jesus Christ, our Lord, Evangelizer and Savior, be at the center of the Church's life today, as yesterday and forever.

May the Virgin most holy, who was always at the side of her divine Son, accompany the pastors and faithful in their pilgrimage toward the Lord.

From the Vatican, 10 November 1992,
memorial of St. Leo the Great, Pope and Doctor of the Church

JOHN PAUL II

Opening Address of the Holy Father

1. Under the guidance of the Spirit, to whom we have fervently appealed to enlighten the work of this important ecclesial assembly, we are inaugurating the Fourth General Conference of the Latin American Episcopate. In doing so, we turn our eyes and our hearts to Jesus Christ, "the same yesterday, today, and forever" (Heb 13:8). He is the beginning and end, the Alpha and Omega (cf. Rv 21:6), the fullness of evangelization, "the very first and the greatest evangelizer; he was so through and through: to perfection and to the point of the sacrifice of his earthly life" (*Evangelii Nuntiandi*, 7).

In this ecclesial gathering, we have a very vivid sense of the presence of Jesus Christ, Lord of history. In his name, the bishops of Latin America met at their previous assemblies: Rio de Janeiro (1955); Medellín (1968); and Puebla (1979). In his name, we are now meeting in Santo Domingo to deal with the issues of "New Evangelization, Human Development, Christian Culture," which encompass the major challenges that the Church will be confronting due to the new situations emerging in Latin America and around the world.

This is a time of grace, my dear brothers, for all of us and for the Church in the Americas. Indeed, it is a time of grace for the universal Church, which is accompanying us with its prayer and with that deep communion of hearts that the Holy Spirit engenders in all the members of the one body of Christ. It is a time of grace and of great responsibility. The third millennium is now within sight. If divine providence has called us together so that we may give thanks to God for the five hundred years of faith and Christian life on the American continent, it is perhaps even more true to say that we have been called together for interior renewal, to "judge the signs of the times" (Mt 16:3). Indeed, the call to the new evangelization is first and foremost a call to conversion. For through the witness of a Church that is ever more faithful to its own identity and that manifests itself with ever greater vitality, the individuals and peoples of Latin America and of the whole world will be able to continue finding Jesus Christ, and in him the truth of their calling and their hope, and the way to a nobler humanity.

Looking toward Christ, keeping "our eyes fixed on Jesus, the leader and perfecter of faith" (Heb 12:2), we follow the path traced by the Second Vatican Council. The thirtieth anniversary of its solemn inauguration was yesterday. Hence, in inaugurating this splendid assembly, I want to recall

41

those heartfelt words pronounced by my venerable predecessor Pope Paul VI at the opening of the second session of the council:

> Christ!
> Christ, our beginning.
> Christ, our life and our guide.
> Christ, our hope and our end. ...
> May no other light hover over this assembly
> than that of Christ, light of the world.
> May no other truth draw our minds,
> than the words of the Lord, our one Master.
> May no other hope sustain us,
> than that which bolsters our weakness through his
>   word.

I. JESUS CHRIST, YESTERDAY, TODAY, AND FOREVER

2. This conference is meeting to celebrate Jesus Christ, to thank God for his presence in these lands of the Americas, where the message of salvation began to spread five hundred years ago. It is meeting to celebrate the planting of the Church, which has furnished the New World with such abundant fruits of holiness and love during these five centuries.

Jesus Christ is the eternal truth who became manifest in the fullness of time. It was specifically to transmit the good news to all peoples that he founded his Church with the specific mission to evangelize: "Go into the whole world and proclaim the Gospel to every creature" (Mk 16:15). These words can be said to contain the solemn proclamation of evangelization. Thus, the Church began the great task of evangelization on the day when the apostles received the Holy Spirit. St. Paul expresses it in a crisp, emblematic expression: *"Evangelizare Iesum Christum,"* "to proclaim Jesus Christ" (Gal 1:16). This is what the disciples of the Lord have done in all ages and throughout the world.

3. The year 1492 marks a key date in this unique process. On October 12 — exactly five centuries ago today — Admiral Christopher Columbus, with the three caravels from Spain, arrived at these lands and planted the cross of Christ. Nevertheless, strictly speaking, evangelization began with the second journey of the explorers, who were accompanied by the first missionaries. Thus, began the sowing of the precious gift of faith. How can we fail to thank God for that, along with you, my dear brother bishops, you who today embody in Santo Domingo all the particular churches of Latin America! How can we fail to give thanks for the abundant fruits of the seed sown over the course of these five centuries by so many dauntless missionaries!

With the coming of the gospel to the Americas, the history of salvation expands, the family of God grows and multiplies "so that the grace bestowed in abundance on more and more people may cause the thanksgiving to overflow for the glory of God" (2 Cor 4:15). The peoples of the New World were "new peoples . . . entirely unknown to the Old World until 1492," but they were "known to God from all eternity, and he had embraced them with the Fatherhood that the Son had revealed in the fullness of time (cf. Gal 4:4)" (*Homily*, January 1, 1992). In the peoples of the Americas, God has chosen for himself a new people whom he has brought into his redemptive plan and made sharers in his Spirit. Through evangelization and faith in Christ, God has renewed his covenant with Latin America.

Thus, we thank God for the throng of evangelizers who had to leave their homeland and who gave their life in order to sow the new life of faith, hope, and love in the New World. They were not drawn by the legend of El Dorado or personal interests, but by the pressing call to evangelize some brothers and sisters who did not yet know Jesus Christ. They proclaimed "the kindness and generous love of God our savior" (Ti 3:4) to peoples, some of whom even offered human sacrifices to their gods. With their lives and their word, they gave witness to that humanity that results from encounter with Christ. By their witness and their preaching, the number of men and women who were opened to the grace of Christ multiplied like "the stars in the sky and as countless as the sands on the seashore" (Heb 11:12).

4. Since the first steps of evangelization, the Catholic Church, prompted by fidelity to the Spirit of Christ, has been a tireless defender of the Indians, a protector of the values present in their cultures and a promoter of humane treatment in the face of the abuses of sometimes unscrupulous colonizers. The denunciation of injustices and abuses through the work of Montesinos, las Casas, Córdoba, Fray Juan del Valle, and so many others was like a cry that led to laws based on acknowledgment of the sacred value of the person. The Christian conscience flourished with prophetic courage in that cathedral of dignity and freedom known as the School of Vitoria at the University of Salamanca (cf. *Speech*, May 14, 1992) and in so many outstanding defenders of the natives in both Spain and Latin America. Their names are well known, and they have been recalled with admiration and gratitude on the occasion of the fifth centenary anniversary.

I myself suggested that an international symposium be held on the history of the evangelization of the Americas, organized by the Pontifical Commission for Latin America, to determine the outlines of historical truth, placing in relief the continent's Christian roots and Catholic identity. The data of history show that a valid, fruitful, and admirable labor of evangelization took place, thereby opening the way to the truth about God and the human being in the Americas — so much so, indeed, that the evangelization itself became a kind of tribunal for holding accountable those responsible for such abuses.

I have been able to witness the fruitfulness of the gospel seed deposited in these blessed lands during the apostolic journeys that the Lord has allowed me to make to your particular churches. How can I fail to show openly my ardent gratitude to God, for I have been allowed to become familiar with the living reality of the Church in Latin America! On my journeys to this continent and on your *ad limina* visits as well as in various other encounters—which have strengthened the bonds of episcopal collegiality and shared responsibility in pastoral care for the whole Church—I have been able to verify many times the vitality of the faith of your ecclesial communities. I have also been able to measure the breadth of the challenges facing the Church, which is inseparably linked to the fate of the peoples of the continent.

5. This general conference is meeting to trace guidelines for an evangelizing activity that will place Christ in the heart and on the lips of all Latin Americans. This is our task: to make the truth about Christ and the truth about the human being penetrate ever more deeply into all strata of society and to transform it (cf. *Speech to the Pontifical Commission for Latin America*, June 14, 1991).

In its deliberations and conclusions, this conference must know how to combine the three doctrinal and pastoral elements that constitute the three axes of the new evangelization: Christology, ecclesiology, and anthropology. The challenges to the Church's evangelizing activity in the Americas today must be met through a deep and solid Christology, and on the basis of a sound anthropology and a clear and correct ecclesiological vision. As a sign of deep communion and shared responsibility for the Church, I now want to share with you some observations along the lines of the conference's main themes that may be of help in your ministry as pastors generously committed to the flock that the Lord has entrusted to you. My intention is to present some doctrinal and pastoral priorities from the standpoint of the new evangelization.

II. NEW EVANGELIZATION

6. The new evangelization is the central idea within the whole set of issues to be addressed in this conference.

Since my meeting in Haiti with the bishops of CELAM in 1983, I have been giving particular emphasis to this expression in order to arouse a new fervor and new concerns for evangelization in the Americas and the whole world, that is, in order to give pastoral work "a fresh forward impulse, capable of creating, with a Church still more firmly rooted in the undying power and strength of Pentecost, a new period of evangelization" (*Evangelii Nuntiandi*, 2).

The new evangelization does not consist in a "new gospel," which would always arise from ourselves, our culture, our analysis of human need. Hence, it would not be "gospel" but mere human invention, and there would be no salvation in it. Nor does it consist of trimming away from the gospel everything that seems difficult for the contemporary mind-set to accept. Culture is not the measure of the gospel; rather Jesus Christ is the measure of all culture and all human endeavor. No, the new evangelization does not arise from the desire "to curry favor with human beings" or to "please people" (Gal 1:10), but from responsibility for the gift that God has made to us in Christ, in which we accede to the truth about God and about the human being, and to the possibility of true life.

The starting point for the new evangelization is the certainty that in Christ are "inscrutable riches" (Eph 3:8) that are not exhausted by any culture or any age and that we human beings can always approach in order to be enriched (cf. *Final Declaration* of the Special Assembly for Europe of the Synod of Bishops, 3). That wealth is first and foremost Christ himself, his person, for he himself is our salvation. By approaching him through faith and being incorporated into his body, which is the Church, we human beings of any period and any culture can find the answer to those ever old and ever new questions with which we human beings face the mystery of our existence and which we bear indelibly engraved in our hearts from creation and from the wound of sin.

7. Newness does not touch the content of the gospel message, which is unchangeable, for Christ is the same "yesterday, today and forever" (Heb 13:8). Hence, the gospel is to be preached with complete faithfulness and purity as it has been guarded and transmitted by the tradition of the Church. To evangelize is to announce a person, who is Christ. Indeed, "there is no true evangelization if the name, the teaching, the life, the promises, the kingdom and the mystery of Jesus of Nazareth, the Son of God, are not proclaimed" (*Evangelii Nuntiandi*, 22). Hence, reductive Christologies, whose errors I have pointed out on several occasions (cf. *Opening Address*, Puebla Conference [January 28, 1979], I, 4), cannot be accepted as instruments for the new evangelization. When evangelization takes place, the unity of the Church's faith must shine forth not only in the authentic magisterium of the bishops but also in service to truth by pastors of souls, theologians, catechists and all those who are committed to proclaiming and preaching the faith.

In this regard, the Church stimulates, esteems, and respects the vocation of the theologian, whose "role is to pursue in a particular way an ever deeper understanding of the word of God contained in the inspired Scriptures and handed on by the living tradition of the Church" (Congregation for the Doctrine of the Faith, instruction, *On the Ecclesial Vocation of the Theologian* [May 24, 1990], 6). That noble and necessary vocation arises within the Church and presumes that the theologian is a believer and has an attitude of faith to which he or she must bear witness in the community. "The right conscience of the Catholic theologian presumes not only faith in the word of God . . . but also love for the Church, from whom he receives his mission, and respect for her divinely assisted magisterium" (ibid., 38).

Theology is thus called to provide a great service to the new evangelization.

8. Certainly, it is the truth that makes us free (cf. Jn 8:32). However, we must certainly point out that some positions on what constitutes truth, freedom, and conscience are unacceptable. Some have even gone so far as to justify dissent by invoking "theological pluralism sometimes to the point of a relativism which calls the integrity of the faith into question." Some think that "the documents of the magisterium reflect nothing more than a debatable theology" (ibid., 34); "in opposition to and in competition with the authentic magisterium, there thus arises a kind of 'parallel magisterium' of theologians" (ibid.). Furthermore, we cannot ignore the fact that "attitudes of general opposition to church teaching which even come to expression in organized groups," contestation and discord, besides "presenting serious harm to the community of the Church," are also an obstacle to evangelization (cf. ibid., 32).

The confession of faith "Jesus Christ yesterday, today, and forever," found in the Letter to the Hebrews—which is, as it were, the backdrop of the topic of this fourth conference—draws our attention to the words of the next verse: "Do not be carried away by all kinds of strange teaching" (Heb 13:9). You, beloved pastors, have to be especially watchful for the faith of simple people lest it be disoriented and confused.

9. All evangelizers must also pay particular attention to catechesis. At the outset of my pontificate, I sought to give new impetus to this pastoral work with the apostolic exhortation *Catechesi Tradendae*, and recently I have approved the *Catechism of the Catholic Church*, which I present as the best gift that the Church can make to its bishops and to the entire people of God. It is a valuable tool for the new evangelization, compiling all the doctrine that the Church must teach.

I likewise trust that the biblical movement will continue to provide its benefits in Latin America and that Sacred Scripture will increasingly nourish the life of the faithful. To that end, it is essential that pastoral agents tirelessly delve more deeply into the word of God, living it and transmitting it to others faithfully, that is, taking into account "the living tradition of the whole Church . . . along with the harmony which exists between elements of the faith" (*Dei Verbum*, 12). Likewise, the liturgical movement must give a renewed impetus to the inner experience of the mysteries of our faith, leading to the encounter with the risen Christ in the Church's liturgy. It is in the celebration of the word and the sacraments, but especially in the eucharist, the apex and source of the Church's life and of all evangelization, that there is effected our saving encounter with Christ, to whom we are mystically united and become his Church (cf. *Lumen Gentium*, 7). Therefore, I exhort you to give a new impetus to the respectful, vital, and participatory celebration of liturgical assemblies, with that profound sense of faith and contemplation of the mysteries of salvation that is so rooted in your peoples.

10. The newness of the evangelizing activity that we have called for is a

matter of attitude, style, effort, and planning, or as I proposed in Haiti, of ardor, methods, and expression (cf. *Address* to Bishops of CELAM, March 9, 1983). An evangelization new in its ardor means a solid faith, an intense pastoral charity, and a steadfast fidelity, that under the action of the Spirit generate a spirituality, an irrepressible enthusiasm for the task of announcing the gospel. In New Testament terminology, it is that "parrhesia" that ignites the apostle's heart (cf. Acts 5:28-29; cf. *Redemptoris Missio*, 45). This parrhesia must also be the seal of your apostolate in the Americas. No one can silence you, for you are heralds of truth. The truth of Christ must enlighten your minds and hearts with the active, tireless, and public proclamation of Christian values.

However, the new times demand that the Christian message reach people today through new methods of apostolate and that it be expressed in language and forms that are accessible to Latin Americans, who need Christ and thirst for the gospel. How does one make accessible, penetrating, valid, and deep the response to people today without in any way altering or changing the content of the gospel message? How does one reach the heart of the culture that we want to evangelize? How does one speak of God in a world in which there is a growing process of secularization?

11. As you have indicated in the meetings and conversations that we have held during these years both in Rome and in my visits to your particular churches, today the simple faith of your peoples is being assaulted by secularization, with the consequent weakening of religious and moral values. In urban environments there is a growing cultural tendency to trust only in science and technological progress and to be hostile to faith. Certain "models" of life are pitted against gospel values. Under the pressure of secularism, some even treat faith as though it were a threat to human freedom and autonomy.

Nevertheless, we cannot forget that recent history has demonstrated that when the truth about God and the truth about the human being are denied, under the cover of certain ideologies, it becomes impossible to build a society with a human face. It is to be hoped that the fall of those regimes of so-called real socialism in Eastern Europe will lead people in this continent to realize that the value of such ideologies is ephemeral. The roots of the crisis of Marxist collectivism have not been merely economic, since the truth about the human being is necessarily very closely connected to the truth about God, as I have emphasized in the encyclical *Centesimus Annus* (41).

The new evangelization must therefore be a response that is integral, timely, and flexible, that strengthens the Catholic faith in its fundamental truths and in its individual, family, and societal dimensions.

12. Like the Good Shepherd, you are to feed the flock entrusted to you and defend it from rapacious wolves. A source of division and discord in your ecclesial communities are — as you well know — the sects and "pseudospiritual" movements mentioned in the *Puebla Conclusions* (628), whose

aggressiveness and expansion must be faced. As many of you have pointed out, the advance of the sects highlights a pastoral vacuum, often caused by a lack of formation that leads to the undermining of Christian identity. A further effect is that large masses of Catholics who are without adequate religious attention — among other reasons because of a shortage of priests — are at the mercy of very active sectarian proselytizing campaigns. It may also happen, however, that the faithful do not find in pastoral agents that strong sense of God that such agents should be transmitting in their lives. "Such situations may be the occasion for many poor and simple persons to become easy prey for the sects, as unfortunately is happening. In the sects, they are looking for a religious meaning to life that they perhaps do not find in those who should be abundant examples of it" (apostolic letter, *Los Caminos del Evangelio,* 20).

Moreover, we should not underestimate a particular strategy aimed at weakening the bonds that unite Latin American countries and so to undermine the kinds of strength provided by unity. To that end, significant amounts of money are offered to subsidize proselytizing campaigns that try to shatter such Catholic unity.

The worrisome phenomenon of the sects must be countered with pastoral action centered on the whole person, on his or her communal dimension and yearning for a personal relationship with God. It is a fact that where the Church's presence is dynamic, such as in parishes where there is a steady formation in the word of God; where the liturgy is active and people participate; where there is a solid Marian piety, true solidarity in the social field, a notable pastoral concern for the family, youth, and the sick, we see that the sects or parareligious movements do not become established or do not make progress.

Because of its eminently Catholic roots, the deep-seated popular religiosity of your faithful, with its extraordinary values of faith and piety, of sacrifice and solidarity, when properly evangelized and joyfully celebrated and directed toward the mysteries of Christ and the Virgin Mary, may serve as antidote to the sects and help safeguard fidelity to the message of salvation.

III. HUMAN DEVELOPMENT

13. Since the Church is aware that the human being — not an abstract being, but the concrete human being in history — "is the route that it must traverse in carrying out its mission" (*Redemptor Hominis,* 14), stimulating human development must be the logical outcome of evangelization, which tends toward the comprehensive liberation of the person (cf. *Evangelii Nuntiandi,* 29-39).

When you look at this concrete human being, pastors of the Church, you are well aware how problematic is the current social condition of Latin

America, where large segments of the population are poor and excluded. Accordingly, in solidarity with the cry of the poor, you feel called to act as the good Samaritan (cf. Lk 10:25-37), since love for God is shown in love for the human person. The apostle James thus reminds us with those very serious words, "If a brother or sister has nothing to wear and no food for the day, and one of you says to them, 'Go in peace, keep warm and eat well,' but you do not give them the bodily necessities, what good is it?" (Jas 2:15-16).

Concern for the social dimension is "part of the Church's evangelizing mission" (*Sollicitudo Rei Socialis*, 41) and is also "an essential part of the Christian message, since this doctrine points out the direct consequences of that message in the life of society and situates daily work and struggles for justice in the context of bearing witness to Christ the savior" (*Centesimus Annus*, 5).

As Vatican Council II states in the pastoral constitution *Gaudium et Spes*, the problem of human development cannot be considered apart from human relationship with God (cf. nos. 43, 45). Indeed, to pit authentic human development and God's plan for humankind against one another is a grave distortion, the product of a secularistic cast of thought. Genuine efforts at human betterment must always respect the truth about God and the truth about the human being, and respect both God's rights and the rights of the human being.

14. Beloved pastors, you are in close contact with the anguished situation of so many brothers and sisters who lack what is needed for a genuinely human life. Despite progress in some fields, poverty remains a reality and is even increasing. Problems are mounting with the decline in purchasing power of money due to sometimes uncontrolled inflation and deteriorating trade relations, with consequent lower prices paid for certain raw materials and the crushing weight of international debt, whose social consequences are so dreadful. The serious problem of growing unemployment adds to the suffering by preventing people from putting bread on the table and blocking their access to other basic goods (cf. *Laborem Exercens*, 18).

Since I am vividly aware of how serious this situation is, I have continually issued calls for an active, just, and urgent international solidarity. This duty of justice applies to the whole of humankind, but especially to the rich countries, which cannot shirk their responsibility toward developing countries. Such solidarity is a demand of the universal common good that ought to command respect from all members of the human family (cf. *Gaudium et Spes*, 26).

15. The world cannot feel serene and satisfied in the face of the chaotic and disturbing scene we see before us: nations, segments of the population, families, and individuals growing ever richer and more privileged opposite peoples, families, and a vast number of individuals mired in poverty, victims of hunger and illness who lack decent housing, sanitation, and access to culture. All of that eloquently testifies to a real disorder and an institu-

tionalized injustice. Sometimes it is augmented by delays in taking the required measures, inertia and imprudence, or even the violation of ethical principles in administration, as in the case of corruption. All of this requires "changes of mentality, behavior and structures" (*Centesimus Annus*, 60) so as to bridge the chasm between the rich and poor countries (cf. *Laborem Exercens*, 16; *Centesimus Annus*, 14) as well as the profound differences among citizens of the same country. In short, the new ideal of solidarity must come to prevail over the obsolescent will to dominate.

However, the proposal to resolve the problem by reducing demographic growth without any concern for the morality of the means employed for that purpose is deceptive and unacceptable. The point is not to reduce at any cost the number of those invited to the banquet of life; what is needed is to augment resources and distribute wealth with greater justice so that all may participate equitably in the goods of creation.

Solutions must be sought on a worldwide scale by establishing a true economy of communion and participation in goods on both international and national levels. In that regard, one factor that can make a notable contribution to overcoming the pressing problems today affecting this continent is Latin American integration. Those in charge of governments have a grave responsibility to promote the process — already under way — of integrating peoples whom a common geography, the Christian faith, language and culture have already drawn together in the course of history.

16. In continuity with the Medellín and Puebla conferences, the church reaffirms the preferential option on behalf of the poor. That option is not exclusive or excluding, since the message of salvation is intended for all. It is "an option, moreover, that is based essentially on God's word, and not on criteria provided by human sciences or opposed ideologies, which often reduce the poor to abstract sociopolitical and economic categories. But it is a firm and irrevocable option" (*Address to the Roman Curia* [December 21, 1984], 9).

As the *Puebla Conclusions* says, "When we draw near to the poor in order to accompany them and serve them, we are doing what Christ taught us to do when he became our brother, poor like us. Hence, service to the poor is the privileged, though not the exclusive, gauge of our following of Christ. The best service to our fellows is evangelization, which disposes them to fulfill themselves as children of God, liberates them from injustices, and fosters their integral advancement" (*Puebla Conclusions*, 1145). Such gospel criteria for service to the needy will avoid any temptation toward complicity with those responsible for the causes of poverty or dangerous ideological deviations that are incompatible with the Church's doctrine and mission.

The genuine praxis of liberation must always be inspired by the doctrine of the Church as set forth in the two instructions by the Congregation for the Doctrine of Faith (*Libertatis Nuntius*, 1984; *Libertatis Conscientia*, 1986), which must be kept in mind when the topic of liberation theologies comes up for discussion. However, the Church can in no way allow any ideology or political current to snatch away the banner of justice, for it is one of the primary demands of the gospel and, at the same time, a fruit of the coming of God's kingdom.

17. As the *Puebla Conclusions* already pointed out, some human groups are especially mired in poverty; such is the case of indigenous people (cf. 1265). It has been my intention to deliver a special message expressing solidarity and closeness to them as well as to African Americans. I will give that message tomorrow to a group of representatives of their communities. As a gesture of solidarity, the Holy See has recently created the *Populorum Progressio* Foundation, which has a special fund for small farmers, Indians, and other human groups in the rural sector, who are especially vulnerable in Latin America.

In this same line of pastoral care for the most vulnerable groups of people, this general conference might consider the desirability of celebrating in the near future a meeting of representatives of the episcopacies of the Americas—which might even have a synodal character—in order to increase cooperation among the various local churches in different fields of pastoral action. In the framework of the new evangelization and as an expression of episcopal communion, such a meeting could also deal with issues of justice and solidarity among all the nations of the Americas. On the threshold of the third Christian millennium and after the fall of many ideological barriers and borders, the Church feels that it has an inescapable duty to unite even more closely all the peoples that make up this great continent. It likewise feels that its own religious mission requires it to give impetus to a spirit of solidarity among all of them, particularly in finding ways to solve the dramatic situations of the vast sectors of the population who aspire to a legitimate overall progress and more just and decent living conditions.

18. There is no genuine human development, true liberation, or preferential option for the poor unless it is based on the very foundations of the dignity of the person and of the surroundings in which the person must develop, according to the Creator's design. Hence, among the topics and options that require the entire attention of the Church, I cannot fail to recall those of the family and of life: two things that are closely interrelated, since the family is "the sanctuary of life" (*Centesimus Annus*, 39). Indeed, "the future of humankind is forged in the family; hence, every person of good will must by all means strive to save and promote family values and requirements" (*Familiaris Consortio*, 86).

Despite the problems now besieging marriage and the institution of the family, it can still serve as the "first and vital cell of society" (*Apostolicam Actuositatem*, 11); it can create great energies that are necessary for the good of humankind. Hence, we must "proclaim with joy and conviction the 'good news' on the family" (*Familiaris Consortio*, 86). That good news must be announced here in Latin America, where alongside the high regard shown for the family, common-law arrangements are unfortunately very widespread. In view of this reality and the growing pressures in favor of divorce, it is necessary to promote adequate measures on behalf of the family core in order to safeguard the stability of the union of life and love within marriage in accordance with God's plan, and a suitable education for the children.

Closely connected to this problem is the serious phenomenon of street children in large Latin American cities, whose lives are sapped by hunger and disease and who are vulnerable and subjected to so many dangers, including drugs and prostitution. Here is yet another issue that must compel your pastoral concern, recalling Jesus' words: "Let the children come to me" (Mt 19:14).

Life, from its conception in the mother's womb until its natural end, must be defended firmly and courageously. There must be created in the Americas a culture of life that can counter the anti-culture of death that threatens to prevail in some nations, as manifested in abortion, euthanasia, war, guerrilla warfare, kidnapping, terrorism, and other forms of violence or exploitation. Within this spectrum of assaults against life, drug trafficking stands at the fore, and those in authority must counter it with all available lawful means.

19. Who will deliver us from these signs of death? The experience of the contemporary world has increasingly demonstrated that ideologies cannot overthrow the evil that holds human beings in bondage. The only one who can free from this evil is Christ. As we celebrate five centuries of evangelization, we turn our gaze with feeling toward that moment of grace when Christ was given to us once and for all. The painful situation of so many of our Latin American sisters and brothers does not lead us to despair. On the contrary, it makes more urgent the task confronting the Church: to reawaken within the heart of each baptized person the grace that has been received. "For this reason I remind you," wrote St. Paul to Timothy, "to stir into flame the gift of God that you have through the imposition of my hands" (2 Tm 1:6).

Just as the people of the new covenant were born in the acceptance of the Holy Spirit at Pentecost, so only will that acceptance be able to bring forth a people capable of generating renewed and free human beings conscious of their dignity. We cannot forget that comprehensive human advancement is critically important for the development of the peoples of Latin America. For "a people's development does not derive primarily from money, material assistance or technological means, but from the formation of consciences and the gradual maturing of ways of thinking and patterns of behavior. The human being is the principal agent of development, not money or technology" (*Redemptoris Missio*, 58). Latin America's greatest wealth is its peoples. By "awakening their consciences through the gospel," the Church contributes to the awakening of dormant energies that can be put to work in building a new civilization (cf. ibid.).

IV. CHRISTIAN CULTURE

20. Although the gospel is not identified with any particular culture, it certainly should provide cultures with inspiration to transform themselves from within by enriching them with the Christian values that derive from faith. Indeed, the evangelization of cultures represents the deepest and most comprehensive way to evangelize a society, since the message of Christ thereby permeates people's awareness and is projected into the "ethos" of a people, its essential attitudes, its institutions and all its structures (cf. *Address to Medellín Intellectuals and to the University World* [July 5, 1986], 2).

CELAM has devoted considerable study and reflection to the topic of "culture" in recent years. The Church also directs its attention to this important topic "since the new evangelization must be projected toward the 'coming' culture, toward all cultures, including indigenous cultures" (cf. *Angelus*, June 28, 1992). To proclaim Jesus Christ in all cultures is the Church's central concern and the object of its mission. In our time, it demands, first, that cultures be discerned as a human reality to be evangelized and, consequently, the pressing need for a new kind of collaboration among all those responsible for the work of evangelization.

21. In our day, we can see a cultural crisis of unsuspected dimensions. It is true that the existing cultural substratum offers a good number of positive values, many of them the result of evangelization. At the same time, however, it has eliminated fundamental religious values and has introduced deceitful notions that from a Christian standpoint are unacceptable.

The absence of those fundamental Christian values in the culture of modernity has not only obscured the transcendent dimension and inclined many people—even in Latin America—toward religious indifference, but it is also the key reason for the social disillusionment that has given rise to the crisis of that culture. As a result of the autonomy introduced by rationalism, today values tend to be based primarily on a subjective social consensus that often leads to positions contrary even to natural ethics. Consider the drama of abortion, abuses in genetic engineering, and attacks on life and on the dignity of the person.

The plurality of options available today demands that there be a deep pastoral renewal through the gospel discernment of the prevailing values, attitudes, and collective behavior patterns which often are a decisive factor in choosing either good or evil. Our times require special effort and sensitivity in order to inculturate the message of Jesus in such a way that Christian values can transform the various focal points of culture, purifying them if necessary, and making possible the consolidation of a Christian culture that can renew, extend, and unify past and present historic values so as to respond adequately to the challenges of our time (cf. *Redemptoris Missio*, 52). One such challenge to evangelization is that of intensifying the dialogue between the sciences and faith so as to create a true Christian humanism. The point is to show that science and technology help civilize and humanize the world insofar as they are imbued with the wisdom of God. In this regard, I want to encourage actively universities and centers of advanced study, and particularly those that belong to the Church, to renew their efforts in the dialogue between faith and science.

22. The Church views with concern the split existing between gospel values and modern cultures, for these cultures run the risk of turning inward in a kind of agnostic self-enclosure with no reference to the moral dimension (cf. *Address to the Pontifical Council for Culture*, January 18, 1983). In this regard, Pope Paul VI's words retain all their validity: "The rift between the gospel and culture is undoubtedly an unhappy circumstance of our times, just as it has been in other eras. Accordingly, we must devote all our resources and all our efforts to sedulous evangelization of human culture or, rather, of the various human cultures. They must be regenerated through contact with the gospel. But this contact cannot be effected unless the good news is proclaimed" (*Evangelii Nuntiandi*, 20).

The Church, which regards the human being as its "way" (cf. *Redemptor Hominis*, 14), must know how to respond adequately to the present crisis of culture. In response to the complex phenomenon of modernity, there must be generated a cultural alternative that is fully Christian. If true culture expresses the universal values of the person, what can project more light on the situation of human beings, their dignity and purpose, their freedom and destiny than the gospel of Christ?

At this moment, marking a half-millennium of the evangelization of your peoples, I invite you, dear brothers, with the ardor of the new evangelization and animated by the Spirit of Christ, to make the Church present at the cultural crossroads of our time, in order to imbue with Christian values the very roots of the "coming" culture and of all existing cultures. In this regard, you must devote special attention to indigenous and African American cultures, drawing on and highlighting everything that is deeply human and humanizing within them. Their view of life, which acknowledges the sacredness of the human being, their deep respect for nature, and their humility, simplicity, and solidarity are values that must stimulate the effort to carry out a genuine inculturated evangelization, one that also promotes progress and leads always to the adoration of God "in spirit and truth" (Jn 4:23). Acknowledging such values, however, does not exempt you from proclaiming at all times that "Christ is the one savior of all, the only one able to reveal God and lead to God" (*Redemptoris Missio*, 5).

"The evangelization of culture is an effort to understand the mind-sets and attitudes of the contemporary world and to shine the light of the gospel on them. It is the intention to reach all levels of human life in order to make it more worthy" (*Address to the World of Culture*, Lima, May 15, 1988). However, this effort at understanding and shedding light must always be accompanied by the proclamation of the good news (cf. *Redemptoris Missio*,

46). Thus, the gospel's penetration of cultures will not be a mere external adaptation, but a "a profound and all-embracing one, which involves the Christian message and also the Church's reflection and practice" (ibid., 52), and will always respect the characteristics and integrity of the faith.

23. Since communication between persons is an important aspect of the creation of culture, modern mass media are extremely important in this regard. It must certainly be one of your priorities to intensify the Church's presence in the world of the media. I am reminded of the ominous words of my venerated predecessor, Pope Paul VI: "The Church would feel guilty before God if she did not avail herself of those powerful instruments that human skill is constantly developing and perfecting" (*Evangelii Nuntiandi*, 45).

Care must be taken, however, in the use of the media for religious education and the spread of religious culture. This responsibility weighs particularly on publishing houses sponsored by Catholic institutions. They ought "to be the object of particular concern for local ordinaries so that their publications always conform to church teaching and make an effective contribution to the good of souls" (Congregation for the Doctrine of the Faith, instruction, *On Some Aspects of the Use of the Instruments of Social Communication in Promoting the Doctrine of the Faith* [March 30, 1992], 15, 2).

Certain social and cultural phenomena emerging to defend human beings and their environment also represent the inculturation of the gospel, and they are to be illuminated by the light of faith. Such is the case of the ecology movement, which advocates according nature its due respect and opposes the disordered exploitation of resources that leads to a deteriorating quality of life. The conviction that "God intended the earth and all that it contains for the use of every human being and people" (*Gaudium et Spes*, 69) must be the inspiration for a system for using resources that is more just and better coordinated on a worldwide scale. The Church endorses concern for the environment and urges governments to protect this inheritance according to the criteria of the common good (cf. *25th World Day of Peace Message*, January 1, 1992).

24. The challenge represented by the "coming" culture does not weaken our hope, however, and we thank God that in Latin America, the gift of Catholic faith has reached very deeply into its peoples, shaping the Christian soul of the continent during these five hundred years and inspiring many of its institutions. The Church in Latin America has indeed been able to make its way into the culture of the people and has known how to place the gospel message at the basis of its thinking, its fundamental principles of life, its criteria for judgment, and its norms for activity.

We now face the formidable challenge of the ongoing inculturation of the gospel in your peoples, a topic that you must take up clearsightedly and in depth during the next few days. Latin America provides an example of a perfectly inculturated evangelization in St. Mary of Guadalupe. Certainly, since the beginning of the Christianization of the New World in the light of the gospel of Jesus, genuine indigenous cultural values have been incarnated in the figure of Mary. In the *mestizo* face of the Virgin of Tepeyac is summed up the great principle of inculturation: the deep transformation of genuine cultural values through their integration into Christianity and the rooting of Christianity in the various cultures (cf. *Redemptoris Missio*, 52).

V. A New Era under the Sign of Hope

25. These then, beloved brothers and sisters, are some of the challenges facing the Church at this moment of new evangelization. Faced with this panorama full of questions but also full of promise, we must ask ourselves what path the Church in Latin America must follow so that in this next stage of its history its mission may produce the fruits that the Lord of the harvest expects (cf. Lk 10:2; Mk 4:20). Your assembly must sketch the countenance of a living and dynamic Church growing in faith, becoming holier, loving, suffering, committing itself and awaiting its Lord, as we are reminded by Vatican II, which is an obligatory reference point in the life and mission of every pastor (cf. *Gaudium et Spes*, 2).

A difficult task awaits you during the next few days, but it is marked by the sign of hope that comes from the risen Christ. It is your mission to be heralds of hope, as the apostle Peter tells us (cf. 1 Pt 3:15). That hope is based on God's promises, in fidelity to his word, and its unshakable certainty is Christ's resurrection, his ultimate victory over sin and death, the primary proclamation and the root of all evangelization, the foundation for all promotion of human development, the principle of all genuine Christian culture, which can only be the culture of resurrection and life enlivened by the breath of the Spirit of Pentecost.

Beloved brothers in the episcopacy, in the unity of the local Church, which springs from the eucharist, is found the whole episcopal college with Peter's successor at its head, as something that belongs to the very essence of the local church (cf. Congregation for the Doctrine of the Faith, *Letter to Bishops on Some Aspects of the Church Understood as Communion*, 14). Parishes and Christian communities are to flourish around the bishop and in perfect communion with him like vigorous cells of diocesan life. Therefore the new evangelization demands that the whole life of the diocese be renewed. Parishes, apostolic movements, associations of the faithful and all ecclesial communities in general must always be evangelized and evangelizing. Basic Christian communities in particular must always be characterized by a decisive universal and missionary thrust that instills in them a renewed apostolic dynamism (cf. *Evangelii Nuntiandi*, 58; *Puebla Conclusions*, 640-642). These communities must be stamped with a clear ecclesial identity and find in the eucharist, presided over by a priest, the center of their life and communion among their members, in close union with their pastors and full harmony with the Church's magisterium.

26. An indispensable condition for the new evangelization is that there be many qualified evangelizers available. Hence, the promotion of priestly and religious vocations as well as those of other pastoral agents must be a priority for bishops and a commitment for the whole people of God. Throughout Latin America, vocational pastoral work must be given a decided impetus, and issues concerning seminaries and training centers for men and women religious must be faced, along with the problem of ongoing training for the clergy and a better distribution of priests among the various local churches, and especially now, the valuable work of permanent deacons. There are appropriate guidelines for all of this in my postsynodal apostolic exhortation, *Pastores Dabo Vobis.*

With regard to men and women religious, who carry the burden of a good deal of the pastoral work in Latin America, I want to mention the apostolic letter *Los Caminos del Evangelio*, which I addressed to them June 29, 1990. Here, I would also like to recall secular institutes, with their dynamic vitality in the midst of the world, and the members of societies of apostolic life, which carry out a vast missionary activity.

Today, the members of religious congregations, both male and female, must be more centered on work that is specifically evangelizing, unfolding the whole wealth of pastoral initiatives and tasks that flow from their various charisms. Faithful to their founders, they must be characterized by a deep sense of church and a witness of close and faithful collaboration in pastoral activity, which is to be under the leadership of diocesan ordinaries, and in particular aspects, of bishops' conferences.

As I recalled in my *Letter to Contemplative Women in Latin America* (December 12, 1989), the Church's evangelizing activity is sustained by such sanctuaries of the contemplative life, which are so numerous throughout the continent. They give witness to the radical nature of consecration to God, which must always be in the forefront of our options.

27. In my postsynodal apostolic exhortation *Christifideles Laici*, on the calling and mission of lay people in the Church, I especially wanted to emphasize that in the "grand, demanding and splendid enterprise" of the new evangelization, the work of lay people, and particularly catechists and "delegates of the word," is indispensable. The Church expects a great deal of all those lay people who, enthusiastically and with the efficacy of the gospel, are involved through the new apostolic movements. Those movements, which reflect the need for a greater presence of the faith in the life of society, must be coordinated by means of overall pastoral planning. At this moment, when I have invited all to work with apostolic zeal in the vineyard of the Lord, without excluding anyone, "lay faithful must feel that they play a vital and responsible role in this enterprise (new evangelization), called as they are to proclaim and live the gospel by serving the values and demands of people and society" (no. 64). The Latin American woman, who

passes on the faith, is worthy of all praise. Her role in the Church and in society must be properly highlighted (cf. apostolic letter, *Mulieris Dignitatem*). Special pastoral concern should be devoted to the sick, bearing in mind the evangelizing power of suffering (cf. apostolic letter, *Salvifici Doloris*, February 11, 1984).

I issue a special call to the youth of Latin America. They—who are so numerous on a continent that is young—will be the protagonists in the life of society and of the Church in the new Christian millennium that is now upon us. The beauty of the Christian calling must be presented to them in their own language, and they must be offered high and noble ideals that can sustain them in their aspirations for a more just and familial society.

28. All are called to build the civilization of love on this continent of hope. Furthermore, Latin America, which has received the faith transmitted by the churches of the Old World, must prepare to spread Christ's message around the world "out of its poverty" (cf. *Messages to the Third and Fourth Latin American Missionary Congresses*, Santa Fe de Bogota [1987] and Lima [1991]). "The moment has come to commit all of the Church's energies to the new evangelization and to the mission *ad gentes*. No believer in Christ, no institution of the Church, can avoid this supreme duty: to proclaim Christ to all peoples" (*Redemptoris Missio*, 3). This moment has also come for Latin America. "Faith is strengthened when it is given to others! The new evangelization of Christian peoples," and in the churches of the Americas, "will find inspiration and support in commitment to the Church's universal mission" (ibid., 2). The greatest sign of gratitude for receiving Christ five hundred years ago and the greatest sign of its Christian vitality is to become committed to mission.

29. Beloved brothers in the episcopacy, as successors of the apostles, you must devote your tireless endeavors to the flock "of which the Holy Spirit has appointed you overseers, in which you tend the Church of God" (Acts 20:28). Moreover, as members of the episcopal college, in true, close, and heartfelt unity with Peter's successor, you are called to maintain communion with and concern for the whole Church. On this occasion, as members of the Fourth General Conference of the Latin American Episcopate, you bear a historic responsibility.

By virtue of faith, the revealed word, the action of the Spirit and through the eucharist over which the bishop presides, the local church has a special relationship of mutual interiority with the universal Church, for in it is present and truly operating the Church of Christ, which is one, holy, catholic, and apostolic (cf. *Christus Dominus*, 11). In it must shine forth that holiness of life to which every evangelizer is called; it must give witness to an intense experience of the mystery of Jesus Christ, which is strongly felt and sensed in the eucharist, in steadfast listening to the word, in prayer, in sacrifice, in generous surrender to the Lord, which in priests and other consecrated persons is given a special expression in celibacy.

We must not forget that the primary form of evangelization is witness (cf. *Redemptoris Missio*, 42-43), that is, proclaiming the message of salvation through one's works and the consistency of one's life, thus making it incarnate in the everyday history of human beings. From its origins, the Church became present and operative not only through the explicit proclamation of the gospel of Christ, but also and above all through the radiance of Christian life. Hence, the new evangelization requires a consistency of life, a dense witness of charity under the sign of unity, in order that the world may believe (cf. Jn 17:23).

30. Jesus Christ, the faithful witness, the pastor of the pastors, is in our midst, for we have gathered in his name (cf. Mt 1:20). With us is the Spirit of the Lord, who guides the Church to the fullness of truth and rejuvenates it with the revealed word, as in a new Pentecost.

In the communion of saints, a vast array of Latin American saints is watching over the labors of this important ecclesial encounter. They evangelized this continent with their word and their virtues, and many of them made it fruitful with their blood. They are the supreme fruits of evangelization.

As she did in the upper room of Pentecost, the mother of Jesus and mother of the Church is with us. Her affectionate presence in every corner of Latin America and in the hearts of her children is the assurance of the prophetic thrust and gospel zeal that must accompany your labors.

31. "Blessed are you who believed that what was spoken to you by the Lord would be fulfilled" (Lk 1:45). These words that Elizabeth addresses to Mary, who is bearing Christ, are applicable to the Church, of which the mother of the Redeemer is type and model. Blessed are you, Americas, Church of the Americas, who also bear Christ, you have received the proclamation of salvation and have believed "what was spoken to you by the Lord!" The faith is your joy, the source of your happiness. Blessed are you, men and women of Latin America, adults and young people who have known the Redeemer. You can say along with the Church and with Mary that the Lord "has looked upon his handmaid's lowliness" (Lk 1:48). Blessed are you, poor of the earth, for the kingdom of God has come to you!

"What was spoken to you by the Lord will be fulfilled." Be faithful to your baptism. In this celebration of centuries, stir up again the enormous grace you have received. Turn your heart and your gaze back to the center, the source, to him who is the foundation of all happiness, the fullness of all. Open up to Christ, receive the Spirit, so that in all your communities a new Pentecost may take place! And from you will emerge a new and joyful humanity, and you will again experience the power of the Lord's right arm, and "what was spoken to you by the Lord will be fulfilled." What he has told you, Americas, is his love for you, his love for your men and women, for your families, your peoples. And that love will be fulfilled in you, and you will again find yourself, you will find your own countenance; "all ages will call you blessed" (Lk 1:48).

Church of the Americas, today the Lord is passing alongside you. He calls you. In this moment of grace, say your name once more, renew his covenant with you. If only you would listen to his voice so that you may know true and complete joy, and enter into your rest (cf. Ps 94:7,11)!

Let us conclude by calling on Mary, star of the first and of the new evangelization. To her, who always hoped, we entrust our hope. In her hands, we place our pastoral concerns and all the tasks of this conference, entrusting to her mother's heart its success and its projection into the future of the continent. May she help us to proclaim her Son:

"Jesus Christ . . . yesterday, today, and forever!"

Amen.

Foreword

We are happy to fulfill our duty of presenting the Santo Domingo document to God's pilgrim people in Latin America and the Caribbean. It is the hope-giving fruit of the Fourth General Conference of Latin American Bishops held last October.

This conference, convoked, inaugurated, and presided over by our Holy Father, John Paul II, labored in warm and deep communion with the vicar of Christ. His opening address was the basic reference point and convergence point for the pastors who took part. It is fitting to observe that this fourth conference was held thirty-seven years after Rio de Janeiro, twenty-four after Medellín, and thirteen after Puebla.

The pastors who gathered in Santo Domingo have drawn together and brought up to date the rich legacy of the past at a wonderful moment: as the first five hundred years of the evangelization of the continent are being commemorated, and as one millennium of Christianity is drawing to a close and another is beginning. It is also a moment when our peoples have been harshly battered by a number of problems and are yearning for a word of hope from the Church.

That is what the Santo Domingo document seeks to be: a word of hope. It is also intended to be an effective instrument for a new evangelization, and a renewed message of Jesus Christ, who is the foundation for human development, and principle of an authentic Christian culture.

The *Santo Domingo Conclusions* are not the result of hasty improvisation. They must be read in the light of the three issue areas indicated by the Holy Father and as the outgrowth of a long and fruitful preparation, which is documented in the contributions made by the bishops' conferences and in a number of books published by the *Consejo Episcopal Latinoamericano* (CELAM).

Other important documents are published here along with the *Santo Domingo Conclusions:*

— the Holy Father's opening address and his letter authorizing the publication of the document;
— messages from the pope to indigenous people and to African Americans; and
— the message of the fourth conference to the peoples of Latin America and the Caribbean.

In its revision of the text prepared in Santo Domingo, the Holy See has introduced only a few stylistic corrections and some brief editing changes for the sake of clarification.

This new pastoral tool, which contains the elements for a comprehensive evangelization plan, is now in the hands of the bishops' conferences and the local Churches of the Americas. In it, they will be able to find the challenges and pastoral directions most applicable to their specific needs.

May Mary, Mother of the Church and queen of our continent, shed light on the journey that our American continent is now undertaking toward a new evangelization, which is to be projected into greater commitment to comprehensive human development, and is to permeate the cultures of Latin American peoples with the light of the gospel.

+ NICOLAS DE JESUS CARDINAL LOPEZ RODRIGUES
Metropolitan Archbishop of Santo Domingo
and Primate of the Americas
President of CELAM

+ JUAN JESUS CARDINAL POSADAS OCAMPO
Archbishop of Guadalajara
First Vice-President of CELAM

+ TULIO MANUEL CHIRIVELLA VARELA
Archbishop of Barquisimeto
Second Vice-President of CELAM

+ OSCAR ANDRES RODRIGUEZ MARADIAGA, SDB
Auxiliary Bishop of Tegucigalpa
President of the CELAM Economic Committee

+ RAYMOND DAMASCENO ASSIS
Auxiliary Bishop of Brasilia
Secretary General of CELAM

Santafé de Bogotá
November 22, 1992
Feast of Jesus Christ, King of the Universe

Message of the Fourth General Conference to the Peoples of Latin America and the Caribbean

I. INTRODUCTION

Summoned by the Holy Father John Paul II to the Fourth General Conference of the Latin American Episcopate, which he inaugurated, we, the representatives of the episcopates of Latin America and the Caribbean and the pope's collaborators in the Roman Curia, gathered in Santo Domingo. Bishops from other parts of the world also took part as did priests, deacons, religious, and lay people as well as observers from other Christian churches. **1**

An important historic date suggested the fourth conference: the five-hundredth anniversary of the beginning of the evangelization of the New World. Since that time the word of God has made the cultures of our people fruitful and has become an integral part of their history. Therefore, through a lengthy preparation that included a novena of years which the Holy Father inaugurated here in Santo Domingo, we have come together with this spirit of the pope's, that is, in the humility of truth, giving thanks to God for the many great lights and asking his forgiveness for the undeniable shadows that have darkened this period. **2**

The Fourth General Conference of the Latin American Episcopate has sought to provide a basic outline for a new impetus to evangelization that will put Christ into the hearts, on the lips, and in the activities and lives of all Latin Americans. Our task is to ensure that the truth about Christ, the Church, and humanity penetrates the strata of society ever more deeply, seeking its gradual transformation. Our work has mainly focused on the new evangelization. **3**

Our meeting is closely related to and in continuity with those of the same kind that preceded it: the first was held in Rio de Janeiro, Brazil, in 1955; the second in Medellín, Colombia, in 1968; and the third in Puebla, Mexico, in 1979. We fully confirm the same choices that marked those meetings and embody their more substantive conclusions. **4**

These events were a valuable ecclesial experience which has led to a rich episcopal teaching that is useful to the churches and the society of our continent. We now add to these guidelines the commitment to evangelize, **5** which emerges from this meeting, and which we humbly and joyfully offer to our peoples.

6   The motherly presence of Our Lady, inseparably united to the Christian faith in Latin America and the Caribbean, has always been our guide on the path of faith, and especially at this time it sustains us in our work and encourages us in the face of today's pastoral challenges.

II. LATIN AMERICA AND THE CARIBBEAN: BETWEEN FEAR AND HOPE

7   The great majority of our peoples live in critical conditions. We come across this daily in the apostolate and we have expressed it clearly in many documents. Therefore, when we are overwhelmed with grief, God's words to Moses echo in our ears: "I have witnessed the affliction of my people in Egypt and have heard their cry of complaint against their slave drivers, so I know well what they are suffering. Therefore I have come down to rescue them from the hands of the Egyptians and lead them out of that land into a good and spacious land" (Ex 3:7-8).

8   This plight could jeopardize our hope. However, the Holy Spirit's action gives us a vigorous and solid motive for hope: faith in Jesus Christ, who died and is risen, who keeps his promise to be with us always (cf. Mt 28:20). This faith shows him to us as attentive and solicitous to all human need. We seek to carry out what the Son teaches: to assume the pain of humanity and to strive to convert it into the way of redemption.

9   Our hope would be in vain if it were not active and effective. Jesus' message would be a fallacy if there were a division between faith and action. We urge those who are suffering to open their hearts to the message of Jesus, who has the power to give new meaning to their lives and suffering. Faith, combined with hope and charity in the exercise of apostolic activity, should be transplanted in a "good and spacious land" for those who are suffering today in Latin America and the Caribbean.

10   The present time reminds us of the gospel episode of the paralytic, who had lain sick for thirty-eight years near the pool that could cure him, without anyone helping him into the water. Our task of evangelization aims at putting into practice Jesus' words to the sick man: "Pick up your mat and walk" (Jn 5:1-8).

11   We wish to convert our desire to evangelize into concrete action that makes it possible for people to overcome their problems and recover from their pain—to pick up their mats and walk—and to have primary responsibility for their own lives through their saving encounter with the Lord.

III. HOPE CONVERTED INTO MISSION

1. The New Evangelization

12   Since the Holy Father's visit to Haiti in 1983, we have felt inspired to conduct a renewed, more effective pastoral activity in our individual

churches. The name "new evangelization" has been given to this global project that looks forward to a new Pentecost (cf. John Paul II, *Opening Address*, 6-7).

St. Luke's account of the disciples on the road to Emmaus shows us the risen Jesus proclaiming the good news. It can be a model for the new evangelization.   13

2. *Jesus Christ Yesterday, Today and Forever: Jesus Reaches Out to Pilgrim Humanity (Lk 24:13-17)*

While the sad and bewildered disciples of Emmaus were on their way   14
back to their village, the Master drew near to accompany them on their way. Jesus seeks people and accompanies them in order to assume their joys, hopes, hardships, and sadness.

Today, too, as pastors of the Church in Latin America and the Carib-   15
bean, in fidelity to our divine Master, we wish to renew his spirit of closeness and support for all our brothers and sisters; we proclaim the value and dignity of each person and intend to shed the light of faith on their history and their daily journey. This is a basic element of the new evangelization.

3. *Human Development: Jesus Walks with People (Lk 24:17-24)*

Jesus not only draws near to those on their way. He goes farther: He   16
becomes the way for them (cf. Jn 14:6) and penetrates the depth of their existence, feelings, and behavior. Through simple and direct dialogue, he gets to know their immediate concerns. The same risen Christ accompanied the steps, aspirations and searching, the problems and hardships of his disciples as they went back to their village.

Here, Jesus put into practice with his disciples what he had taught a   17
lawyer one day: The wounds and the groans of the dying man lying by the wayside are the urgent problems on our own way (cf. Lk 10:25-37). The parable of the Good Samaritan concerns us directly as it regards all our brothers and sisters, especially sinners for whom Jesus shed his blood. Let us remember in particular those who are suffering: the sick, the elderly who live in solitude, and abandoned children. Let us also look at those who are the victims of injustice: the marginalized; the poor; inhabitants of the slums of great cities; indigenous people and African Americans; farm workers; those without land or work or home; women whose rights are not recognized. Other forms of oppression also make demands on us: violence; pornography; drug trafficking and abuse; terrorism; kidnapping; and many other acute problems.

4. *Culture: Jesus Enlightens Humanity's Way through the Scriptures (Lk 24:25-28)*

The Lord's presence does not end in mere human solidarity. The inner   18
drama of the two travelers was that they had lost all hope. This despair

was dispelled by explaining the Bible; the good news that they heard from Jesus passed on the message he had received from his Father.

19   Explaining the Scriptures to them, Jesus corrected the errors of a purely temporal messianism and of all those ideologies which enslave humanity. Explaining the Scriptures to them, he clarified their situation and opened up vistas of hope to them.

20   The road Jesus took with his disciples bore the imprint of God's plan for all his creatures and for human existence.

21   We urge all pastoral workers to deepen their study and meditation on God's word in order to live it and faithfully hand it on to others.

22   We reaffirm the need to find new methods so that those who shape a pluralistic society may fulfill the gospel's ethical demands, above all those of the social order. The Church's social doctrine is an essential part of the Christian message. Its teaching, spread, deepening, and application are necessary requirements for the new evangelization of our peoples.

5. New Enthusiasm: Jesus Makes Himself Known
in the Breaking of the Bread (Lk 24:28-32)

23   The scriptural explanation, however, was not sufficient to open their eyes and make them see reality from the faith perspective. Doubtless it moved them deeply, but the ultimate gesture by which they could recognize him as living and risen from the dead was the concrete sign of breaking bread.

24   At Emmaus, moreover, a home was opened up for the pilgrim. Christ revealed his intimacy to his traveling companions, and in the act of sharing they recognized the one who throughout his life had given himself to his brothers and sisters and sealed the gift of his whole life with his own death on the cross.

25   At the end of these days of prayer and reflection, we return to the homes which form our particular churches to share with our brothers and sisters, especially those who participate most closely in our ministry: our priests and our deacons, to whom we wish to express special affection and gratitude. May the celebration of the eucharist increasingly enflame their hearts to put into practice the new evangelization, human development, and Christian culture.

6. Mission: Jesus Is Proclaimed by the Disciples (Lk 24:33-35)

26   The meeting between the Master and the disciples was over. Jesus disappeared from their sight. Spurred on by fresh enthusiasm, they joyfully set out on their missionary task. They left the village and went to find the other disciples. An experience of faith finds expression in community. Therefore, the disciples went back to Jerusalem to meet their brothers and sisters and tell them how they had met the Lord. On the basis of faith lived in a community, they became preachers of a totally new reality: "The Lord

is risen and is again among us." Faith in Jesus of itself implies mission.

For Latin America (and the Caribbean) which received Christ five hun- **27** dred years ago, the greatest mark of its appreciation for the gift it has been given and of its Christian vitality is to be committed to missionary activity (*Opening Address*, 28) within and beyond its frontiers.

IV. PASTORAL PRIORITIES

With great hope, and taking into account the significant contributions **28** received from the bishops conferences and many other church organizations, the Fourth General Conference proposes the following guidelines for pastoral activity. To undertake our work, we were given direction and support by the Holy Father, who for a long time had been encouraging this conference.

First of all, we declare that the Church in Latin America and the Car- **29** ibbean adheres in faith to Jesus Christ, the same yesterday, today, and forever (cf. Heb 13:8).

So that Christ may be the center of our people's life, we call all the **30** faithful to a new evangelization and appeal especially to the laity, and particularly the young people among them. At this moment, we hope that many young people, supported by effective vocational guidance, may respond to the Lord's call to the priesthood and the consecrated life.

• A renewed catechesis and a living liturgy in a Church constantly concerned with mission will increasingly attract and sanctify all Christians, particularly those who are distant and indifferent to the Church.

• The new evangelization will intensify the missionary apostolate in all our churches and will make us feel responsible for going beyond our frontiers to bring to other peoples the faith that reached us five hundred years ago.

As an expression of the new evangelization, we also commit ourselves **31** to working for the integral development of the Latin American and Caribbean peoples, with the poor as our main concern.

• In this human development, the family, where life originates, will occupy a privileged and fundamental place. Today it is urgently necessary to promote and protect life from the many attacks upon it from various sectors of modern society.

We should promote an evangelization that penetrates to the deepest **32** roots of our peoples' common culture, paying special attention to the growing urban culture.

• We have devoted particular attention to an authentic incarnation of the gospel in the indigenous and African American cultures of our continent.

• For this inculturation of the gospel, effective educational programs and the use of the modern means of communications are most important.

V. GREETINGS AND GOOD WISHES

33   We do not wish to conclude this message without addressing an affectionate word to some of the people and groups who have a special place in the Church or in society.

34   Our special greetings go to our priests and deacons, our dedicated coworkers in the episcopal mission, who have been present every day in our thoughts and prayers. We sincerely hope that, as always, they will help us to communicate the conclusions of this conference to the people of our particular churches. We assure them of our paternal and fraternal affection and our gratitude for their devoted, tireless commitment to the ministry.

35   With the same solicitude, let us remember the men and women religious, the members of secular institutes, pastoral workers, catechists, community leaders, members of basic ecclesial communities and ecclesial movements, and the extraordinary ministers, who will certainly draw renewed enthusiasm for their ecclesial work from the conclusions of this conference.

36   Our grateful thoughts are turned to the many missionaries who have proclaimed the gospel on our continent from the very beginning, in conditions of great hardship and with many sacrifices, even to the extent of offering their lives.

37   The presence at our meeting of observers from sister Christian churches gave us encouragement and joy. To them, and through them to all those churches with whom we share faith in Jesus Christ the savior, we offer our fraternal greeting and our prayer that, when God wishes it, we may fulfill the spiritual testament of Jesus Christ: "That all may be one ... that the world may believe" (Jn 17:21).

38   To the indigenous peoples, the original inhabitants of these lands, the bearers of a host of cultural riches that are the basis of our present culture, and to the descendants of thousands of families from various regions of Africa, we express our respect and the desire to serve them as ministers of the gospel of our Lord Jesus Christ.

39   We are united with the builders and leaders of society — governors, legislators, magistrates, political and military leaders, educators, business people, trade union leaders, and many others — and all peoples of good will who work to promote and protect life in raising the dignity of men and women, in safeguarding their rights, and in seeking and guaranteeing peace far from any form of arms race. From this conference, we exhort them in the exercise of their respective missions to be committed to the service of the people on behalf of justice, solidarity, and integral development, guided by indispensable ethical principles in their decisions.

40   We would like the teaching we impart on the Lord's behalf to be echoed in the families of Latin America and the Caribbean. We ask them, the sanctuaries of life, to sow the seed of the gospel in the hearts of their children through a proper upbringing. At a time when the culture of death

threatens us, they will find here a source "that will become a fountain within [them], leaping up to provide eternal life." Through their example and their words, parents are the great evangelizers of the "domestic church," and whether or not this Santo Domingo Conference bears fruit depends to a great extent on them. That is why, together with our greetings, we want to express our closeness and support to them.

We urge representatives of the world of culture to intensify their efforts   **41**
to foster education, the master key to the future. The soul of social dynamism, it is the right and the duty of all to lay the foundations for an authentic integral humanism (cf. John Paul II, *Mass at the Columbus Lighthouse*, 7).

We cordially invite all those who work in social communications to make   **42**
themselves the tireless spokesmen of reconciliation, the steadfast promoters of human and Christian values, and to inspire hope, peace, and solidarity among peoples.

VI. CONCLUSION

Full of confidence, therefore, we entrust this message to the people of   **43**
God in Latin America and the Caribbean. With the same sentiments we offer it to all men and women, especially to the young people of the continent, called to be actively involved in the life of society and the Church in the new Christian millennium already at the door. We offer it also to those who, although they do not share our Christian, Catholic faith, adhere to the message of this Santo Domingo assembly and recognize its call to the Christian and gospel humanism that they respect and live.

To our brothers and sisters in the faith, this message is intended to be   **44**
an explicit profession of faith in Jesus Christ and his good news. In this Jesus, who is the same "yesterday, today, and forever" (Heb 13:8), we have the certitude of finding inspiration, light, and strength for a fresh spirit of evangelization. In him are also found the motives and directions for new efforts toward the authentic human development of nearly 500 million Latin Americans. He will always help us to give our people's cultural values a Christian mark, identity, and the wealth coming from unity in diversity.

We would like to propose to everyone the conclusions of the Santo   **45**
Domingo Conference as a premise for the continued rejuvenation of our predecessors' ideal of the "Great Homeland." We are convinced that the Christian and Catholic roots which our countries have in common will serve as the basis for the unity Latin America desires.

There are very active seeds of division in America. This American land   **46**
is far from being the united continent we desire. Now, besides its primarily religious objective, the new evangelization launched by the Fourth General Conference offers the necessary elements for the birth of the Great Homeland:

• The indispensable **reconciliation** whereby, in the logic of the Our

Father, past and present divisions will be healed, former and recent injustices will be mutually forgiven, past and present offenses will be forgiven and peace will be restored.

• **Solidarity**, people helping others to bear their burden and sharing with them their own aspirations: "The new ideal of solidarity must prevail over the old desire to control" (*Opening Address*, 15).

• To achieve the **integration** of our countries, the barriers of isolation, discrimination, and mutual indifference must be overcome: "Latin American integration is a factor which can significantly help in overcoming the pressing problems which affect the continent today" (*Opening Address*, 15, 17).

• Deep **communion** in the Church concerning the political will for progress and well-being.

47   The social and spiritual heritage contained in these four key words — **reconciliation, solidarity, integration,** and **communion** — could be transformed into Latin America's greatest resource. These are the wishes and prayers of the bishops of the Fourth General Conference of the Latin American Episcopate. It is also the best gift that God's grace could grant us. We think that this heritage is the task and duty of one and all.

48   We entrust our work to Our Lady of Guadalupe, Star of the New Evangelization. She has walked with our peoples from the very first proclamation of Christ. We implore her today to enflame our hearts in order to proclaim, with new methods and new expressions, that Jesus Christ is the same "yesterday, today, and forever" (Heb 13:8).

Fourth General Conference of Latin American Bishops
Santo Domingo, Dominican Republic
October 12–18, 1992

CONCLUSIONS

New Evangelization
Human Development
Christian Culture

"Jesus Christ . . . the same yesterday, today, and forever."
(Heb 13:8)

Part I

Jesus Christ,
Gospel of the Father

Called together by Pope John Paul II and under the impulse of the Spirit   **1**
of God our Father, we bishops participating in the Fourth General Conference of the Latin American Episcopates, in continuity with earlier such
meetings in Rio de Janeiro, Medellín, and Puebla, proclaim our faith and
our love for Jesus Christ. He is the same "yesterday, today, and forever"
(Heb 13:8).

Gathered together in a new upper room, as it were, around Mary, the
Mother of Jesus, we thank God for the priceless gift of faith and for the
countless gifts of his mercy. We ask forgiveness for being unfaithful to his
kindness. Encouraged by the Holy Spirit, we are preparing to set in motion
with new ardor a new evangelization, one that is to issue in a greater

commitment to comprehensive human development and permeate the cultures of Latin American peoples with the light of the gospel. It is the Spirit who must give us the wisdom to discover the new methods and new expressions that may make the one gospel of Jesus Christ more comprehensible to our brothers and sisters today and thereby to respond to new questions.

2   As we consider with the eyes of faith the implanting of the cross of Christ on this continent five centuries ago, we understand that it was he, the Lord of history, who extended the proclamation of salvation to inconceivable proportions. The family of God grew, and the number of those who give thanks multiplied to the glory of God (cf. 2 Cor 4:15; OA 3). God chose for himself a new people among the inhabitants of these lands. Although they were unknown to the old world, they were well "known to God from all eternity, and he had embraced them with the fatherhood that the Son had revealed in the fullness of time" (OA 3).

3   Jesus Christ is truly the center of God's loving plan. Hence with the epistle to the Ephesians we reaffirm: "Praised be the God and Father of our Lord Jesus Christ, who has bestowed on us in Christ every spiritual blessing in the heavens! God chose us in him before the world began to be holy and blameless in his sight, to be full of love; he likewise predestined us through Christ Jesus to be his adopted sons . . ." (Eph 1:3-5).

We celebrate Jesus Christ, who died for our sins and is risen for our justification (see Rom 4:25), who lives among us and is our "hope of glory" (Col 1:27). He is the image of the invisible God, the first-born of all creatures. He sustains creation, and all human paths converge on him; he is the Lord of ages. Beset by problems and crosses, we nevertheless intend to continue to serve as witnesses on our continent to God's love and prophets of that imperishable hope. We want to "inaugurate a new age under the sign of hope" (OA V).

1. PROFESSION OF FAITH

4   We bless God who in his merciful love "sent forth his son born of a woman" (Gal 4:4) to save all people. Jesus Christ thus became one of us (cf. Heb 2:17). Anointed by the Holy Spirit (see Lk 1:15), in the fullness of time he proclaimed the good news, "This is the time of fulfillment. The reign of God is at hand! Reform your lives and believe in the gospel!" (Mk 1:15). This reign ushered in by Jesus first of all reveals God's self to us as "a loving Father full of compassion" (RM 13), who invites all, men and women, to enter it.

In order to emphasize this aspect, Jesus has drawn near particularly to those who were on the margins of society, and has proclaimed to them the "good news." At the outset of his ministry, he announces that he has been sent to "bring glad tidings to the poor" (Lk 4:18). To all who suffer rejection and contempt, who are aware of what they lack, Jesus says "Blessed are you who are poor" (Lk 6:20). Thus the needy and sinners can sense that

God loves them, that they are the object of his enormous affection (cf. Lk 15:1-32).

Entry into the reign of God takes place through faith in the word of 5
Jesus, which is sealed through baptism and witnessed by following him and sharing his life, death, and resurrection (cf. Rom 6:9). Entering God's reign thus demands a profound conversion (see Mk 1:15; Mt 4:17), a break with any kind of selfishness in a world marked by sin (see Mt 7:21; Jn 14:15; RM 13); in other words, embracing the proclamation of the Beatitudes (see Mt 5: 1-10).

The mystery of the reign, which has been hidden in God from ages and generations past (cf. Col 1:26) and is now present in the life and words of Jesus and identified with his person, is the Father's gift (see Lk 12:32; Mt 20:23). It consists of the gratuitously offered communion of the human being with God (see EN 9; Jn 14:23), which begins in this life and reaches fulfillment in eternity (see EN 27).

God's love is attested in fraternal love (cf. 1 Jn 4:20) from which it is inseparable: "Yet if we love one another God dwells in us, and his love is brought to perfection in us" (1 Jn 4:12). "The kingdom's nature . . . is one of communion among all human beings—with one another and with God" (RM 15).

In order to bring about the reign, Jesus "named twelve as his companions 6
whom he would send to preach. . ." (Mk 3:14). To them he revealed the "mysteries" of the Father and made them his friends (cf. Jn 15:15). They were to continue the very mission that he had received from his Father (see Jn 20:21). He also made Peter the foundation of the new community (see Mt 16:18).

Before going to the Father, Jesus instituted the sacrament of his love, the eucharist (see Mk 14:22), the commemoration of his sacrifice. In this way, the Lord remains in the midst of his people to feed them with his body and blood, strengthening and expressing the communion and solidarity that ought to reign among Christians as they journey along earth's paths in the hope of fully encountering him. Spotless victim offered to God (see Heb 9:14), Jesus is likewise the priest who takes away sin through a single sacrifice (see Heb 10:14).

He and he alone is our salvation, our justice, our peace, and our reconciliation. In him we were reconciled to God and it is through him that the "ministry of reconciliation" (cf. 2 Cor 5:19) has been entrusted to us. He tears down any wall separating human beings and peoples (cf. Eph 2:14). Therefore today, in this period of new evangelization, we want to reiterate with the apostle Saint Paul: "Be reconciled to God!" (2 Cor 5:20).

We confess that Jesus, truly risen and ascended into heaven, is Lord, 7
consubstantial with the Father; in him "the fullness of deity resides in bodily form" (Col 2:9); seated at the Father's right hand, he is worthy of our adoration. "The resurrection gives a universal scope to Christ's message, his actions, and his whole mission" (RM 16). Christ rose in order to com-

municate his life to us. From his fullness we have all received grace (cf. Jn 1:16). Jesus Christ, who died to free us from sin and death, has risen to make us God's children in him. If he has not risen "our preaching is void of content and your faith is empty too" (1 Cor 15:14). He is our hope (cf. 1 Tm 1:1; 3:14-16), since he can save those who approach God, and is ever ready to intercede on our behalf (cf. Heb 7:25).

As Jesus had promised, the Holy Spirit was poured out over the apostles as they were gathered with Mary in the upper room (see Acts 1:12-14; 2:1). With the granting of the Spirit on Pentecost, the Church was sent to proclaim the gospel. Since that day, as God's new people (cf. 1 Pt 2:9-10) and body of Christ (cf. 1 Cor 12:27; Eph 4:12) it exists for the sake of the kingdom, of which it is seed, sign, and instrument (see RM 18) until the end of time. From that moment until the present, through preaching and baptism, the Church begets new children of God who are conceived by the Holy Spirit and born of God (see LG 64).

8   In the communion of the apostolic faith, which was confessed in Palestine through Peter — "You are the Messiah, the Son of the living God" (Mt 16:16) — today we make our own the words of Paul VI, of which John Paul II reminded us as we initiated our labors: "Christ! Christ, our beginning. Christ, our life and our guide. Christ, our hope and our end. . . . May no other light hover over this assembly than that of Christ, light of the world. May no other truth draw our minds than the words of the Lord, our one Master. May we have no other aspiration than to be utterly faithful to him. May no other hope sustain us, than that which bolsters our weakness through his word . . . " (OA 1).

Yes, we confess that Jesus Christ is true God and true human being. He is the only Son of the Father, made human in the womb of the Virgin Mary, through the Holy Spirit, who came into the world to free us from all slavery to sin, to give us the grace of filial adoption, and to reconcile us to God and to other human beings. He is the living gospel of the Father's love. In him, humankind finds the measure of its dignity and the meaning and direction of its development.

9   We acknowledge the dramatic situation in which sin places the human being. For although the human being was created good, in God's own image, and is the lord who is responsible over creation, by sinning that same human being now stands at odds with God, is internally divided, has broken solidarity with neighbor, and has destroyed the harmony of nature. Thus we acknowledge the source of the individual and collective evils that grieve us in Latin America: wars, terrorism, drugs, dire poverty, oppression and injustice, institutionalized lying, the marginalization of ethnic groups, corruption, assaults on the family, abandoned children and old people, campaigns against life, abortion, the utilization of women, the pillaging of the environment — in a word, everything that typifies a culture of death.

Who will free us from these forces of death? (cf. Rom 7:24). Only the grace of our Lord Jesus Christ, offered once more to the men and women of Latin America, as a call to conversion of heart. The renewed evangelization that we are now undertaking must be an invitation to the conversion of personal and collective conscience alike (cf. OA 18) so that we Christians may be the soul, as it were, in all realms of society (cf. *Letter to Diognetus* 8).

Identified with Christ living in each individual (cf. Gal 2:20), and led by   **10**
the Holy Spirit, the children of God receive the law of love in their hearts. Thus they are enabled to respond to the demand that they be perfect like the Father in heaven (cf. Mt 5:48), following Jesus Christ and carrying their cross every day, even to the point of giving their lives for him (cf. Mk 8:34-36).

We believe in the one, holy, catholic, and apostolic Church, and we love   **11**
it. It was established by Jesus Christ "on the foundation of the apostles" (Eph 2:20) whose successors, the bishops, preside over the various local Churches. United in communion among themselves and presided over in charity by the bishop of Rome, they serve their local Churches and thus Christ's Church is alive and active in each of them. "The first beneficiary of salvation is the Church. Christ won the Church for himself at the price of his own blood and made the Church his co-worker in the salvation of the world" (RM 9).

The Church is present as a pilgrim on this continent, and it takes the form of a community of brothers and sisters under the guidance of the bishops. Gathered by the Holy Spirit (cf. CD 11) around the word of God and the eucharistic table, the faithful and pastors alike are sent to announce the gospel, by announcing Jesus Christ and offering the witness of fraternal love.

"The pilgrim Church is of its very nature missionary since it draws its   **12**
origin from the mission of the Son and the mission of the Holy Spirit, in accordance with the plan of God the Father" (AG 2). Evangelization is its *raison d'être;* it exists in order to evangelize (cf. EN 15). The moment has come for Latin America, now providentially prompted by a new evangelical ardor, to carry its faith to those peoples that still do not know Christ, fully confident that "faith is strengthened when it is given to others" (OA 28).

Today, the Church intends to carry out a new evangelization that may transmit, strengthen, and make mature among our peoples their faith in God, Father of our Lord Jesus Christ. This evangelization must "always contain — as the foundation, center, and, at the same time, summit of its dynamism — a clear proclamation that, in Jesus Christ, the Son of God made man, who died and rose from the dead, salvation is offered to all men, as a gift of God's grace and mercy" (EN 27).

By its own inherent strength, the Christian proclamation tends to heal,   **13**
strengthen, and advance human beings and to establish a fraternal community, by renewing humanity itself and endowing it with its full human dignity, through the newness of baptism and life according to the gospel (cf. EN 18). Evangelization promotes integral development, by demanding

that all fully respect their rights and fully observe their duties so as to create a just and solidary society en route to its completion in the ultimate reign. The human being is called to collaborate with Jesus Christ and be his instrument in evangelization. In Latin America — a continent both religious and long-suffering — we urgently need a new evangelization, one that can announce forthrightly the gospel of justice, love, and mercy.

We know that through the incarnation Christ has been united in some fashion to every human being (cf. GS 22). He is the perfect revelation of the human being to the human being, and it is he who unveils the grandeur of the human vocation (cf. GS 22). Jesus Christ takes his place at the heart of humankind and invites all cultures to let themselves be drawn toward fulfillment by his spirit by elevating in them what is good and purifying what bears the mark of sin. All evangelization must therefore mean inculturating the gospel. Every culture can thus become Christian, that is, point toward Christ and draw inspiration from him and his message (cf. John Paul II, *Address to the Second Assembly of the Pontifical Commission for Latin America* [June 14, 1991], 4). Jesus Christ is indeed the standard for every culture and every human endeavor. The inculturation of the gospel is an imperative of following Jesus and it is necessary in order to restore the disfigured countenance of the world (cf. LG 8). This effort takes place within the striving and aspiration of each people, strengthening its identity and liberating it from the powers of death. Hence we can confidently proclaim: Men and women of Latin America, open your hearts to Jesus Christ! He is the way, the truth, and the life. One who follows him walks not in darkness! (cf. Jn 14:8; 8:12).

14   We believe that Christ the Lord is to return to bring God's reign to its fullness and hand it over to the Father (cf. 1 Cor 15:24), when all creation has been transformed into the "new heavens and a new earth where ... the justice of God will reside" (2 Pt 3:13). There we will attain the perfect communion of heaven, enjoying the eternal vision of the Trinity. With sin, the devil, and death finally defeated, men and women who have remained faithful to the Lord will attain their full humanity as they share in the divine nature itself (cf. 2 Pt 1:4). Then Christ will recapitulate and fully reconcile creation; all will be his, and God will be all in all (cf. 1 Cor 15:28).

15   We want to confirm the faith of our people by proclaiming that the Virgin Mary, Mother of Christ and of the Church, is the first of the redeemed and the first believer. A woman of faith, Mary has been fully evangelized; she is the most perfect disciple and evangelizer (cf. Jn 2:1-12). In her testimony of prayer, of hearing the word of God, and of being ready to serve the reign faithfully, even to the cross, she is the model for all disciples and evangelizers. Her maternal figure played a decisive role in aiding the men and women of Latin America to acknowledge their own dignity as children of God. Mary is the distinguishing feature of our continent's culture. Mother and educator of the newborn Latin American people, Saint Mary of Guadalupe, through Blessed Juan Diego, "provides an example of a perfectly

inculturated evangelization" (OA 24). She has preceded us in the pilgrimage of faith and on the road to glory, and she accompanies our peoples
who lovingly call on her until we all finally come together with her Son.
We joyfully and gratefully accept the magnificent gift of her motherhood
and her tender protection, and we aspire to love her just as Jesus Christ
loved her. We therefore invoke her as Star of the first — and of the new —
evangelization.

2. FIVE HUNDRED YEAR ANNIVERSARY
OF THE FIRST EVANGELIZATION

"In the peoples of the Americas, God has chosen for himself a new   16
people whom he has . . . made sharers in his Spirit. Through evangelization
and faith in Christ, God has renewed his covenant with Latin America"
(OA 3).

1492 marked an all-important point in this process of preaching the good
news. For "what the Church is celebrating in this commemoration is not
more or less debatable historical events, but something magnificent and
permanent that cannot be underestimated: the coming of the faith, the
proclamation and spread of the gospel message on this continent. Moreover
it celebrates it in the deepest and most theological meaning of that term,
namely as Jesus Christ, Lord of history and of the destinies of humankind
is celebrated," (John Paul II, *Sunday Address* [January 5, 1991], 2).

God's creative, caring, and saving presence was already with these peo-   17
ples. The "seeds of the Word," present in the deep religious sense of pre-
Colombian cultures, was awaiting the fruitful sprinkling of the Spirit. Along
with other aspects that needed to be purified, these cultures at their core
offered positive elements such as openness to God's action, the sense of
gratitude for the fruits of the earth, the sacred character of human life and
esteem for the family, the sense of solidarity and shared responsibility for
work performed in common, the importance of worship, belief in a life-
beyond earth, and so many other values that enrich the Latin American
soul (see John Paul II, *Message to Indigenous People* [October 13, 1992], 1).
This natural religiosity predisposed the indigenous peoples of the Americas
to receive the gospel more readily, even though some evangelizers were not
always disposed to recognize those values.

Consequently, the encounter between Iberian Catholicism and the cul-   18
tures of the Americas gave rise to a special process of amalgamation (*mes-*
tizaje). While that process had conflictive aspects, it highlights our
continent's Catholic roots as well as its unique identity. That amalgamation
process, which is also observable in many forms of popular religiosity and
mestizo art, represents the joining of what is perennial in Christianity with
what is specific to the Americas. From the very outset it has spread throughout our continent.

History teaches us that "a valid, fruitful and admirable labor of evangelization took place, thereby opening the way to the truth about God and the human being in the Americas—so much so, indeed, that the evangelization itself became a kind of tribunal for holding accountable those [sometimes unscrupulous colonizers who were] responsible for such abuses" (OA 4).

19   Initially, it was members of religious orders who led the way in the work of evangelization. That work, however, under the inspiration of the Holy Spirit, was a combined effort by the whole people of God, bishops, men and women religious, and lay faithful. Among these latter we should also note that baptized indigenous themselves were involved, and that as time went on, they were joined by African American catechists.

Men and women of holy lives were the privileged instruments of that initial evangelization. The pastoral means they employed were tireless preaching of the word, the celebration of the sacraments, catechesis, devotion to Mary, the practice of the works of mercy, denouncing injustice, the defense of the poor, and a special concern for education and human development.

20   The great evangelizers defended the rights and dignity of the native people and rebuked "the outrages committed against the Indians in the time of the conquest" (*Message to Indigenous People,* 2). The bishops also exemplify the same stance of prophetic condemnation which is combined with the proclamation of the gospel in their councils and other meetings, in letters to the kings of Spain and Portugal, and in decrees on pastoral visitation.

Hence, "at the time of this five-century anniversary how could the Church, which in its religious, priests, and bishops has always stood alongside the indigenous people, forget the enormous suffering inflicted on the populations of this continent during the period of conquest and colonization? We must recognize the full truth about the abuses committed, due to the lack of love in those people who were unable to recognize in the indigenous people their brothers and sisters and children of the same God and Father" (*Message to Indigenous People,* 2). Regrettably, this suffering has in some ways lasted until our own day.

One of the saddest episodes in the history of Latin America and the Caribbean was the forced transfer of an enormous number of Africans as slaves. Government and private bodies from almost all the countries of the Atlantic side of Europe and of the Americas were involved in the slave trade. The inhuman traffic in slaves, the lack of respect for life, for personal and family identity, and for ethnic groups are a scandalous disgrace in the history of humankind. With John Paul II we want to ask God's pardon for this "unknown holocaust" in which "baptized people who did not live their faith were involved" (*Homily on the Island of Gorée, Senegal*, February 21, 1992; *Message to African Americans*, Santo Domingo, October 12, 1992).

21   When we look at the more recent period of history, we continue to find the living traces of a centuries-old culture at whose core the gospel is present. The lives of saints in the Americas attests especially to that presence. By fully living the gospel, they have been the most authentic, credible, and best qualified witnesses to Jesus Christ. The Church has proclaimed that many have possessed heroic virtue, from Blessed Juan Diego, an Indian, along with Saint Rose of Lima, and Saint Martin de Porres up to Saint Ezequiel Moreno.

On this five-hundred-year anniversary, we express gratitude to the countless anonymous missionaries, pastoral agents, and lay people, many of whom have worked in silence, and especially to those who have even given witness with their blood out of love for Jesus.

Part II

Jesus Christ, Evangelizer, Living in His Church

22   "Go, therefore, and make disciples of all the nations. Baptize them in the name of the Father, and of the Son, and of the Holy Spirit. Teach them to carry out everything I have commanded you. And know that I am with you always, until the end of the world!" (Mt 28:19-20). "These words can be said to contain the solemn proclamation of evangelization" (OA 2).

The Holy Father has called us together to commit the Church in Latin America and the Caribbean to a new evangelization and to "draw up now a new evangelization strategy for the next several years, a comprehensive plan for evangelization" (*Address to the Second Assembly of the Pontifical Commission for Latin America* [June 14, 1991], 4). We want to present some elements that will provide a basis for implementing these guidelines in the local Churches on our continent.

The new evangelization, which is the "all encompassing element" or the "central idea" that has shed light on our conference, will serve as the basis for our understanding of the true dimension of human development, which must respond to "the delicate and difficult situation of Latin America today" (*Letter of Cardinal Gantin,* December 12, 1990). The new evangelization will also be the basis for our consideration of the challenge of the dialogue between the gospel and the various elements that make up our cultures in order to purify and improve those cultures from within by means of the teaching and example of Jesus so as to come to a Christian culture.

CHAPTER 1: NEW EVANGELIZATION

23   All evangelization begins with Christ's command to his apostles and their successors; it develops further in the community of the baptized, within living communities sharing their faith; and it seeks to strengthen the life of filial adoption in Christ, whose primary expression is fraternal love.

After inquiring what we mean by new evangelization, we will better be able to understand that its starting point is in the Church, in the power of the Spirit, in an ongoing conversion process that seeks to witness to unity within the diversity of ministries and charisms, and that lives its missionary commitment with intensity. Only an evangelized Church can evangelize.

The tragic situations of injustice and suffering in Latin America, which have become even more acute since Puebla, demand responses that can be given only by a Church that is a sign of reconciliation and that bears the life and hope that spring from the gospel.

What Is the New Evangelization?   24

The starting point for the new evangelization is the assurance that Christ holds "unfathomable riches" (Eph 3:8) that no age or culture exhausts and to which we human beings can ever turn to be enriched (cf. OA 6). To speak of a new evangelization is to acknowledge that an old one or a first one has already taken place. It would be incorrect to speak of a new evangelization of tribes or peoples who never received the gospel. In Latin America, we can speak in this fashion because a first evangelization took place here five hundred years ago.

To speak of a new evangelization does not mean that the previous one was invalid, sterile, or short-lived. Rather, it means that today Christians face new challenges and new questions that urgently require a response. To speak of a new evangelization, as the pope noted in his opening address to this fourth general conference, does not mean proposing a new gospel different from the first. There is only one gospel, but it can shed new light on those new problems.

The expression "new evangelization" does not mean reevangelizing. In Latin America, the point is not to act as though there were no first evangelization but, rather, to start from the many rich values it has left in place and proceed to complement them by correcting previous shortcomings. The new evangelization has emerged in Latin America as a response to the problems plaguing a continent where a divorce between faith and life leads to situations of injustice, social inequality, and violence that cry out. It means taking up the magnificent endeavor of energizing Latin American Christianity.

For John Paul II, the new evangelization is something operational and dynamic. It is first and foremost a call to conversion (cf. OA 1) and to the hope that rests on God's promises. Its unshakable certainty derives from Christ's resurrection, which is the primary proclamation and the root of all evangelization, the foundation for all human advancement, and the principle of all genuine Christian culture (cf. OA 25). It is also a new realm of vitality, a new Pentecost (cf. OA 30-31) in which the acceptance of the Holy Spirit will give rise to a renewed people made up of free human beings conscious of their dignity (cf. OA 19) and able to forge a truly human history. It is the combination of means, activities, and attitudes that can put the gospel into active dialogue with modernity and with the postmodern, in order to challenge them and to be challenged by them. It is likewise the effort to inculturate the gospel into the present situation of our continent's cultures.

25   The agent of the new evangelization is the whole church community in accordance with its own nature: we bishops, in communion with the pope; our priests and deacons; men and women religious; and all of us men and women who constitute the people of God.

26   The aim of the new evangelization is to form people and communities whose faith is mature and to respond to the new situation we are facing as a result of the social and cultural changes of modernity. It must take into account urbanization, poverty, and marginalization. Our situation bears the marks of materialism, the culture of death, the invasion of the sects, and a variety of religious offers being made. This situation also brings with it new values, yearning for solidarity and justice, religious searching, and the abandonment of all-encompassing ideologies. The addressees of the new evangelization also include the middle class, those groups, populations, and living and working environments that are impacted by science, technology, and the mass media.

It is the task of the new evangelization to arouse a personal acceptance of Jesus Christ and the Church on the part of the vast numbers of baptized men and women whose Christianity is devoid of vitality, who "have lost a living sense of the faith, or even no longer consider themselves members of the Church and live a life far removed from Christ and his gospel" (RM 33).

27   The content of the new evangelization is Jesus Christ, gospel of the Father, who with deeds and words proclaimed that God is merciful to all his creatures; that God loves human beings with a limitless love and has willed to enter into human history through Jesus Christ, who died and rose for us in order to free us from sin and from all its consequences and to make us sharers in his divine nature (John Paul II, *Homily in Veracruz,* Mexico, May 7, 1990). Everything acquires meaning in Christ. He bursts the narrow horizon within which secularism encloses human beings and returns to them their truth and dignity as children of God; he does not allow any temporal reality—neither the state, nor the economy, nor technology—to become for human beings the ultimate reality to which they must submit. In the words of Paul VI, evangelizing means announcing "the name, the teaching, the life, the promises, the Kingdom and the mystery of Jesus of Nazareth, the Son of God" (EN 22).

The renewing power of this evangelization will be found in faithfulness to God's word; it will be welcomed in the church community; and its creative breath will be the Holy Spirit, who creates in unity and diversity, nourishes the wealth of charism and ministry, and projects out into the world through commitment to mission.

28   What form is this new evangelization to take? The pope has answered: It is to be new in its ardor, in its methods, and in its expression.

New in its ardor. Jesus Christ calls us to renew our apostolic ardor. To that end, he sends his Spirit who today is igniting the heart of the Church. The apostolic ardor of the new evangelization springs from being radically conformed to Jesus Christ the first evangelizer. Thus the best evangelizer is the saint, the person of the Beatitudes (cf. RM 90-91). An evangelization that is new in its ardor means a solid faith, intense pastoral charity, and steadfast fidelity, which under the Spirit's action generates a mystique, an enthusiasm that irrepressibly proclaims the gospel and that can awaken credibility so that the good news of salvation may be accepted.

New in its methods. Our situations require new approaches to evangeli-   **29**
zation. Witness and personal encounter, the presence of Christians in everything human, and confidence in the saving proclamation of Jesus (*kerygma*) and in the activity of the Holy Spirit are all essential.

Under the impulse of the creator Spirit, we must draw on imagination and creativity so that the gospel will reach everyone in a pedagogical and compelling way. Since we live in an image culture, we must boldly use the means made available to us by science and technology, while never placing all our trust in them.

Moreover, we must use those means that can make the gospel reach the core of both person and society, down to the very roots of the culture, and "not in a purely decorative way as it were by applying a thin veneer" (EN 20).

New in its expression. Jesus Christ urges us to proclaim the good news in   **30**
a language that will bring the perennial gospel closer to the new cultural realities of today. New expressions must be sought within the inexhaustible riches of Christ so as to make it possible to evangelize those circles affected by urban culture and to inculturate the gospel in the new forms of the culture now taking shape. The new evangelization must be more inculturated into the ways of being and living of our cultures, while keeping in mind the particular features of different cultures, especially indigenous and African American cultures. (It is crucial that we learn to speak in tune with the mentality and culture of our hearers, and in accord with their forms of communication and contemporary means of expression.) The new evangelization will thus follow the thrust of the incarnation of the Word. New evangelization demands that the Church undergo a pastoral conversion. Such a conversion must be in keeping with the council. It affects everything and everybody: in personal and community awareness and practice and in relationships of equality and of authority. It does so with structures and dynamisms that can make the Church ever more clearly present as an effective sign, and as sacrament of universal salvation.

1.1 THE CHURCH CALLED TO HOLINESS

Doctrinal Perspectives. During this fourth general conference, like Mary,   **31**
we have been listening to the word in order to communicate it to our peoples. We have sensed that the Lord Jesus was repeating the call to a

holy life (cf. Eph 1:4) on which our whole missionary activity is based.

The Church, as mystery of unity, finds its source in Jesus Christ. Only in him can it produce the fruits of holiness that God expects of it. Only by participating in his Spirit can it transmit the authentic word of God to human beings. Only holiness of life nourishes and guides true human development and Christian culture. Only with him and in him can it give God, almighty Father, honor and glory throughout all ages.

32 **Call to Holiness.** The Church is a holy community (cf. 1 Pt 2:9) first through the presence within it of the Lamb who sanctifies through his spirit (cf. Rv 21:22ff.; 22:1-5; Eph 1:18; 1 Cor 3:16; 6;19; LG 4). Hence its members must strive day by day to live following Christ and in obedience to the Spirit, "so as to be holy and blameless in his sight . . . full of love" (Eph 1:4). The new men and women that Latin America and the Caribbean need are those who have heard with a good and upright heart (cf. Lk 8:15) the call to conversion (cf. Mk 1:15); those who have been reborn through the Holy Spirit in accordance with the perfect image of God (cf. Col 1:15; Rom 8:29); those who call God "Father" and express their love for him by acknowledging their brothers and sisters (*Puebla Conclusions,* 327); those who are blessed because they share in the joy of the kingdom of heaven; those who are free with the freedom that comes from truth and who stand in solidarity with all human beings, especially those who suffer the most. In the Blessed Virgin the Church has attained the perfection by which she has neither stain nor wrinkle. Holiness "is the key to the renewed ardor of the new evangelization" (John Paul II, *Homily in Salto, Uruguay* [May 9, 1988], 4).

33 **Called Together by the Word.** A holy community called together by the word, the Church has as one of its primary duties to preach the gospel (cf. LG 25). We bishops of the local pilgrim Churches in Latin America and the Caribbean and all of us who are participating in this gathering in Santo Domingo want to assume with the renewed ardor required by our time the call issued by the pope, Peter's successor, to undertake a new evangelization. In doing so, we are quite conscious that evangelizing necessarily means proclaiming with joy the name, teaching, life, promises, reign, and mystery of Jesus of Nazareth, Son of God (cf. EN 22).

Kerygma and catechesis. Because many baptized Latin Americans have not personally accepted Jesus Christ through an initial conversion, the Church in its prophetic ministry must make it a basic priority to proclaim vigorously Jesus dead and risen (*kerygma*) (cf. RM 44), "the root of all evangelization, the foundation for all promotion of human development, and the principle of all genuine Christian culture" (OA 25).

This prophetic ministry of the Church also includes catechesis which, by continually making present God's loving revelation manifested in Jesus Christ, leads incipient faith to maturity and educates the true disciple of Jesus Christ (cf. CT 19). Faith should be nourished on God's word as read and interpreted in the Church and celebrated in the community so that pondering the mystery of Christ may help it to present that mystery as good news in the actual situations in which our peoples find themselves.

The service that theologians provide for the people of God likewise belongs to the prophetic ministry of the Church (cf. OA 7). Their task, which is rooted in God's word and carried out in open dialogue with the pastors and in complete fidelity to the magisterium, is noble and necessary. When carried out in this fashion their efforts can make a contribution to the inculturation of the faith and the evangelization of cultures. It may also serve to nourish a theology capable of energizing pastoral work and promote the whole of Christian life toward the pursuit of holiness. Theological effort thus understood stimulates work on behalf of social justice, human rights, and solidarity with the poorest.

Nevertheless, we are not forgetting that all of "God's holy people" share in Christ's prophetic function, and that it is exercised first by "spread[ing] abroad a living witness to Him, especially by means of a life of faith and charity" (LG 12). The witness of Christian life is the primary and irreplaceable form of evangelization, as Jesus forcefully demonstrated on a number of occasions (cf. Mt 7:21-23; 25:31-46; Lk 10:37; 19:1-10), and as the apostles also taught (cf. Jas 2:14-18).

Liturgical Celebration. The holy Church finds in the life of prayer, praise, and thanksgiving that heaven and earth direct to God for his "mighty and wonderful" works (cf. Rv 15:3f; 7:9-17) the ultimate reason for its own convocation. That is why the liturgy "is the summit toward which the activity of the Church is directed; [and] at the same time ... the fountain from which all her power flows" (SC 10). However, the liturgy is the activity of the whole Christ, Head and members, and as such, it must express the deepest meaning of his sacrifice to the Father: obeying by making its whole life the revelation of the Father's love for human beings. Thus, as the celebration of the Last Supper is essentially connected to Christ's life and sacrifice on the cross and makes it present every day for the salvation of all human beings, so also those who gather around the Lamb praising God are those who show in their lives the witnessing signs of Jesus' self-surrender (cf. Rv 7:13ff.). Hence Christian worship ought to express the twofold thrust of obedience to the Father (glorification) and of charity to brothers and sisters (redemption), for God's glory is that the human being live. Far from alienating people, therefore, worship frees them and makes them brothers and sisters.

When carried out in the Church in this fashion, liturgical service has in itself an evangelizing power that ought to be made very prominent in the new evangelization. In the liturgy, Christ the Savior is made present today. The liturgy is proclamation and realization (cf. SC 6) of the saving deeds that we are enabled to touch sacramentally; hence, it convokes, celebrates, and commissions. The liturgy is an exercise of faith and is profitable for faith whether robust or weak, and even for the nonbeliever (cf. 1 Cor 14:24-25). It sustains commitment to human development since it leads believers to accept their responsibility for building the reign in order to "make it plain that those who believe in Christ, though indeed they are not of this world, are nevertheless the light of the world" (SC 9). Liturgical celebration cannot be something separated from life or parallel to it (cf. 1 Pt 1:15). Finally, it is particularly through the liturgy that the gospel penetrates into the very heart of cultures. The entire liturgical ceremony of each sacrament also has a pedagogical value; the language of signs is the best way for Christ's message to "permeate people's awareness and [be] projected into the *ethos* of a people, its essential attitudes, its institutions and all its structures" (OA, 20; John Paul II, *Address to Intellectuals in Medellín* [July 5, 1986], 2). Hence the forms of liturgical celebration must be apt for expressing the mystery being celebrated and at the same time clear and intelligible to men and women (John Paul II, *Address to UNESCO* [June 2, 1980], 6).

36 **Popular Religiosity.** Popular religiosity is a privileged expression of the inculturation of faith. It involves not only religious expressions but also values, criteria, behaviors, and attitudes that spring from Catholic dogma and constitute the wisdom of our people, shaping their cultural matrix. This way of celebrating the faith, which is so important in the life of the Church in Latin America and the Caribbean, is present in our pastoral concern. Paul VI's words (see EN 48), which the Puebla Conference accepted and developed into clear proposals, are still valid today (cf. *Puebla Conclusions,* 444ff.). We must reaffirm our intention to continue our efforts to understand better and to accompany pastorally our peoples' ways of feeling and living, and of understanding and expressing the mystery of God and Christ, in order that, purified of their possible limitations and distortions, they may come to find their proper place in our local Churches and their pastoral activity.

37 **Contemplation and Commitment.** We want to conclude these words about the Church as mystery of communion, which is fully achieved in the holiness of its members, by calling to mind the contemplative and monastic life as it exists in Latin America today, and thanking God for it. Holiness, which is the unfolding of the life of faith, hope, and charity that is received in baptism, seeks to contemplate the God of love and Jesus Christ his Son. Prophetic activity can be understood and is true and authentic only on the basis of a real and loving encounter with God who lures irresistibly (Am 3:8; Jer 20:7-9; Hos 2:16f.). When a capacity for contemplation is lacking, the liturgy, which is access to God through signs, becomes a shallow activity. We thank God for the presence of men and women dedicated to contemplation in a life based on the evangelical counsels. They are a living sign of the holiness of the whole people of God. They also constitute a powerful call to all Christians to grow in prayer which gives expression to ardent, committed faith; to faithful love contemplating God in the inner life of the Trinity and in God's saving action in history; and to unshakable hope in him who is to return to draw us into the glory of his Father who is likewise our Father (cf. Jn 20:17).

Pastoral Challenges. These observations on the holiness of the Church,   **38**
its prophetic character, and its vocation to celebration lead us to recognize
certain challenges that we regard as fundamental. They must be met in
order that the Church in Latin America and the Caribbean may fully be
the mystery of communion of human beings with God and with one another.
Prayer groups, apostolic movements, new forms of life and of contemplative
spirituality, as well as various expressions of popular religiosity are spreading within the Church. Many lay people are becoming aware of their pastoral responsibility in the various forms it takes. Interest in the Bible is
growing, thus demanding a biblical pastoral activity adequate to offer the
laity criteria for responding to the subtle accusations and appeals of a
fundamentalist interpretation or to the tendency to withdraw from life in
the Church and take refuge in sects.

Very often our own Catholics are unaware of the truth about Jesus Christ   **39**
and of the fundamental truths of the faith; sometimes this ignorance goes
along with a loss of the sense of sin. Popular religiosity, its wonderful
positive features notwithstanding, has not been purified of elements foreign
to genuine Christian faith nor does it always lead to personal acceptance
of Christ risen from the dead.

We do little preaching about the Spirit, who is at work in our hearts and   **40**
converts them, thus opening the way to holiness, the development of the
virtues, and the strength to take up Christ's cross each day (cf. Mt 10:38;
16:24).

All of this obliges us to insist on the importance of the initial procla-   **41**
mation (*kerygma*) and on catechesis. We thank God for the efforts of so
many catechists, male and female, who carry out their service in the Church
with sacrifice, which is often sealed with their lives. As pastors, however,
we must acknowledge that much remains to be done. Religious ignorance
is still widespread; catechesis does not reach everyone, and it often reaches
people superficially with contents missing or in a purely intellectual way
that lacks the power to transform people's lives and their environments.

The practice of "spiritual direction" has largely disappeared. Besides   **42**
being a condition for the maturing of priestly and religious vocations, it is
utterly essential for preparing more committed lay people.

A great deal remains to be done in the liturgy in order to assimilate into   **43**
our celebrations the liturgical renewal stimulated by Vatican II and to help
the faithful to make the celebration of the eucharist express their personal
and communal commitment to the Lord. We are not yet fully aware of the
significance of the centrality of the liturgy as the source and culmination
of the Church's life. Many people are losing the sense of the "day of the
Lord" and of its inherent demand for the eucharist; there is still little
participation of the Christian community; and we see some people attempting to make use of the liturgy with no regard for its true ecclesial sense.
Serious and ongoing liturgical formation in keeping with the instructions
and documents of the magisterium (cf. apostolic letter *Vicesimus Quintus*

Annus, 4) has been neglected on all levels. The process of a sound inculturation of the liturgy is still being neglected, and consequently liturgical
celebrations are still for many people a ritualistic and private matter that
does not make them conscious of the transforming presence of Christ and
of his Spirit, nor does it translate into a commitment in solidarity to transform the world.

44   Consequently, in many Catholics—ourselves or some of our pastoral
agents sometimes included—faith and life are out of joint. Lack of doctrinal
formation and a shallow life of faith make many Catholics an easy target
for the secularism, hedonism, and consumerism invading modern culture—
or in any case, it prevents them from evangelizing that culture.

45   **Pastoral Directions.** The new evangelization demands a renewed spirituality which, illuminated by the light of the faith that is being proclaimed,
may encourage genuine human development through God's wisdom and
be the leaven of a Christian culture. We think it is necessary to continue
and to augment the doctrinal and spiritual formation of the faithful starting
with the clergy, men and women religious, catechists, and pastoral agents,
clearly emphasizing the primacy of God's grace which saves through Jesus
Christ in the Church, through living charity and through the efficacy of the
sacraments.

46   Jesus must be proclaimed in such a way that encountering him leads to
the acknowledgment of sin in one's own life and to conversion, in a deep
experience of the grace of the Spirit received in baptism and confirmation.
Hence we must restore appreciation for the sacrament of penance, and its
pastoral practice must extend into spiritual direction for those people who
demonstrate that they are mature enough to benefit from it.

47   We must endeavor to have all members of God's people take on the
contemplative dimension of their baptismal dedication and "learn to pray"
by imitating the example of Jesus Christ (cf. Lk 11:1), so that prayer may
always be made a part of the apostolic mission in the Christian community
and in the world. To the many people who are Christians, and yet look to
practices foreign to Christianity for answers to their yearnings for an interior life, we should be able to offer the Church's rich teaching and long
experience.

48   Such an evangelization presenting Christ and his divine life in us must
demonstrate the utter need to make our behavior fit the model he offers
us. The effectiveness of the new evangelization demands that the lives of
Christians be consistent with their faith. The specific conditions in which
contemporary people are living must be known so that the faith can be
presented to them in a light-giving fashion. It also requires a clear preaching
of Christian morality that encompasses personal and family as well as social
behavior. The practice of small communities receiving good pastoral attention is a good means for learning to live the faith in close communion with
life and with a missionary projection. Apostolic movements also make a
very significant contribution in this area.

49   The new evangelization must emphasize a *kerygmatic* and missionary

catechesis. The vitality of the church community demands that there be more catechists and pastoral agents who have a solid knowledge of the Bible, enabling them to read it in the light of tradition and the Church's magisterium and, thus, shed light on their own personal situation and that of their community and society on the basis of God's word. They will be especially effective instruments for inculturating the gospel. Our catechesis must follow a continual path from infancy to maturity and should use the most fitting means for each age and situation. Catechisms are very important aids to catechesis; they are both the way to, and fruit of, a process of inculturating the faith. The *Catechism of the Catholic Church*, announced by John Paul II, will guide the preparation of our future catechisms.

The prophetic function of the Church — proclaiming Jesus Christ — must always evidence the signs of true "courage" (*parrhesia:* cf. Acts 4:13; 1 Thes 2:2), completely free of any of this world's powers. The Church's social teaching, which is the basis for, and the stimulus to, the authentic preferential option for the poor, must form part of any preaching and any catechesis. **50**

Our local Churches, which reach full expression in the liturgy, and above all in the eucharist, ought to promote a serious and continuing liturgical formation for God's people at all levels, so that they may live the liturgy spiritually, consciously, and actively. This formation ought to take into account the living presence of Christ in the celebration, its paschal and festive value, the active role of the assembly, and its missionary thrust. There should be a special concern to develop and give serious formation to those whose responsibility it is to lead prayer and the celebration of the word when there is no priest. Finally, we think that Sunday, the liturgical seasons, and the celebration of the liturgy of the hours must be given all their meaning and their evangelizing power. **51**

Community celebration ought to help integrate into Christ and his mystery the events of one's life; it should bring about a growth in fraternity and solidarity; it should be attractive to all. **52**

We must develop a liturgy that, in complete fidelity to the spirit that Vatican II sought to recover in all its purity, may strive to adopt the forms, signs, and actions proper to the cultures of Latin America and the Caribbean, within the norms laid down by the Church. In this task, special emphasis must be given to appreciating popular piety, which finds expression especially in devotion to the Blessed Virgin, pilgrimages, and shrines, and in religious feast days illuminated by the word of God. If we pastors do not make major efforts to accompany the expressions of our popular religiosity by purifying them and opening them to new situations, secularism will make further inroads into our Latin American people and the inculturation of the gospel will be made more difficult. **53**

1.2 VITAL, DYNAMIC CHURCH COMMUNITIES

"That all may be one as you Father, are in me, and I in you; I pray that they may be one in us, that the world may believe that you sent me" (Jn **54**

17:21). Such is Jesus Christ's prayer for his Church. He has prayed that the Church embody unity, according to the model of trinitarian unity (cf. GS 24). Thus did the first Christians in Jerusalem strive to live.

Conscious that the historic moment we are living demands that we "sketch the countenance of a living and dynamic Church growing in faith, becoming holier, loving, suffering, committing itself and awaiting its Lord" (OA 25), we want to turn to discover the risen Lord, who today lives in his Church, entrusts himself to it, sanctifies it (cf. Eph 5:25-26), and makes it a sign of union of all human beings among themselves and with God (cf. LG 1).

We want to reflect this "countenance" in our local Churches, parishes, and other Christian communities. We seek to impart an evangelizing drive to our Church, one that grows out of an experience of communion and participation that is already being felt in various kinds of communities on our continent.

1.2.1 The Local Church

55   Local Churches have as their mission to extend "the presence and evangelizing activity of Christ" (*Puebla Conclusions,* 224) to the various communities since they are "formed in the likeness of the universal Church; in and from these Churches there exists the one unique catholic Church" (LG 23).

The local Church is called to embody the driving force of communion and mission. "Communion and mission are profoundly connected with each other; they interpenetrate and mutually imply each other, to the point that communion represents both the source and the fruit of mission. ... It is always the one and the same Spirit who calls together and unifies the Church and sends her to preach the gospel to the ends of the earth" (CL 32).

The local Church is likewise "organic communion ... characterized by a diversity and a complementarity of vocations and states in life, of ministries, of charisms and responsibilities" (CL 20).

"In the unity of the local Church, which springs from the eucharist, is found the whole episcopal college with Peter's successor as its head, as something that belongs to the very essence of the local Church. Parishes and Christian communities are to flourish around the bishop and in perfect communion with him like vigorous cells of diocesan life" (OA 25).

In keeping with its nature and its mission of gathering the people of God in a place or region, the local Church has firsthand knowledge of the life, culture, and problems of its members and is called to use all its energies under the impulse of the Spirit to carry out the new evangelization, human development, and the inculturation of the faith in that location (cf. RM 54).

56   As a rule, our dioceses do not have enough well-trained pastoral agents.

Many do not yet have a genuine and clear pastoral planning process. We must move further along the path of communion and participation, which is often hindered by the lack of a sense of Church and of a genuine missionary spirit.

Hence it is absolutely necessary that we: 57

• Increase the number of people working in the various fields of pastoral action and provide them with adequate training in accordance with the ecclesiology of Vatican II and subsequent official church teaching.

• Set in motion comprehensive, organic planning processes to encourage the involvement of all members of the people of God, of all communities, and all the various charisms, and to guide them toward the new evangelization, including mission "to the nations."

1.2.2 The Parish

The parish — community of communities and movements — gathers   58
human anxieties and hopes and awakens and guides communion, participation, and mission. It is "not principally a structure, a territory, or a building but rather 'the family of God, a fellowship afire with a unifying spirit.' ... The parish is founded on a theological reality, because it is a eucharistic community. ... The parish is a community of faith and an organic community, that is, constituted by the ordained ministers and other Christians, in which the pastor — who represents the diocesan bishop — is the hierarchical bond with the entire particular Church" (CL 26).

If the parish is the Church present amidst people's homes, it thereby lives and works deeply within the fabric of human society and in close solidarity with its aspirations and problems.

The parish has the mission of evangelizing; celebrating the liturgy; promoting human development; and furthering the inculturation of the faith in families, in Christian base communities, apostolic groups, and movements, and in society through all of these. As organic and missionary communion, the parish is a network of communities.

The process of parish renewal in both pastoral agents and the partici-   59
pation of lay believers is still proceeding slowly. The questions facing urban parishes urgently demand solutions so that they can respond to the challenges of the new evangelization. The normal operating principles of parish activity are out of phase with the pace of modern life.

Our work must take the following directions: 60

• Renew parishes through structures that make it possible to subdivide pastoral activity into small church communities in which the responsibility of lay believers can come to the fore.

• Upgrade the formation and participation of the laity by training them to embody the gospel in the specific situations where they live or engage in activity.

• In urban parishes, joint planning in homogenous areas should be emphasized so that styles of activity for the new evangelization can be set up.

• Renew their ability to display both a welcoming attitude and missionary drive toward those believers who remain afar, and multiply the physical presence of the parish by creating chapels and small communities.

1.2.3 Christian Base Communities

61   The Christian base community (= CBC) is a living cell of the parish which, in turn, is understood as an organic and missionary community. The CBC, which is ordinarily made up of a small number of families, is called to live as a community of faith, worship, and love; it must be led by lay people, men and women adequately trained within the community process itself; the leaders must be in communion with their parish and the bishop.

"Basic Christian communities ... must always be characterized by a decisive universal and missionary thrust that instills in them a renewed apostolic dynamism" (OA 25). "These communities are a sign of vitality within the Church, an instrument of formation and evangelization, and a solid starting point for a new society based on a 'civilization of love' " (RM 51).

62   When they lack a clear ecclesiological foundation and are not sincerely seeking communion, such communities cease being ecclesial and may fall victim to ideological or political manipulation.

63   We see a need to:
• Reaffirm the validity of basic Christian communities by developing in them a spirit of mission and solidarity and seeking to integrate them into the parish, the diocese, and the universal Church, in keeping with the teachings of *Evangelii Nuntiandi* (58).
• Develop plans for pastoral activity to strengthen the training of the lay leaders who serve these communities in close communion with the pastor and the bishop.

1.2.4 The Christian Family

64   The Christian family is a "domestic church," the primary evangelizing community. "Despite the problems now besieging marriage and the institution of the family, it can still serve as the first and vital cell of society; it can create great energies that are necessary for the good of humankind" (OA 18). Pastoral work with families must be made a priority and, indeed, a basic, felt, real, and operative priority: *basic,* insofar as such work is on the frontlines of the new evangelization; *felt,* that is, a priority that the whole diocesan community accepts and assumes; *real,* insofar as the bishop and his parish priests will stand by it in a concrete and firm way; *operative* in the sense that it ought to be incorporated into joint-planned pastoral activity. Such pastoral activity must be up-to-date in its use of pastoral and

scientific tools. Religious communities and movements in general must accept family pastoral work from within their own charisms.

1.3 IN THE UNITY OF THE SPIRIT, WITH A VARIETY OF MINISTRIES AND CHARISMS

Baptism makes us God's people and living members of the Church.   **65**
Through the action of the Holy Spirit, we share in all the wealth of grace that the Risen One bestows on us.

It is this same Spirit who enables us to recognize Jesus as Lord and leads us to build up the unity of the Church from the various charisms that he entrusts to us for "the common good" (1 Cor 12:3-11). This is our nobility and our responsibility: to be bearers of the saving message to others.

Thus, Christ's salvific ministry (cf. Mt 20:28; Jn 10:10) is made present   **66**
through the service of each one of us. We exist and serve in a Church with a wealth of ministries.

1.3.1 Ordained Ministries

The ministry of bishops in communion with Peter's successor, together   **67**
with that of priests and deacons, is essential in order that the Church respond to God's saving design with the proclamation of the word, cele-bration of the sacraments, and pastoral leadership. The ordained ministry is always a service to humankind for the sake of the reign. We have received "the power of the Holy Spirit" (Acts 1:8) in order to be witnesses to Christ and instruments of new life.

Today, we turn to listen to the voice of the Lord, who is calling and sending us the challenges of the present moment. We want to remain faith-ful to the Lord and to the men and women to whose service we have been dedicated, especially to the poorest.

a) The Challenge of Unity. The council reminded us that our ministry   **68**
has a community dimension: episcopal collegiality, priestly communion, and unity among deacons. We already have bodies for coordination at the con-tinental level and in each one of our local Churches. The effort to achieve unity with those religious who share in our pastoral work in every diocese is impressive. Nevertheless, we recognize that there are reasons for concern in our local Churches: divisions and conflict that do not always reflect the unity desired by the Lord. Furthermore, due to the shortage of ministers and the overload of work that some people have to bear in exercising their ministry, many remain isolated.

Hence we have to embody reconciliation in the Church, and we must travel further along the road of unity and communion among ourselves as pastors and with the persons and communities that have been entrusted to us.

We therefore propose: **69**

• To maintain those structures that exist to enhance communion between ordained ministers, devoting particular attention to the various subsidiary functions and without impugning lines of authority as established in church law. Such structures can be reexamined and reshaped as the need arises and in keeping with the lessons of experience to make their scope and nature more clear. Such arrangements include bishops conferences, ecclesiastical provinces and regions, priests councils, and, on a continent-wide level, CELAM.

• We especially want to encourage the spirit of unity and communion in the initial training of future pastors and the ongoing training of bishops, priests, and deacons.

70   **b) The Need for a Deeper Spiritual Life.** The priesthood proceeds from the depths of the inexpressible mystery of God. Our priestly life springs from the love of the Father, the grace of Jesus Christ, and the sanctifying and unifying action of the Holy Spirit. That life is played out in service to a community so that all may become receptive to Christ's saving action (cf. Mt 20:28; PDV 12).

The 1990 Synod of Bishops and the post-synodal statement *Pastores Dabo Vobis* have clearly outlined the characteristic features of a priestly spirituality with deep insistence on pastoral charity (cf. PDV, ch. 3).

71   We therefore propose:

• To seek in our liturgical and private prayer and in our ministry an ongoing and deep spiritual renewal so that Jesus Christ may be ever present on our lips, in our hearts, and in the lives of each of us.

• To grow in the witness of holiness of life to which we are called with the aid of the means we already have at hand: "gatherings for priestly spirituality, such as spiritual exercises, days of retreat or spirituality" (PDV 80), and other means indicated in that post-synodal papal document.

72   **c) Pressing Need for Ongoing Formation.** Saint Paul urges his disciple to revive the gift he has received through the laying on of hands (cf. 2 Tm 1:6). John Paul II has reminded us that the Church needs to present credible models through priests who are convinced and fervent ministers of the new evangelization (cf. PDV 8, and ch. 6).

There is a growing awareness of the inherent need for ongoing formation, understood and undertaken as a path of conversion and a means for remaining faithful. The concrete implications of such formation on the commitment of the priest to the new evangelization demand that specific channels be created and developed to assure that it take place. It is ever more obvious that the growth process must be accompanied, striving to make it possible to take on and respond to the challenges that secularism and injustice pose to that growth process. We should devote equal attention to priests who are old or sick.

73   We consider it important:

• To prepare proposals and programs for the ongoing formation of bishops, priests, and deacons; national clergy commissions; and priests councils.

• To encourage all ordained ministers to be in continual formation structured in accordance with the guidelines of the papal magisterium, and to support them as they do so.

d) Utter Need to Be Close to Our Communities. The good shepherd knows his sheep and they know him (cf. Jn 10:14). As servants of communion we want to watch over our communities, generously surrendering ourselves and being models for the flock (cf. 1 Pt 5:1-5). We want our humble service to make all feel that we are making present Christ the head, the good shepherd, and the bridegroom of the Church (cf. PDV 10).

By being close to each individual person, pastors can share with them their situations of suffering and ignorance, of being poor and outcast, and their yearnings for justice and liberation. This is an entire program for living out more fully our role as ministers of reconciliation (cf. 2 Cor 5:18), by offering each individual reasons for hope (cf. 1 Pt 3:15) on the basis of Jesus Christ's saving proclamation (cf. Gal 5: 1).

• We bishops propose to better organize a ministry of accompanying our priests and deacons in order to support those who are in especially difficult contexts.

• All of us ministers want to maintain a humble presence within our communities and to be close to them so that all may feel God's mercy. We want to be witnesses of solidarity with our brothers and sisters.

e) Concern for Permanent Deacons. The ministry of deacons is important for our service of communion to Latin America. In a very privileged way, they are signs of the Lord Jesus, "who has come, not to be served by others, but to serve, to give his own life as a ransom for the many" (Mt 24:12).

Because he is both an ordained minister and very much a part of complex human situations, the permanent deacon has a broad field for service on our continent in a new evangelization that may respond to the needs of human development and gradually lead to a culture of solidarity by presenting the word and the Church's social teaching.

• We want to recognize our deacons more for what they are than for what they do.

• We want to accompany our deacons in discernment so that they may obtain both initial and ongoing training appropriate for their situation.

• We will continue to reflect on the spirituality specific to deacons, which is based on Christ the servant, so that with a deep sense of faith they may live out their commitment to the Church and their incorporation into the diocesan body of priests.

• We want to aid married deacons so that they may be faithful to their twofold sacramentality — that of matrimony and of holy orders — and so that their wives and children many live and share the diaconate with them. Their experience of work and their role as parents and spouses make them very well qualified co-workers for addressing the various situations demanding attention in our local Churches.

• We propose to create the space necessary so that deacons may help

74

75

76

77

in developing the services that the Church provides, by detecting and developing leaders, and promoting the shared responsibility of all in working toward a culture of reconciliation and solidarity. The deacon is the only kind of ordained minister who can reach some situations and places, especially isolated rural areas and densely populated urban areas.

1.3.2 Vocations to the Priestly Ministry and Seminaries

78   "In those days he departed to the mountain to pray, and he spent the night in prayer to God. When day came, he called his disciples to himself, and from them he chose Twelve, whom he also named apostles . . ." (Lk 6:12-13; Mk 3:13-14).

"At the sight of the crowds, his heart was moved with pity for them because they were troubled and abandoned, like sheep without a shepherd" (Mt 9:36-38).

Within a Church of "communion for mission," the Lord who calls us all to holiness calls some to priestly service.

79   **a) Pastoral Work for Vocations: A Priority.** The facts before us are undeniable: priestly vocations are on the rise, and there is a growing interest in pastoral activity aimed at clearly presenting to young people the possibility of a call from the Lord.

However, those young people who are called cannot isolate themselves from contemporary changes in the family as well as cultural economic and social changes. Family breakdown can hinder one from experiencing love in a way that helps prepare for lifelong generous self-surrender. A contagious "permissive" consumer society does not encourage a life of austerity and sacrifice. Thus, it can happen that vocational motivation may be undercut by nonevangelical urgings even without the candidate's intention.

80   Hence we think it is important to:

• Build vocational pastoral work into the overall pastoral work of the diocese and closely relate it to pastoral activity with families and youth. There is an urgent need to prepare pastoral workers, to find resources for this field of pastoral work, and to support the commitment of lay people to the promotion of consecrated vocations.

• Base vocational pastoral work on prayer, frequenting the sacraments of the eucharist and penance, catechesis for confirmation, Marian devotion, accompaniment through spiritual direction, and a specific missionary commitment. These are the main means that will help young people in their discernment.

• Make efforts to encourage vocations to arise out of all the cultures present in our local Churches. The pope has invited us to devote attention to vocations from native peoples (cf. *Message to Indigenous Peoples,* 6; *Message to African Americans,* 5).

81   • There is still a place for minor seminaries and similar kinds of centers when properly adapted to present conditions for young people in their last

years of high school, when a strong desire for choosing the priesthood begins to emerge. In some countries and under very adverse family conditions, such institutions are necessary if young people are to grow in their Christian experience and make a mature vocational option.

Since there is a resurgence of vocations among adolescents, we have the **82** task of furnishing them with adequate encouragement, discernment, and formation.

• In our vocational pastoral work, we will keep the words of the Holy Father very much in mind: "An indispensable condition for the new evangelization is that there be many qualified evangelizers available. Hence the promotion of priestly and religious vocations ... must be a priority for bishops and a commitment for the whole people of God" (OA 26).

b) Seminaries. The fact that major seminaries are springing up on our **83** continent and that the number of students in them is growing is a sign of joy and hope.

Efforts are generally made to establish a climate favorable to spiritual direction and to be up-to-date in training future priests, especially in preparing them for pastoral work.

Nevertheless, we are concerned about the difficulty of finding a training team adequate to the needs of each seminary. The quality of training suffers as a result.

Due to the environment from which they come, candidates are often marked by very secularized ways of life or come to the seminary with limitations in their human or intellectual formation or even in the foundations of their Christian faith.

In view of these situations we propose to: **84**

• Fully assume the guidelines of the post-synodal exhortation *Pastores Dabo Vobis* and on that basis reexamine our basic *Norms for Priestly Formation* in each country.

• Select and train those who provide formation, by taking advantage of courses provided by CELAM and other institutions. Before a seminary is opened there must be assurance that a formation team will be available.

• Examine the direction of the formation provided in each of our seminaries to assure that it fits the needs of the new evangelization, which in turn has consequences for human development and the inculturation of the gospel. While maintaining the standards of a serious overall formation, particular concern must be directed to the challenge represented by the priestly formation of those candidates who come from indigenous and African American cultures.

• Strive for a comprehensive formation that from the seminary onward may pave the way for the priest's ongoing formation.

1.3.3 Religious Life

As a gift from the Holy Spirit to his Church, one that belongs to the **85** Church's inner life and its holiness (cf. LG 44; EN 69), religious life is expressed in the heroic witness of many women and men religious, who on the basis of their unique covenant with God make the gospel's power present in even the most difficult situations. By faithfully living out the evangelical counsels, they share in Christ's mission and mystery; they irradiate the values of the reign; they glorify God; they provide encouragement to the church community itself; and they challenge society (cf. Lk 4:14-21; 9:1-6). The evangelical counsels are deeply paschal, since they entail being identified with Christ in his death and resurrection (see John Paul II, *Los Caminos del Evangelio* [*The Paths of the Gospel*], 17).

Through its experience of giving witness, religious life "must always be evangelizing so that those in need of the light of faith may accept the word of salvation with joy; so that the poor and the most forgotten may feel the closeness of fraternal solidarity; so that the outcast and abandoned may experience Christ's love; so that those who have no voice may feel that they are heard; so that those treated unjustly may find protection and aid" (John Paul II, *Homily in the Cathedral in Santo Domingo* [October 10, 1992], 8). The Virgin Mary, who is so deeply a part of the Christian identity of our Latin American peoples (cf. *Puebla Conclusions,* 283), is the model of life for those who have taken vows and a firm support for their fidelity.

On the basis of Vatican II and motivated by Medellín and Puebla, religious have been striving for renewal. They have sought to "return to the sources" and to the original inspiration of their orders and congregations (cf. PC 2). The role played by major superiors is very important for religious life. While respecting the purpose and spirit of each order or congregation, they deal with common issues and assure that the proper cooperation with the shepherds of the Church takes place (cf. CIC 708).

Since it is God's special gift to his Church, religious life must be ecclesial, and it enriches local Churches. Latin America's religious are renewing their allegiance to the pope. There must be an effort at greater mutual awareness between the various forms of religious life and the local Churches, based on the provisions of *Mutuae Relationes.*

86   Contemplative life is uniquely fruitful for evangelization and mission. Its entire life gives witness to the primacy of God's absoluteness. We are happy to see that the number of vocations to this kind of life is on the rise and that it is being extended to other countries.

87   The experience of secular institutes is significant, and they are growing. Through their consecration, they seek to harmonize the authentic values of the contemporary world with the following of Jesus as lived from within a secular situation. They should therefore occupy an important place in the effort of new evangelization for the sake of human development and the inculturation of the gospel.

88   Societies of apostolic life also make a generous contribution to this task of evangelization, and they are called to continue with their specific features.

89   Another form of consecration is that of virgins dedicated to God by the

bishop of the diocese; they are mystical spouses of Jesus Christ who devote themselves to serving the Church (cf. CIC 604.1).

The woman who has taken vows helps permeate with the gospel our process of comprehensive human development, and she imparts a drive to the Church's pastoral work. She is often in the more difficult mission sites and is especially sensitive to the cry of the poor. Hence she must be given greater responsibilities in the planning of pastoral and charitable activity.

"The work of evangelization in Latin America," says the pope, "has been largely the fruit of your missionary service. ... In our own time as well, men and women religious represent a primary evangelizing and apostolic force on the Latin American continent" (*Los Caminos del Evangelio*, 2.3).

In his letter to Latin American religious (*Los Caminos del Evangelio*, June 29, 1990), the Holy Father poses the following challenges: to continue "in the very front lines of preaching, always testifying to the gospel of salvation" (24); "to evangelize on the basis of a deep experience of God" (25); "to keep alive the charisms of your founders" (26); to evangelize in close collaboration with bishops, priests, and lay people, providing an example of renewed communion (cf. 27); to be in the forefront of the evangelization of cultures (cf. 28); to respond to the need to evangelize beyond our own borders.

Pastoral Directions. This fourth conference lays down the following commitments and pastoral guidelines with regard to religious life:

• Recognize religious life as a gift to our local Churches.

• Encourage the calling to holiness in religious women and men, by appreciating that their very existence and witness impart value to their life. Hence we want to respect and promote fidelity to each founding charism as a contribution to the Church.

• Engage in dialogue in mixed commissions and other bodies foreseen in the Holy See's document *Mutuae Relationes* in order to deal with the various tensions and conflicts on the basis of ecclesial communion. It is our intention that knowledge of the theology of religious life be encouraged in our seminaries and that in religious houses of formation particular importance be given to the theology of the local Church presided over by the bishop, and also to becoming familiar with the specific spirituality of the diocesan priest.

• We want to encourage initiatives by major superiors on behalf of initial and ongoing formation and spiritual accompaniment of men and women religious so that they may be able to respond to the challenges of the new evangelization. We will try to foster a missionary spirit so as to awaken in religious a yearning to serve beyond our borders.

• Support and assume the specific way of being and the missionary presence of religious in the local Church, especially when their option for the poor places them in front-line positions that are more difficult or entail a more committed form of involvement.

• Strive to assure that men and women religious who are working pas-

90

91

92

93

torally in a local Church always do so in complete communion with the bishop and the priests.

1.3.4 The Lay Faithful in the Church and in the World

94   The people of God is made up primarily of lay Christian believers. As Church—as both agents and addressees of the good news of salvation—they are called by Christ to exercise an utterly necessary evangelizing task in the world, which is God's vineyard. The words of the Lord are addressed to them today: "Go into the whole world and proclaim the gospel to every creature" (Mk 16:15; cf. CL 33). By virtue of baptism, the faithful are inserted into Christ and are called to live out the threefold priestly, prophetic, and royal function. The pastors in their particular churches should continually encourage them in their vocation.

95   a) **Lay People Today in Our Churches.** One of the signs of the times that we observe today is a large number of lay people committed to the Church; they exercise a variety of ministries, services, and functions in Christian base communities and are active in church movements. They are ever more aware of their responsibility in the world and in mission "to the nations." Thus, a sense of evangelization is growing among lay Christians. Young people are evangelizing young people; the poor are evangelizing the poor. Committed lay people indicate that they feel a need for formation and spirituality.

96   Nevertheless, it is obvious that the bulk of those baptized have not yet become fully aware that they belong to the Church. They feel that they are Catholic, but they do not feel that they are Church. Few make Christian values part of their cultural identity, and hence they feel no need to be committed to the Church and to evangelization. Consequently, the realms of work, politics, the economy, science, art, literature, and the media are not guided by gospel principles. Thus, there is an inconsistency between the faith people claim to profess and their real commitment in life (cf. *Puebla Conclusions,* 783).

It is also obvious that lay people are not always sufficiently accompanied by their pastors as they discover and mature in their own vocation. Because a certain clerical mentality persists in many pastoral agents—clergy and even lay—(cf. *Puebla Conclusions,* 784), and many lay people devote themselves to tasks within the Church and do not have an adequate formation, they are unable to respond effectively to the challenges of society today.

97   b) **The Challenges Facing Lay People.** The pressing needs of the present moment in Latin America and the Caribbean demand:

That all lay people be active agents of the new evangelization, human development, and Christian culture. Further development of the laity must be an ongoing process free of any clericalism, and it must not be reduced to matters within the Church.

That baptized people who are not evangelized be the primary targets of new evangelization. Such will truly be the case only if lay people conscious of their baptism respond to Christ's call to become active agents of the new evangelization.

In the context of ecclesial communion, there is an urgent need to encourage lay people to strive for holiness and to exercise their mission.

c) **Main Pastoral Directions.**

• Deepen the experience of the Church as communion which leads us **98** to shared responsibility for the Church's mission. Encourage the participation of lay people in pastoral councils on the various levels within the Church's structure. Avoid having lay people reduce their activity to the realm of internal church matters by urging them to move into social and cultural circles and, within those circles, to be a driving force for transforming society in the light of the gospel and the Church's social teaching.

• Encourage the formation of lay councils in full communion with their pastors and yet sufficiently independent, so that they may serve as places for coming together, dialogue, and service and thus help strengthen the unity, spirituality, and organization of the laity. Such lay councils are also places for formation and may be set up in each diocese in the Church in every country. They can include apostolic movements, as well as lay people who are committed to evangelization but are not members of apostolic groups.

• Encourage comprehensive, gradual, and ongoing training of lay people **99** through agencies that may serve to "train trainers." They may also schedule courses and set up diocesan and national training centers, while devoting special attention to the formation of the poor.

• As an immediate pastoral objective, we will strive as pastors to intensify formation for lay people who are prominent in the areas of education, politics, the media, culture, and labor. We will encourage a specific line of pastoral work aimed at each of these areas so that people in those areas will feel that they have the full support of their pastors. Among those included will be the military, whose task it is to be ever at the service of the freedom, democracy, and peace of their peoples (cf. GS 79).

• Bearing in mind that all Christians are called to holiness, the pastors are to endeavor to provide all the proper means for helping lay people to have a genuine experience of God. They will also encourage the publication of materials specifically on lay spirituality.

• Encourage lay people to be organized on all levels of the pastoral **100** structure, based on criteria of communion and participation and respecting "the freedom for lay people in the Church to form such groups" (CL 29-30).

d) **Ministries Conferred on Lay People.** The Puebla document gathered **101** up our continent's experience of lay ministries and provided clear guidelines in order to encourage, in keeping with the charisms of each person and the needs of each community, "special creativity . . . to establish ministries or services that can be exercised by the laity to meet the needs of evangelization" (*Puebla Conclusions,* 833; cf. 804-805; 811-817). The 1987 Synod of Bishops and the apostolic exhortation *Christifideles Laici* have insisted that it is important to show that these ministries "find their foundation in the sacraments of baptism and confirmation" (CL 23).

In keeping with the Holy Father's guidelines, we want to continue to encourage such experiences. They offer broad scope for lay participation (cf. CL 21-23) and meet the needs of many communities. Without this precious collaboration, those communities would be left without anyone to accompany them in catechesis and prayer, and to encourage them in their social and charitable commitments.

We believe that "new expressions and new methods" for our evangelizing mission are finding broad areas in which they can be embodied in the "ministries, offices, and roles" that some carefully chosen and trained lay people may exercise (cf. CL 23). One such appropriate form might be that a whole family be given the pastoral responsibility for guiding other families, and that it be properly trained for that role.

102   e) **Church Movements and Associations.** In response to situations of secularism, atheism, and religious indifference, and as a fruit of the aspiration and need for the religious (cf. CL 4), the Holy Spirit has prompted the rise of movements and associations of lay people that have already produced much fruit in our Churches.

These movements give priority to the word of God and praying together, and they are particularly attentive to the action of the Spirit. Sometimes the experience of a shared faith leads to a need for a Christian sharing in goods, which is a first step toward an economy of solidarity.

Associations for the apostolate are legitimate and necessary (cf. AA 18). In accordance with the council, "Catholic Action" occupies a special place because of its deep connection to the local Church (cf. AA 20; CL 31). Since there is a danger that some movements and associations may become closed in on themselves, it is crucially important to bear in mind the "criteria of ecclesiality" indicated in the post-synodal exhortation *Christifideles Laici* (cf. 30). Such movements must be accompanied by a more clearly defined process of inculturation. The formation of movements with more of a Latin American stamp should be encouraged. "The Church expects a great deal of all those lay people who, enthusiastically and with the efficacy of the gospel, are involved through the new apostolic movements. Those movements, which reflect the need for a greater presence of the faith in the life of society, must be coordinated by means of overall pastoral planning" (OA 27).

103   f) **Lay People, a Pastoral Priority.** Because it is so important that the laity be present in the task of the new evangelization, which leads to human development and ultimately permeates the whole of the culture with the power of the Risen One, we can state that as a result of this fourth conference, one of the main lines of our pastoral work must be that of a Church in which lay Christian believers are the active agents. A mature, committed,

well-organized laity always in formation is the sign of local Churches that
have taken the commitment to new evangelization very seriously.

1.3.5 Women

In Christ, fullness of time, the equality and complementarity with which   **104**
man and woman were created (cf. Gn 1:27) become possible, since "there
is not male and female; for you are all one in Christ Jesus" (Gal 3:26-29).
Jesus welcomed women; he restored their dignity to them, and after his
resurrection he entrusted to them the mission of announcing him (cf. MD
16). "Born of a woman" (Gal 4:4), Christ gives us Mary, who goes before
the Church, eminently and uniquely standing as the model of Virgin and
Mother (cf. LG 63). She forges history through her free cooperation, which
attains the greatest degree of sharing with Christ (cf. *Puebla Conclusions*
293). Mary has played a very important role in the evangelization of Latin
American women; she has also made them effective evangelizers, as wives,
mothers, women religious, workers, farmers, and professional people. She
continually inspires them with the courage to give their lives; to bend over
to help those in pain; to resist and to give hope when life is most threatened;
to find alternatives when paths are being blocked; and to do so as an active
and free partner who energizes society.

Situation. In our age, society and the Church have become increasingly   **105**
aware that woman and man are equal in dignity. Although this equality is
acknowledged theoretically, it is often ignored in practice. The new evangelization should firmly and actively promote the enhancement of women's
dignity. Hence, we must delve more deeply into women's role in the Church
and in society.

• Today various reductionistic claims about woman's nature and mission
are being propagated: her specifically feminine dimension is denied; her
dignity and rights are slighted; she is made an object of pleasure and has
a secondary role in the life of society. In response we want to set forth the
gospel teaching on woman's dignity and calling, emphasizing her role "as
mother, defender of life, and educator of the home" (*Puebla Conclusions,*
846).

A greater solidarity between men and women is gaining ground today,   **106**
both within the family and in the building of the world, but further advances
must be made toward real equality and toward the discovery that both find
fulfillment in reciprocity.

In the family, in church communities, and in the various organizations
within a country, it is women who most communicate, sustain, and promote
life, faith, and values. For centuries, they have been the "guardian angel
of the Christian soul of the continent" (John Paul II, *Homily in Santo
Domingo* [October 11, 1992], 9). Such acknowledgment clashes scandalously
with the fact that women are frequently excluded, their dignity is imperiled,
and they are often subject to violence. She who gives and defends life is

denied a decent life. The Church feels called to take a stand for life and to defend it in women.

107   **Pastoral Commitments.** We regard the following lines of action as urgent:

• Courageously denounce assaults against Latin American and Caribbean women, especially farming and indigenous women, migrants, and workers, including assaults against their dignity committed by the mass media. Promote comprehensive formation so that people will become truly conscious of the dignity men and women have in common. Prophetically proclaim woman's true essence, drawing from the gospel the light and hope of what she is in fullness without reducing it to passing cultural fashions. Create spaces in which women may discover their true values, esteem them, and openly offer them to society and to the Church.

108   • Make priests and lay leaders more conscious so that they may accept and appreciate women in the church community and in society, not only for what they do but especially for what they are. Encourage a stance of critical analysis toward media messages with regard to the stereotypes they present about femininity. In the light of the gospel of Jesus carry out a discernment among the movements struggling for women from various perspectives so as to energize their positive aspects, shed light on what might seem confused, and criticize what is contrary to human dignity. When we read the Scriptures, forcefully proclaim what the gospel means for women and develop a reading of God's word that may uncover the features that woman's calling contributes to the plan of salvation.

109   • In education, develop new languages and symbols that will not reduce anyone to the category of object but rather will restore the value of each individual as a person; in educational programs eliminate material that discriminates against women by debasing their dignity and identity. It is important to implement educational programs on love and sex from a Christian perspective and to try to find ways in which interpersonal relations between man and woman will be based on mutual respect and esteem, acknowledgement of differences, dialogue, and reciprocity. Women must be incorporated responsibly into the decision-making process in all areas in both family and society. It is important that we have female leadership and that the woman's presence in organizing and leading the new evangelization in Latin America and the Caribbean be promoted. We must encourage the development of a kind of pastoral work that may advance indigenous women socially, educationally, and politically.

110   • Condemn whatever affects woman's dignity by attacking life, such as abortion, sterilization, birth-control programs, and violence in sexual relationships; foster the means for assuring a decent life for those women who are most vulnerable: domestic servants, migrants, peasant women, indigenous, African American women, poor and exploited working women; intensify and renew pastoral accompaniment of women in difficult situations:

separated, divorced, single mothers, children and women forced into prostitution by hunger, deceit, and abandonment.

1.3.6 Adolescents and Youth

Jesus has gone through the same life-stages as every human person: **111**
childhood, adolescence, youth, adulthood. He reveals himself as the way,
the truth, and the life (cf. Jn 14:5). When he was born, he took on the
condition of a poor child and was subject to his parents; he had scarcely
been born when he was persecuted (cf. Mt 2:13). That very Jesus, revelation
of the Father who wills life in abundance (cf. Jn 10:10), restores the life of
his friend Lazarus (cf. Jn 22), of the young son of the widow of Naim (cf.
Lk 7:7-17), and of Jairus's young daughter (cf. Mk 5:21-43). Today he
continues to call young people in order to give their lives meaning.

The mission of Latin American adolescents and young people who are
on their way toward the third Christian millennium is to prepare themselves
to be the men and women of the future, responsible and active in social,
cultural, and church structures. Thus prompted both by the Spirit of Christ
and their own creative spark to join in the effort to devise original solutions,
they may help bring about a kind of development that is ever more human
and more Christian (John Paul II, *Homily in Higüey, Dominican Republic*
[October 12, 1992], 4).

Situation. Many young people suffer the effects of poverty, and of rejec- **112**
tion by society, of joblessness and underemployment, of an education that
does not meet the needs of their lives; they suffer from drug traffic, guer-
rillas, gangs, prostitution, alcoholism, and sexual abuse; many are tran-
quilized by advertising and propaganda and are alienated by cultural
imposition and by a concern for short-term results that has created new
problems for adolescents and young people in their process of emotional
maturing.

Yet we find that some adolescents and young people stand up to the
prevailing consumerism and become sensitive to people's infirmities and to
the pain of the poorest. They strive to take their place in society by rejecting
corruption and creating genuinely democratic areas for participation. More
and more are joining together in ecclesial groups, movements, and communities to pray and engage in a variety of missionary and apostolic activities. Adolescents and young people are brimming with vital questions.
Their challenge is to have a comprehensive personal and community life-
direction that can give meaning to their lives so that they may thereby
achieve their potential. A further challenge is the need to accompany them
along the way as they grow in their faith and their work in the Church, and
in their concerns to bring about the needed change in society through
organized pastoral activity.

Young Catholics organized into groups in the Latin American Church **113**
ask their pastors to accompany them spiritually and to support them in

their activities. What they most need in each country, however, are clear pastoral directions that may help establish comprehensive pastoral youth activity.

114   **Pastoral Commitments.** We propose to implement the following pastoral actions:

• Reaffirm the "preferential option" for young people announced at Puebla not merely in feelings but practically. That should entail a concrete option for a comprehensive pastoral activity with young people, involving accompaniment and real support, along with mutual dialogue among young people, pastors, and communities. To truly make an option for young people requires greater personal and material resources on the part of parishes and dioceses. Such pastoral work with youth must always have a vocational dimension.

115   In order to make that option we propose that there be pastoral activity:

• That meets the needs for emotional maturing and the need to accompany adolescents and young people throughout the process of human formation and the growth of faith. Special importance is to be given to the sacrament of confirmation so that its celebration will lead young people to apostolic commitment and to be evangelizers of other young people.

• That develops an ability to be aware of, and respond critically to, the impact that culture and society have on them and helps them become committed to the Church's pastoral work and to the changes needed in society.

116   • That energizes a spirituality of following Jesus, brings faith and life together, and promotes justice and solidarity, and that fosters an overall thrust that can give hope and create a new culture of life.

117   • That takes on new ways of celebrating faith proper to youth culture and fosters creativity and the pedagogy of signs, while always respecting the essential elements of the liturgy.

118   • That proclaims in commitments assumed and in everyday life that the God of life loves young people and desires that they have a different future in which they will not be frustrated and excluded and in which a full life may be available to everybody.

119   • That can open participatory areas for adolescents and young people in the Church itself. That the pedagogy used in the educational process be experiential, participatory, and transforming. That it foster active involvement through the methodology of see, judge, act, review, and celebrate. Such a process must integrate the growth of faith into the human growth process, taking into account various elements such as sports, celebration, music, and theater.

• Such pastoral activity should keep in mind and strengthen all those organic processes that are valid and that the Church has extensively analyzed since Puebla. It will take special care to give prominence to pastoral work with youth in those particular *milieux* where adolescents and young people live and act: peasants, indigenous people, African Americans, workers, students, residents in the poor outskirts of cities, the marginalized, the military, and young people in critical situations.

• Through its word and witness, the Church must primarily present Jesus Christ in an attractive and inspiring way to adolescents and young people so that he may be their way, truth, and life and thus respond to their yearnings for personal fulfillment and their need to find a meaning to life itself.

• In order to respond to the contemporary cultural situation, youth pas- **120** toral activity must present the gospel ideals forcefully and in a way that is attractive and accessible to young people in their lives. It should foster the creation and leadership of energetic and gospel-oriented groups and communities of young people. Such groups may serve to sustain the educational process of adolescents and young people and sensitize and commit them to respond to the challenges of human development, solidarity, and building the civilization of love.

1.4 TO PROCLAIM THE REIGN TO ALL PEOPLES

Christ reveals the Father to us and draws us into the mystery of the **121** trinitarian life through the Spirit. Everything passes through Christ who becomes way, truth, and life. Through baptism we receive divine filiation; having all become children of God, we peoples of Latin America have all become brothers and sisters to one another.

We have been drawn into the mystery of trinitarian communion because Christ has become one with us by taking on the condition of a slave and everything that is part of our human condition — except sin — in order to transform it, give it life, and make it ever more human and divine. In this fashion, Christ now enters into the heart of our peoples and takes up and transforms those peoples.

When we are incorporated into him, he communicates his life of love to us, as the vine to the branches, by pouring out his Spirit, who enables us to forgive, to love God above all things, and to love all our brothers and sisters without regard for race, nation, or economic situation. Thus, Jesus Christ is the seed of a new reconciled humankind.

In Latin America many people live in poverty, which often reaches **122** shocking levels. Even in limit-situations, however, we are able to love one another, to live in unity despite our differences, and to provide the world with our radiant experience as brothers and sisters.

We joyfully testify that in Jesus Christ we have integral liberation for **123** each one of us and for our peoples: liberation from sin, death, and slavery, which consists of forgiveness and reconciliation.

Jesus calls us together in his Church, which is sacrament of evangelizing communion. There we are to live the unity of our Churches in charity and to communicate and proclaim this communion to the whole world through the word, the eucharist, and the other sacraments. The Church lives in order to evangelize; its life and vocation are realized when it becomes witness, when it prompts conversion and leads men and women to salvation (cf. EN 15). "Thus the Church began the great task of evangelization on the day when the apostles received the Holy Spirit" (OA 2).

124   Jesus Christ gives us life in order to communicate it to all. Our mission demands that in union with our peoples we be open to receive this life in fullness in order to communicate it abundantly to the churches entrusted to us, and beyond our borders as well. We ask forgiveness for our frailties, and we implore the grace of the Lord so that we may be more effective in carrying out the mission that we have received. We invite everyone, renewed in the Spirit, to also proclaim Jesus Christ and become missionaries of life and of hope for all our brothers and sisters. The new evangelization must be able to awaken a new missionary fervor in a Church that is ever more rooted in the perennial strength and power of Pentecost (cf. EN 41).

1.4.1 Projecting the Mission "to the Nations"

125   Arising out of the Father's saving love, the mission of the Son with power of the Holy Spirit (cf. Lk 4:18), which is the very essence of the Church (cf. AG 2) and fundamental object of this fourth general conference, is our primary responsibility.

In his encyclical on mission, John Paul II has led us to discern three ways of carrying out this mission: pastoral care in situations where faith is alive, the new evangelization, and missionary activity "to the nations" [*ad gentes*] (cf. RM 33).

We are renewing this latter sense of mission fully aware that new evangelization is impossible without a projection toward the non-Christian world, for as the pope points out: "It is in commitment to the Church's universal mission that the new evangelization of Christian peoples will find inspiration and support" (RM 2).

We are pleased that we can say that, out of our poverty, people have responded to the challenge of the mission "to the nations" proposed at Puebla and have shared the wealth of our faith with which the Lord has blessed us. We nevertheless acknowledge that awareness of mission to the nations is still insufficient or weak. Latin American Missionary Congresses (COMLAS), national missionary congresses, missionary groups and movements, and aid received from sister churches have served to motivate us to become aware of this gospel demand.

Pastoral Challenges.

126   • There has not been enough insistence that we must be better evangelizers.

• We become enclosed in our own local problems and forget our apostolic commitment to the non-Christian world.

• We pass our missionary commitment on to some of our brothers and sisters to discharge for us.

The root of all this is the lack of an explicit program of missionary   **127**
formation in most seminaries and houses of formation.

We invite each local Church in Latin America to: **128**

• Bring the energy of mission into its ordinary pastoral activity, with the support of a diocesan mission run by a missionary team and moved by a living spirituality toward a creative and generous missionary action.

• Establish a positive relationship with the missionary activities of the papacy which should be put in the hands of a capable person and have the backing of the local Church.

• Encourage all of God's people to provide missionary cooperation, translated into prayer, sacrifice, witness of Christian life, and financial support.

• Incorporate into programs of priestly and religious formation specific courses in missiology, and instruct candidates for the priesthood on how important it is that the gospel be inculturated.

• Train native pastoral agents with a missionary spirit along the lines indicated in the encyclical, *Redemptoris Missio*.

• Courageously agree to send missionaries—whether priests, religious, or lay people. Coordinate human and material resources in order to strengthen the processes of training, sending, accompaniment, and reincorporation of missionaries.

1.4.2 Reinvigorating the Faith of Those Baptized Who Are Afar

Our God is a Father rich in mercy. God respects the freedom of his sons   **129**
and daughters and awaits the moment of return, going forth to meet those who have strayed far from their home (cf. Lk 15).

Pastoral Challenge. Many baptized people in Latin America and the   **130**
Caribbean do not steer their lives by the gospel. Many draw away from the Church and do not identify with it. These include many young people and those who are more critical of what the Church does, although they are not the only ones. Other people become uprooted from their religious environment when they move away from their native region.

Pastoral Guidelines. As pastors of the Church, we are concerned about   **131**
this situation. We are likewise pained to observe that many of our faithful are unable to communicate to others the joy of their faith. Jesus Christ asks us to be the "salt of the earth," and leaven in the dough. Hence, while not neglecting to care for those who are near, the Church—both pastors and faithful—must go out to meet those who are far away.

The doors of many of these distant brothers and sisters are waiting for the Lord to knock (cf. Rv 3:20) through Christians who take on their baptism and confirmation in a missionary spirit and go out to meet those who have wandered far from the Father's house. Hence, we make these suggestions:

• Develop a new missionary drive toward these believers and go out to meet them. The Church must not remain content with those who accept and follow it more easily.

• Preach the *kerygma* to them in a lively and joyful manner.

• Organize missionary campaigns that can unveil the ever contemporary newness of Jesus Christ, especially through house visits and popular missions.

• Take advantage of those moments in which the baptized have contact with the Church, such as the baptism of their children, first communion, confirmation, illness, marriage, and funerals, in order to unveil to them the ever contemporary newness of Jesus Christ.

• Strive to approach through the media those who cannot be reached directly.

• Motivate and encourage ecclesial communities and movements to redouble their evangelizing service within the pastoral direction taken by the local Church.

1.4.3 Uniting All Brothers and Sisters in Christ

132   "That they may all be one, as you, Father, are in me and I in you, that they may also be in us, that the world may believe that you have sent me" (Jn 17:21). This prayer of Christ is the basis for Vatican II's deploring of the scandal of divisions among Christians (cf. UR 1), and it demands that we find the most effective ways to attain unity in truth.

133   **Pastoral Challenge.** The great challenge before us is this division between Christians, a division that for various reasons has been aggravated over the course of history.

• Confusion over the issue as the result of a deficient religious formation, among other reasons.

• Proselytizing fundamentalism by sectarian Christian groups who hinder the sound ecumenical path.

134   • We may regard the whole Jewish people as being in a situation similar to that of separated Christians. Dialogue with them is also a challenge to our Church.

135   **Pastoral Guidelines.** We therefore join John Paul II in saying: "Ecumenism is a priority for the Church's pastoral activity in our age." In order to respond adequately to this challenge we make these suggestions:

• Consolidate ecumenical work and spirit in truth, justice, and charity.

• Deepen relationships of convergence and dialogue with those Churches who pray the creed of Nicea-Constantinople, who share the same sacraments and who revere Holy Mary, Mother of God, even if they do not acknowledge the primacy of the Roman pontiff.

• Intensify ecumenical theological dialogue.

• Encourage prayer in common for Christian unity and especially the week of prayer for the unity of believers.

• Promote ecumenical formation in training courses for pastoral agents, especially in seminaries.

• Encourage study of the Bible between theologians and scholars in the Church and in Christian denominations.

• Maintain and strengthen programs and initiatives in the way of joint cooperation in the social realm and in promoting shared values.

• Appreciate CELAM's division for ecumenism (SECUM) and collaborate with its endeavors.

1.4.4 Engaging in Dialogue with Non-Christian Religions

"God, in an age-long dialogue, has offered and continues to offer salvation to humankind. In faithfulness to the divine initiative, the Church too must enter into a dialogue of salvation with all men and women" (DP 38). The Church is well aware that the dialogue it promotes has a witnessing character while at the same time the person and nature of the dialogue partner is to be respected (cf. *Puebla Conclusions* 1114). **136**

Pastoral Challenges.

• The importance of deepening a dialogue with the non-Christian religions on our continent, and especially with indigenous and African American religions, which have been ignored or shunted aside for a long time. **137**

• The existence of prejudice and misunderstanding as an obstacle to dialogue.

Pastoral Directions. In order to intensify interreligious dialogue, we think it is important to: **138**

• Foster a change of attitude on our own part, leaving aside historical prejudices in order to establish a climate of trust and familiarity.

• Promote dialogue with Jews and Muslims despite the problems that the Church suffers in countries where these are the majority religions.

• Deepen knowledge of Judaism and Islam among pastoral agents.

• Encourage pastoral agents to develop a knowledge of other religions and manifestations of religion existing on our continent.

• Seek activities on behalf of peace, the promotion and defense of human dignity, and cooperation in defending creation and ecological balance as a way of coming together with other religions.

• Seek occasions for dialogue with African American and indigenous religions while being alert to discover in them the "seeds of the Word" with true Christian discernment, offering them the complete proclamation of the gospel and avoiding any kind of religious syncretism.

1.4.5 Fundamentalist Sects

The problem of the sects has reached dramatic proportions and has become truly worrisome, particularly due to increasing proselytism. **139**

140   Fundamentalist sects are religious groups that insist that only faith in Jesus Christ saves, that the only basis for faith is Scripture interpreted personally in a fundamentalist manner, and hence excluding the Church; they emphasize the end of the world and the proximity of judgment.

They are characterized by their very enthusiastic proselytizing through persistent house visiting and large-scale distribution of Bibles, magazines, and books; their presence and the opportunistic help they provide at times of personal or family crisis; and their great technical skill in using the media. They have at their disposal immense funding from other countries and the tithes they oblige all their members to pay.

Other features are a rigorous moralism, prayer meetings with a participatory and emotional Bible-based worship, and their aggressive stance toward the Church; they often resort to defamation and to material inducements. Although they are only weakly committed to the temporal realm, they tend to become involved in politics with a view to taking power.

Such fundamentalist sects have grown enormously in Latin America since the time of Puebla.

141   **Pastoral Challenges.** Provide an effective pastoral response to the advance of the sects by making the Church's evangelizing activity more present in the vulnerable sectors such as migrants, those populations unattended by priests or in which there is a great deal of religious ignorance, and simple people or those with material needs and family problems.

Pastoral Directions.

142   • Strive to make the Church ever more communitarian and participatory through ecclesial communities, family groups, Bible circles, and ecclesial movements and associations so that the parish becomes a community of communities.

• Bring Catholics to personal acceptance of Christ and to the Church by proclaiming the risen Lord.

• Develop a catechesis that can properly instruct the people by explaining the mystery of the Church, which is sacrament of salvation and communion, the mediation of the Virgin Mary and the saints, and the mission of the hierarchy.

• Foster a ministerial Church by increasing the number of ordained ministers and encouraging properly trained lay ministers so as to enhance evangelizing service throughout God's people.

143   • Reaffirm the Church's identity by cultivating its characteristic features such as:

   a) Devotion to the mystery of the eucharist, sacrifice and paschal banquet;
   b) Devotion to the Blessed Virgin Mary, mother of Christ and mother of the Church;
   c) Communion and obedience to the Roman pontiff and to one's own bishop;
   d) Devotion to God's word as read in the Church.

• Strive to make the contemplative dimension and holiness a priority in   **144**
all pastoral planning, so that the Church may bring about God's presence
in contemporary human beings who so long for him.

• Create the conditions so that all ministers of God's people may offer   **145**
a witness of life and charity, spirit of service, and a welcoming spirit, especially at moments of suffering and crisis.

• Promote a lively and participatory liturgy projecting outward toward
life.

• Calmly and objectively provide the people with ample instruction on   **146**
the features and differences of the various sects and on how to answer
unjust accusations against the Church.

• Promote home visiting by trained lay people and organize a specific
form of pastoral work aimed at welcoming Catholics back to the Church.

1.4.6 New Religious Movements or Free Religious Movements

In phenomenological terms, these are social and cultural groups whose   **147**
drive comes from poor segments of society but also from the middle and
upper classes in Latin America, who find a way of expressing their identity
and human yearnings in syncretistic religious forms. From the standpoint
of Catholic faith, these phenomena can be regarded as signs of the times
and as a warning that the Church is absent from some circles and must
reexamine its evangelizing activity.

Several currents or kinds of phenomena can be distinguished:

• Para-Christian or semi-Christian forms, such as the Jehovah's Witnesses and Mormons. Each of these movements has its own characteristics,
but they share a proselytizing approach, millenarianism, and an organiza-
tional style similar to those of businesses.

• Esoteric forms that seek special enlightenment and share secret items
of knowledge and a religious concern for the occult. Such is the case of
spiritist, Rosacrucian, gnostic, theosophical, and similar currents.

• Philosophies and kinds of worship that have some oriental aspects but
are rapidly adapting to our continent, such as Hare Krishna, Divine Light,
Ananda Marga, and others, which offer mysticism and a communal experience.

• Groups that spring from the great Asian religions whether Buddhism
(e.g., Seicho no Ié), Hinduism (e.g., yoga), or Islam (e.g., Baha'i), which
are not only a manifestation of immigrants from Asia but are also taking
root in some sectors of our society.

• Socio-religious enterprises, like the Moon sect or the New Acropolis,
which have clear ideological and political aims along with their religious
expressions in media crusades and proselytizing campaigns. They draw on
help or inspiration from the First World; with regard to religion they
emphasize immediate conversion and healing, thus giving rise to the so-
called electronic Churches.

• A vast array of centers for "divine healing," which deal with the spiritual or physical ills of people who have problems or are poor. These therapeutic cults serve their clients individually.

148 Since there are so many of these new religious movements and they differ a great deal from one to another, we want to center our attention on the reasons for their growth (cf. *Puebla Conclusions* 1122) and the pastoral challenges they pose.

149 The explanations offered for why they arouse interest in some people are numerous and varied. Among them we should note:

• The ongoing and deepening social crisis, which arouses a certain collective anxiety and loss of identity and causes people to lose their roots.

• The ability these movements have to adapt to social circumstances and momentarily satisfy some needs of people. A taste for novelty certainly plays a role.

• The fact that the Church has become distant from some groups— whether poor or rich—who are seeking new channels of religious expression, but who also may be evading the commitments entailed in faith.

• Their ability to provide an apparent solution to the desires for "healing" on the part of people who are suffering.

Pastoral Challenges.

150 • Our greatest challenge is to evaluate the Church's evangelizing activity and to determine which circles it reaches and which it does not reach.

• Learn how to respond adequately to the questions people ask themselves on the meaning of life, on the meaning of our relationship with God, in the midst of our ongoing and deepening social crisis.

• Acquire greater knowledge of the identities and cultures of our peoples.

151 **Pastoral Directions.** In the face of these challenges, we propose the following pastoral directions:

• Offer help for discerning life's problems in the light of faith. In this respect, we must restore the value of the sacrament of penance and spiritual direction.

• Strive to adapt our evangelization and celebrations of faith to the cultures and subjective needs of the faithful without falsifying the gospel.

• Engage in a deep reexamination of our pastoral work in order to improve the quality of the means we use and the witness we give.

• Treat religious movements in a differentiated way in accordance with their nature and their attitudes toward the Church.

152 • Foster a living liturgy in which the faithful may be drawn into the mystery.

• Present a Christian anthropology, which provides the meaning of human potential, the meaning of resurrection, and the meaning of our relationships with the universe. Keep in mind that indifferentism must be combatted by adequately presenting the ultimate meaning of the human being. For that purpose a presentation of the last things will be very helpful.

1.4.7 Inviting the Godless and the Indifferent

The phenomenon of unbelief is growing in Latin America and the Car-   **153**
ibbean today. It is of concern to the Church, especially with regard to those
who live as though they were not baptized (cf. EN 56).

One of its forms is *secularism,* which denies God, either because it holds
that all things can be explained in themselves without any need to invoke
God, or because it regards God as inimical and as alienating to human
beings. This secularist position should be distinguished from the process
known as *secularization,* which rightfully maintains that the material realities
of nature and human beings are inherently "good," that their laws must be
respected, and that freedom is for the sake of human self-fulfillment and
is respected by God (cf. GS 36).

The other form is the *indifferentism* of those who either reject any religion
because they regard it as useless or harmful for human life and hence are
uninterested in it, or because they hold that all religions are equal and
therefore none can claim to be the one true religion.

Pastoral Challenges.

• *Secularism* is a serious challenge to the new evangelization since it   **154**
regards God as incompatible with human freedom (cf. OA 11) and religion
as a dehumanizing and alienating stance because it separates human beings
from their earthly responsibility. Moreover, by rejecting dependence on the
Creator, it leads to the idolatries of possession, power, and pleasure and
to a loss of life's meaning by reducing human beings to their merely material
value.

• *Indifferentism* also challenges the new evangelization because it cuts
off the creature's relationship to God at the root, that is, it rejects any
concern for religion and hence for the commitment of faith, or because it
brings the figure of Christ down to where he is simply a teacher of morality
or the founder of a religion alongside others of equal stature, thus denying
that he is the sole, universal, and definitive savior of human beings.

• Likewise, both *indifferentism* and *secularism* undermine morality
because they deprive human behavior of any ethical foundation and hence
easily fall into the relativism and permissiveness that characterize contemporary society.

Many pseudo-religious movements of an orientalist cast and those of the   **155**
occult, divination, or spiritism undermine faith and confuse people by providing false solutions to the great questions about human beings, that is,
their destiny, their freedom, and the meaning of life.

Pastoral Guidelines. The new evangelization demands that we: **156**

• Provide formation in a faith that becomes life, initiating that faith by
proclaiming the *kerygma* to those who are in the dechristianized world (cf.
EN 51 and 52) and fostering it with the joyful witness of genuine faith
communities in which our lay people live out the meaning of the sacraments.

• Cultivate a solid moral conscience so that in the complex circumstances of modern life our faithful may be able to interpret soundly the voice of God in moral matters and develop a gospel sense of sin.

• Educate Christians to see God in their own person, in nature, in all of history, in work, in culture, in the whole secular realm by discovering the harmony that according to God's plan should exist between the order of creation and that of redemption.

• Develop a way of celebrating the liturgy that may integrate the life of human beings into a deep and respectful experience of the unfathomable divine mystery of inexpressible wealth.

• Encourage pastoral activity suitable for the evangelization of university circles, where those who will play a decisive role in shaping culture are now being trained.

CHAPTER 2: HUMAN DEVELOPMENT

157   "Between evangelization and human advancement—development and liberation—there are in fact profound links. These include links of an anthropological order, because the person who is to be evangelized is not an abstract being but is subject to social and economic questions. They also include links in the theological order, since one cannot dissociate the plan of creation from the plan of redemption. The latter plan touches the very concrete situation of injustice to be combatted and of justice to be restored. They include links of the eminently evangelical order, which is that of charity: How in fact can one proclaim the new commandment without promoting in justice and in peace true, authentic human development?" (EN 31).

The ultimate meaning of the Church's commitment to human development, continually reiterated in its social teaching, lies in the firm conviction that "... genuine exterior social union has its origin in the union of minds and hearts ... in faith and love" (GS 42). "Through the gospel message, the Church offers a force for liberation which promotes development precisely because it leads to conversion of heart and of ways of thinking, fosters the recognition of each person's dignity, encourages solidarity, commitment, and service of one's neighbor" (RM 59). "In carrying on these activities, however, she never loses sight of the priority of the transcendent and spiritual realities which are premises of eschatological salvation" (RM 20). By acting in this manner, the Church offers its specific participation to human development, which is the obligation of all.

158   The Church's social teaching is what the magisterium proposes on social matters. It contains principles, criteria, and guidelines for the activity of believers in the task of transforming the world in accordance with God's plan. Teaching the Church's social thought is "part of the Church's evan-

gelizing mission" (SRS 41) and is "a valid instrument of evangelization" (CA 54) because it sheds light on how we are to live our faith.

2.1 HUMAN DEVELOPMENT: A PRIVILEGED DIMENSION
OF THE NEW EVANGELIZATION

Jesus told his disciples to distribute the bread that had been multiplied **159** to the needy crowd, and thus "they all ate and were satisfied" (Mk 6:34-44). He cured the sick, and "he went about doing good" (Acts 10:38). At the end of time he will judge us by love (cf. Mt 25).

Jesus is the good Samaritan (cf. Lk 10:25-37), who embodies charity. Not only is he moved emotionally; he becomes real aid. His action is prompted by the dignity of every human being. The foundation for that dignity lies in Jesus Christ himself as creative Word (cf. Jn 1:3) made flesh (cf. Jn 1:14). In the words of the *Pastoral Constitution on the Church in the Modern World:* "In fact, it is only in the mystery of the Word incarnate that light is shed on the mystery of humankind. For Adam, the first human being, was a representation of the future, namely of Christ the Lord. It is Christ, the last Adam, who fully discloses humankind to itself and unfolds its noble calling by revealing the mystery of the Father and the Father's love" (GS 22).

This dignity was not lost through the wound of sin, but was raised up by God's compassion, which is revealed in the heart of Jesus Christ (cf. Mk 6:34). Hence, while Christian solidarity is certainly service to those in need, it is primarily fidelity to God. This is the basis for the intimate connection between evangelization and human development (cf. EN 31).

Our faith in the God of Jesus Christ and love for our brothers and sisters **160** must be translated into concrete deeds. Following Christ means being committed to live in his manner. This concern for consistency between faith and life has always been present in Christian communities. The apostle Saint James wrote: "What good is it, my brothers, if someone says he has faith but does not have works? If a brother or sister has nothing to wear and has no food for the day, and one of you says to them, 'Go in peace, keep warm, and eat well,' but you do not give them the necessities of the body, what good is it? So also faith of itself, if it does not have works, is dead" (Jas 2:14-17; 26).

The inconsistency between the faith professed and everyday life is one **161** of the causes of poverty in our countries. Christians have not known how to find in their faith the strength necessary to affect the criteria and decisions of those segments of society that provide ideological leadership and organize the common social, economic, and political life of our peoples. "Structures that cause injustice have been imposed on peoples who have a deeply rooted Christian faith" (*Puebla Conclusions,* 437).

As the Church's social teaching points out, development ought to lead **162** man and woman from less human to ever more human conditions until they come to full knowledge of Jesus Christ (cf. PP 20-21). At its root, we discover that this teaching is a true hymn to life—to all life from that of the unborn to that of the outcast.

163   Mary, who became concerned over the need that arose at the wedding feast of Cana, is a model and figure of the Church in facing any kind of human need (cf. Jn 2:3ff). As he did with Mary, Jesus enjoins the Church to strive to show a motherly concern for humankind, and especially for those who suffer (cf. Jn 19:26-27).

2.2 THE NEW SIGNS OF THE TIMES IN THE REALM OF HUMAN DEVELOPMENT

2.2.1 Human Rights

164   The equal dignity of human beings because they are created in God's image and likeness is reinforced and perfected in Christ. In taking on our nature in the incarnation, and especially in his redeeming action on the cross, the Word demonstrates how much each person is worth. Therefore, Christ, God and man, is the deepest source assuring the dignity of the person and his or her rights. Every violation of human rights runs counter to God's plan and is sin.

165   In preaching the gospel—the deep root of human rights—the Church is not usurping a task foreign to its mission. On the contrary, it is obeying the command of Jesus Christ when he made aiding the needy an essential requirement of its evangelizing mission. States do not grant these rights; it is their role to protect and develop them, for they belong to human beings by their very nature.

Pastoral Challenges.

166   • Awareness of human rights has advanced considerably since Puebla, along with significant actions by the Church in this area. At the same time, however, the problem of the violation of some rights has grown, and social and political conditions have worsened. Ideologically motivated interpretations and manipulation by some groups have confused the meaning of human rights, and there obviously is a greater need for legal avenues and procedures for citizen involvement.

167   • Human rights are violated not only by terrorism, repression, and murder, but also by the existence of conditions of extreme poverty and unjust economic structures that give rise to vast inequalities. Political intolerance and indifference toward the situation of widespread impoverishment indicate a contempt for the way people are actually living that we cannot pass over in silence.

• Violence against the rights of children, women, and the poorest groups in society (e.g., small farmers, indigenous people, and African Americans) are worthy of special condemnation. We must also condemn drug trafficking.

Pastoral Directions.

• Promote human rights more effectively and courageously on the basis   **168**
of the gospel and the Church's social teaching, through word, action, and
collaboration, by becoming committed to the defense of individual and
social rights of the human being, of peoples, of cultures, and of the marginal
sectors, as well as of those who are vulnerable or imprisoned.

• Be committed to defending life from the initial moment of conception
to its last breath.

• Participate with discernment in agencies for dialogue and mediation
as well as in institutions to support the various kinds of human rights victims, provided they are serious and are not engaged in manipulation by
employing ideologies that are incompatible with the Church's social teaching.

• Strive resolutely in the light of gospel values to overcome all unjust
discrimination based on race, nationalism, culture, gender, and creed by
endeavoring to eliminate all hatred, resentment, and vindictiveness and by
promoting reconciliation and justice.

2.2.2 Ecology

Creation is the work of the Word of the Lord and the presence of the   **169**
Spirit, who from the beginning was hovering over all that was created (cf.
Gn 1-2). This was God's first covenant with us. When the human being
who is called to enter into this covenant of love refuses to do so, sin affects
the relationship with God and, likewise, with all creation.

Pastoral Challenges.

• The United Nations Conference on the Environment and Development, held in Rio de Janeiro, has brought to the world's attention the
gravity of the ecological crisis.

• Large Latin American cities are sick in their decaying downtown areas
and especially in their shantytowns. In the countryside, indigenous and
peasant populations are deprived of their lands, or they find themselves
forced onto the least productive lands. They continue to slash and burn the
forests in the Amazon and elsewhere on the continent. As a solution to
this crisis, some are proposing sustainable development that seeks to
respond to the needs and aspirations of the present without compromising
the ability to deal with them in the future. The intent is thus to reconcile
economic growth with ecological limits.

With regard to this proposal, we must ask whether all these aspirations
are legitimate and who pays the cost of such development, as well as whom
it is intended to benefit. It cannot be a kind of development that gives
preference to small groups at the expense of the world's great impoverished
majorities.

• Development proposals must be subjected to ethical criteria. An ecological ethic entails abandoning a utilitarian and individualistic morality. It

means accepting the principle that the goods of creation are destined for all and promoting justice and solidarity as utterly necessary values.

Pastoral Directions.

• Since they belong to society, Christians are not free of responsibility for the development models that have brought about current environmental and social disasters.

• Undertake a task of reeducating everyone — starting with children and young people — on the value of life and the interdependence of the various ecosystems.

• Cultivate a spirituality that can recover the sense of God that is ever present in nature. Explain the new relationship established by the mystery of the incarnation, by which Christ assumed all that is created.

• Appreciate the new platform for dialogue created by the ecological crisis, and question wealth and waste.

• Learn from the poor to live in moderation and to share and esteem the wisdom of indigenous peoples on the preservation of nature as a *milieu* of life for all.

170 • Delve more deeply into the Holy Father's statements on the World Day of Peace, especially within a context of "human ecology."

• Urge Christians to undertake dialogue with the North, through the channels of the Catholic Church as well as through ecological and ecumenical movements.

• In his love for the poor and for nature, Saint Francis of Assisi can be an inspiration for this path of reconciliation within creation and of human beings among themselves, which is a path of justice and peace.

2.2.3 The Earth: God's Gift

171   Christians look at the universe not simply as nature in isolation but rather as creation and the Lord's first gift of love for us.

"The Lord's are the earth and its fullness; the world and those who dwell in it" (Ps 24:1) is the affirmation of faith that runs through the Bible and confirms our peoples' belief that the earth is the first sign of God's covenant with humans. Indeed, the biblical revelation teaches us that at creation the human being was placed in the garden of Eden to work it and care for it (cf. Gn 2:15) and use it (cf. Gn 2:16). Limits were pointed out (cf. Gn 2:17) to ever remind the human being that "God is the Lord and creator, that his is the earth and all it contains," and that the human being may use it, not as absolute master but as administrator.

These limits to the use of the land are intended to preserve the justice and right of all to partake in the goods of creation that God destined for the service of every human being who comes into this world.

172   In our continent, we have to take into account two opposed attitudes toward the land, both of which differ from the Christian vision:

a) Within all elements that together form the indigenous community, the land is life, sacred space, and integrating center of community life. They live on the land and with it, and through it they feel in communion with their ancestors and in harmony with God. Hence, the land — their land — is a substantial part of their religious experience and of their own thrust in history. Indigenous people have a natural sense of respect for the land; it is mother earth who nourishes her children and thus, one must care for her, ask her permission to sow, and not mistreat her.

b) The commercial vision looks at the land exclusively in terms of exploitation and profit, even going so far as to drive off and forcefully expel its legitimate owners.

That same commercial attitude leads to speculation with urban property, making the land unavailable for housing for the ever-growing numbers of the poor in our large cities.

Besides these categories, we cannot forget the situation of small farmers who work their land and earn their families' livelihood using traditional technologies.

The attitude proper to the Christian vision is based on Sacred Scripture, which regards the land and the elements of nature primarily as allies of God's people and instruments of our salvation. Jesus Christ's resurrection once more sets humankind before the mission of liberating all of creation, which is to be transformed into a new heaven and a new earth, where righteousness will dwell (cf. 2 Pt 3:13).   **173**

Pastoral Challenges.

• The problematic situation of the land in Latin American and the Caribbean is a challenge to us, since "five centuries in which the gospel has been present ... have not yet brought about an equitable distribution of the goods produced by the land," which "is still unfortunately in the hands of small groups" (John Paul II, *Lenten Message,* 1992). For the most part, the former aboriginal peoples were stripped of their lands, while legislation made it difficult for African Americans to own land. Small farmers today bear the burden of institutional disorder and the consequences of economic crises.   **174**

• In recent years the impact of this crisis has been felt even more forcefully where the modernization of our societies has brought the expansion of international agribusiness, increasing integration between countries, greater use of technology, and a transnational presence. Very often these trends benefit the economically strong segments, but at the cost of small producers and workers.

• The situation of the tenure, administration, and utilization of land in Latin America and the Caribbean is one of the most pressing claims on human development.   **175**

Pastoral Directions.

• Promote a change of attitude about the value of land on the basis of   **176** the Christian world view, which has connections with the cultural traditions of the poor and small farmers.

• Remind the lay faithful that they must influence the agrarian policies of their governments (especially their modernization policies) and peasant and indigenous organizations, so as to attain ways of using the land that are just, more community-oriented, and participatory.

177

• Support all those persons and institutions striving to bring governments and those who own the means of production to create a just and humane agrarian reform and policy, one that can legislate, plan, and provide support for a more just distribution of land and for utilizing it more efficiently.

• Support in solidarity those organizations of small farmers and indigenous people who are struggling through just and legitimate channels to hold onto or reacquire their lands.

• Promote those technical advances required to make the earth productive, while also keeping in mind market conditions and, accordingly, the need to develop an awareness of the importance of technology.

• Encourage theological reflection on the land question, stressing inculturation and an effective presence of pastoral agents in peasant communities.

• Support the organization of mediating groups, such as cooperatives, to serve as a means for the defense of human rights, democratic participation, and community education.

2.2.4 Impoverishment and Solidarity

178

Evangelizing means doing what Jesus Christ did in the synagogue when he stated that he had come to "bring glad tidings" to the poor. He "became poor although he was rich, so that by his poverty you might become rich" (2 Cor 8:9). He challenges us to give an authentic witness of gospel poverty in the way we live and in our church structures, just as he gave it.

Such is the basis for our commitment to a gospel-based and preferential option for the poor, one that is firm and irrevocable but not exclusive or excluding, as was very solemnly affirmed at the Medellín and Puebla Conferences. Like Jesus, we draw inspiration for all community and personal evangelizing activity from such a preferential option (cf. SRS 42 and RM 14; OA 16). The poor Church wants to energize the evangelization of our communities with the "evangelizing potential of the poor" (*Puebla Conclusions*, 1147).

Discovering the face of the Lord in the suffering faces of the poor (cf. Mt 25:31-46) challenges all Christians to a deep personal and ecclesial conversion. Through faith, we find faces emaciated by hunger as a result of inflation, foreign debt, and social injustice; faces disillusioned by politicians who make promises they do not keep; faces humiliated because of their culture, which is not shown respect and is sometimes treated with contempt; faces terrorized by daily and indiscriminate violence; anguished faces of the abandoned children who wander our streets and sleep under our bridges; suffering faces of women who are humiliated and disregarded; weary faces of migrants, who do not receive a decent welcome; faces aged by time and labor of people who lack even the minimum needed to survive decently (CELAM, *Working Document,* 163). Merciful love also means turning toward those who are in spiritual, moral, social, and cultural need.

Pastoral Challenges.

• The growing impoverishment in which millions of our brothers and sisters are plunged — to the point where it is reaching intolerable extremes of misery — is the cruelest and most crushing scourge that Latin America and the Caribbean are enduring. We condemned it at both Medellín and Puebla, and we are now doing so once again with concern and anguish.   **179**

• Statistics eloquently indicate that during the last decade situations of poverty have increased in both absolute and relative numbers. As pastors, we are torn apart by the continual sight of the throng of men and women, children, youth, and the aged who endure the unbearable weight of dire poverty, as well as the various forms of social, ethnic, and cultural exclusion. They are specific, unique, human persons who find their horizons ever more closed and their dignity ignored.

• We look on the impoverishment of our people not simply as an economic and social phenomenon described and measured by the social sciences. We look at it from within the experience of many people whose daily struggle to live we share as pastors.

• Policies of a neoliberal type now prevailing in Latin America and the Caribbean further deepen the negative impact of these mechanisms. The gaps in society have widened as the market has been deregulated in an indiscriminate way; major portions of labor legislation have been eliminated and workers have been fired; and the social spending that protected working-class families has been cut back.

• We have to extend the list of suffering faces that we already noted at Puebla (cf. *Puebla Conclusions,* 31-39), all of them disfigured by hunger, terrorized by violence, aged by subhuman living conditions, and anguished over family survival. The Lord asks us to discover his own face in the suffering faces of our brothers and sisters.

• However, we are happy to note the numerous efforts that various groups and institutions in Latin America and the Caribbean are making to change this situation. The Church, which is called to be ever more faithful to its preferential option for the poor, has played a growing role in such efforts. For that we thank God, and we urge that the path already opened be widened, since there are many more who have yet to tread on it.

Pastoral Guidelines.

• Assume with renewed decision the gospel-inspired and preferential option for the poor, following the example and the words of the Lord Jesus, with full trust in God, austerity of life, and sharing in goods.   **180**

• Give priority to providing fraternal service to the poorest among the poor and helping institutions that take care of them: the handicapped, the sick, old people who are alone, abandoned children, prisoners, people with AIDS, and all those who need the merciful approach of the "good Samaritan."

• Examine personal and community attitudes and behaviors, along with pastoral structures and methods, so that rather than alienating the poor they may facilitate closeness and sharing with them.

• Foster social involvement vis-à-vis the state by demanding laws to defend the rights of the poor.

181 • Make our parishes a space for solidarity.

• Support and encourage those organizations for economic solidarity with which our people are trying to respond to their desperate situations of poverty.

• Press governments to respond to the hardships that are being worsened by the neoliberal economic model whose primary impact is on the poor. When considering these situations, it is important to single out the millions of Latin Americans who are struggling to survive in the informal economy.

2.2.5 Work

182 Given its humanizing and saving significance, the realm of work is one of the areas of greatest concern to us in our pastoral activity. Its origins lie in the human being's co-creative vocation as "image of God" (cf. Gn 1-26), and it has been rescued and elevated by Jesus, the worker and "carpenter's son" (cf. Mt 13:55 and Mk 6:3).

As custodian and servant of the message of Jesus, the Church has always seen human beings as subjects who dignify work, as they achieve their own fulfillment and bring God's work to perfection by making it a hymn of praise to the Creator and service to their brothers and sisters.

The constant teaching by the Church's magisterium that work is, as it were, the "key to the social question" has been confirmed in the recent social encyclicals of John Paul II (*Laborem Exercens; Sollicitudo Rei Socialis; Centesimus Annus*). That teaching particularly highlights "the subjective dimension" of work (LE 6), which is the most eloquent expression of the dignity of the worker.

Pastoral Challenges.

183 • The situation today challenges us to develop a culture of work and solidarity, based on faith in God the Father, who makes us brothers and sisters in Jesus Christ. In the realm of working people, we can observe the following: a decline in their living conditions and respect for their rights; little or no observance of what the law says should be done for the weakest sectors (e.g., children, pensioners, and so forth); a loss of the independence of workers' organizations due to dependencies or self-imposed dependencies of various kinds; abuse by capital, which is unaware of or denies the primacy of labor; few or no job opportunities for young people. It is obvious that there is an alarming lack of work or employment, with all the ensuing economic and social insecurity. Labor is calling for the economy to grow and productivity to increase so as to make possible greater welfare for individuals and their families through a just and fair distribution.

• The rights of working people are part of the moral patrimony of society,   **184** and they should be protected by means of an adequate social legislation along with the judicial component that may be necessary for reliability and continuity in labor relations.

Pastoral Directions.

• Foster and support pastoral work with labor in all our dioceses so as   **185** to promote and defend the human value of work.

• Support organizations of working people to defend their legitimate rights, especially the right to adequate pay and to a just social protection for old age, illness, and unemployment (cf. CA 35).

• Encourage training for workers, business people, and government officials in their rights and duties and help provide places for meeting one another and working together.

2.2.6 Human Mobility

The Word of God becomes flesh in order to unite in a single people   **186** those who were wandering dispersed and to make them "citizens of heaven" (cf. Phil 3:20; Heb 11:13-16).

Thus, God's son becomes a pilgrim and undergoes the experience of the displaced (cf. Mt 2: 13-23) as a migrant living in an insignificant village (cf. Jn 1:46). He trains his disciples to be missionaries by having them undergo the experience of migrants so that they will put their trust only in the love of God, whose good news they bear (cf. Mk 6:6b-12).

Pastoral Challenges.

• In recent years, there is a sharp increase in migration to the two great   **187** countries in the north and also, albeit to a lesser extent, to better-off Latin American countries. We see new phenomena, such as the voluntary repatriation and the deportation of undocumented people. Increased travel and tourism and even religious pilgrimages and the needs of those who make their living at sea, all demand special care on the part of the Church.

• In those countries which for social and economic reasons are especially prone to migration there are generally no social measures to halt it; and in the receiving countries the tendency is to block entry. The serious consequences include family breakdown and the siphoning off of the productive forces of our own peoples, along with the uprooting, insecurity, discrimination, exploitation, and religious and moral degradation of the migrants themselves. Nevertheless, in some instances they manage to become part of Catholic communities and even to revitalize them.

Pastoral Directions.

• Reinforce pastoral attention related to human movement by connect-   **188** ing efforts between dioceses and bishops conferences of the affected regions and by taking care that within the reception and other services provided for migrants, their spiritual and religious wealth be respected.

• Make government circles aware of the issue of migration so as to achieve equity in laws on labor and social security and compliance with international agreements.

189   • Offer migrants a catechesis adapted to their culture and legal aid to protect their rights.

• Present alternatives to small farmers so that they will not feel forced to migrate to the city.

2.2.7 The Democratic System

190   Christ the Lord, who was sent by the Father for the redemption of the world, came to proclaim the good news and begin the reign and, through personal conversion, to bring about a new life according to God and a new kind of common life and social relationship. Faithful to the mission entrusted to it by its founder, the Church is to constitute the community of the children of God and to aid in building a society where the Christian values of the gospel are paramount.

The Church respects the legitimate autonomy of the temporal order and has no specific model for the political system. "The Church values the democratic system inasmuch as it ensures the participation of citizens in making political choices, guarantees to the governed the possibility both of electing and holding accountable those who govern them, and of replacing them through peaceful means when appropriate" (CA 46).

In recent years, the Church in Latin America and the Caribbean has played an active role in this process. In many countries, its activity has laid the groundwork for a common life based on dialogue and respect for the human person. Supported by the magisterium in its social teaching, the Church has been accompanying the people in their struggles and yearnings for greater participation and government based on the rule of law.

191   The people of our continent have been winning freedom, which indeed is inherent in the human person and has been brought to the fore by modernity. Thus, it has been possible to establish democracy as the most accepted system of government, although its exercise is still more formal than real.

Pastoral Challenges.

192   • In some countries democratic common life, which took root after Puebla, has been deteriorating. The reasons include the following: administrative corruption, separation of party leadership from the concerns of the grass roots and the real needs of the community; a lack of programs and disregard for the social, ethical, and cultural dimensions by party organizations; governments elected by the people but not truly directed toward

the common good; a great deal of political patronage and populism, but little participation.

Pastoral Guidelines.

• Proclaim persistently to civil society the values of a genuine pluralistic,   **193**
just, and participatory democracy.

• Teach and urge the people really to become actively involved.

• Create conditions for lay people to learn the Church's social doctrine with a view to acting politically to remedy and improve democracy and truly serve the community.

• Provide guidance for the family, the school, and the various levels of the Church to educate in those values that provide the basis for genuine democracy: responsibility, shared responsibility, participation, respect for the dignity of persons, dialogue, and the common good.

2.2.8 New Economic Order

Conscious that a new economic order affecting Latin America and the   **194**
Caribbean is taking shape, the Church is obliged to make a serious effort at discernment from its own perspective. We must ask ourselves: How far should the freedom of the market extend? What must be its features if it is to serve the development of the vast majority?

According to John Paul II's recent teaching (cf. the encyclical letter   **195**
Centesimus Annus), the free activity of individuals in the market is legitimate. That does not mean that the market can provide all the goods that society needs nor that society can pay for many goods that are necessary. The market economy must keep these limits in mind.

Hence, the Holy Father's teachings point to the need for specific actions by governments so that the market economy will not become an absolute to which everything is sacrificed, thus aggravating inequality and the exclusion of the vast majority. There cannot be a creative and yet socially just market economy unless the whole society and the actors within it are firmly committed to solidarity through a legal framework that safeguards the value of the person, honesty, respect for life and distributive justice, and a real concern for the poorest.

Although by halting inflation and stabilizing the economy, economic   **196**
adjustments may be beneficial in the long run, they tend to produce a sharp drop in the living standards of the poor. The state, therefore, has the obligation to make up for the social costs to the poorest, within the limits of what is possible, but sincerely and generously.

The problem of the foreign debt is not only — or even primarily — eco-   **197**
nomic; rather, it is a human problem for it leads to an ever greater impoverishment and blocks the development and slows the advancement of those who are poorest. We ask ourselves whether the debt is valid, when paying it seriously jeopardizes the survival of our peoples, when the population was not consulted before contracting the debt, and when it has not always

been used for lawful purposes. Hence, as pastors, we make ours the concern of John Paul II when he says that "it is necessary to find—and in fact is partly happening—ways to lighten, defer or even cancel the debt, compatible with the fundamental right of peoples to subsistence and progress" (CA 35).

Pastoral Challenges.

198   • The eighties have been characterized by the scourge of inflation augmented by fiscal deficit, the weight of foreign debt and monetary disorder, devastation of government finances due to the loss of revenue sources, inflation and corruption, and the drop in investment both domestic and foreign, along with other trends.

• Internationally, the ratio between prices for raw materials and finished goods has been increasingly unequal and discriminatory and has had a very negative effect on the economy of our countries. This situation still exists and is tending to become worse.

199   • Impoverishment and the accentuation of the gap between rich and poor have a very serious impact on the vast majority of our peoples as a result of inflation and the lowering of real pay levels, the lack of access to basic services, unemployment, the growth of the informal economy, and scientific and technological dependence.

• A consumeristic and selfish mindset and life style—widely promoted by the media—are spreading, and they hinder or prevent a more just and decent way of organizing society.

• In response to the crisis of economic systems that has led to failures and frustrations, there is a tendency to propose a free market economy as the solution. Many understand it in terms of neoliberalism, and on the basis of narrow or reductive interpretations of person and society, they see it as extending beyond the purely economic sphere.

Pastoral Directions.

200   • Fortify the knowledge, dissemination, and implementation of the Church's social teaching in various circles.

• Foster at various levels and in different sectors of the Church a social pastoral activity whose starting point is the gospel's preferential option for the poor, by being active through proclamation, denunciation, and witness, and by encouraging cooperative undertakings in the context of a market economy.

• Educate in the values of hard work and sharing, of honesty and austerity, of the ethical and religious sense of life so that starting in the family—the first school—new human beings may be formed to live in a more fraternal society, where people will experience that goods are meant for all, in the context of comprehensive development.

201   • Lay the groundwork for a real and efficient economy of solidarity, while assuring that socioeconomic models likewise be created on the local and national levels.

• Encourage the search for and implementation of socioeconomic models that combine free enterprise, personal and group creativity, and the moderating function of the state, while making certain to devote attention to those sectors that are most in need. All of this is to be aimed at achieving an economy of solidarity and participation, reflected in various kinds of property.

• Develop international economic relations that can facilitate technology **202**
transfer in an atmosphere of social reciprocity.

• Denounce those mechanisms of the market economy that do deep damage to the poor. We cannot fail to be present at a time when there is no one to watch over their interests.

• Bear in mind that the informal economy arises out of a need for sur- **203**
vival, although it is vulnerable to illness, inflation, and so forth.

• Remind the lay faithful that they are to bring their influence to bear so that the government can achieve greater stability in economic policies, eliminate administrative corruption, and further extend decentralization in administration, the economy, and education.

• Acknowledge the basic role of the firm, the market, and private property, and the ensuing responsibility toward the means of production and human creativity in a legal framework of social justice (cf. CA 42).

2.2.9 Latin American Integration

Experience has shown that no nation can live and achieve solid devel- **204**
opment in isolation. We all feel the pressing need to bring together what is dispersed and to join our efforts so that interdependence may become solidarity, which in turn may be transformed into fraternity. Hence, these are the values that we single out in speaking about the economic and social reality of the world and of the yearnings for humanization latent in them.

Christians find very deep motivations for continuing this effort. Jesus Christ has made God's reign present: a reign of justice, love, and peace. He has made all of us brothers and sisters by becoming our brother and teaching us to recognize that we are children of one and the same Father (cf. Mk 14:36). He himself has called us to unity: "that they may all be one, as you, Father, are in me and I in you" (Jn 17:21).

The Church is conscious that it plays a unique role and that it has the task of developing a sense of being part of humankind and fostering a culture of solidarity and reconciliation.

It is characteristically human that nations and persons must be inter- **205**
dependent for the sake of a genuine solidarity. We also note that the world-wide trend of nations to associate with one another, which is a sign of the times, is likewise observable in Latin America and the Caribbean.

John Paul II has insisted on the need to transform structures that no **206**
longer meet the needs of peoples and particularly that, "Stronger nations must offer weaker ones opportunities for taking their place in international life" (CA 35). Observing the spectacle of countries that are ever richer

alongside others that are ever poorer he said: "Solutions must be sought on a worldwide scale, by establishing a true economy of communion and participation in goods, on both international and national levels. In that regard, one factor that can make a notable contribution to overcoming the pressing problems today affecting this continent is Latin American integration. Those in charge of governments have a grave responsibility to promote the process—already underway—of integrating peoples whom a common geography, Christian faith, language and culture have already drawn together in the course of history" (OA 15).

Pastoral Challenges.

207   • Our own nations find themselves isolated and splintered, at the very moment when the economy of the planet is undergoing globalization, and large blocs are being established or reestablished.

208   • The establishment of large blocs threatens to isolate the whole continent to the extent that it does not respond to their economic interests.

• There is a breakdown within our countries as the result of discrimination against races or groups and of the economic, political, and cultural predominance of particular interests that also impede a broader opening.

• The same lack of communion between the local Churches of one nation to another, or between neighboring countries on the continent, weakens the integrating power of the Church itself.

Pastoral Directions.

209   • Foster and accompany efforts to integrate Latin America as a "great homeland" from a perspective of solidarity, which further requires a new international order.

• Promote justice and participation within our nations by educating in those values, condemning situations that contradict them, and giving the witness of relating fraternally.

• Encourage initiatives and strengthen such structures and agencies for collaboration within the Church as may be necessary or useful, while respecting the various areas of authority. In this sense, take up the Holy Father's suggestion about a meeting of the episcopates from throughout the Americas.

2.3 THE FAMILY AND LIFE: ESPECIALLY URGENT CHALLENGES IN HUMAN DEVELOPMENT

2.3.1 The Family, Sanctuary of Life

210   With joy and conviction, the Church announces the good news with regard to the family. In it the future of humankind is being forged, and it represents the crucial frontier of the new evangelization. That is what we proclaim here in Latin America and the Caribbean at a moment in history when the family is suffering from many forces that are attempting to destroy or distort it.

Certainly, the most fitting place for speaking about the family is in connection with the local Church, the parish, and ecclesial communities, since the family is the domestic church. Due to the enormous problems facing human life today, however, we are including this topic in the section devoted to human development.

Of course, we acknowledge that there are different kinds of families in both the countryside and the cities, each in its own cultural context. Everywhere, however, the family is leaven and sign of divine love and of the Church itself, and therefore it must be open to God's plan.

As God originally disposed, marriage and family are institutions of divine origin and not the result of human will. When the Lord says, "From the beginning it was not so" (Mt 19:8), he is referring to the truth about marriage, which according to God's plan rules out divorce. **211**

Man and woman, being image and likeness of God (cf. Gn 1:27) who is love, are called to live in marriage the mystery of trinitarian communion and relationship. "God inscribed in the humanity of man and woman the vocation, and thus the capacity and responsibility, of love and communion" (FC 11). Man and woman are called to love in the totality of their body and spirit. **212**

Jesus Christ is the new covenant; in him, marriage reaches its true grandeur. A model for every family was established through his incarnation and his family life with Mary and Joseph in their home in Nazareth. Through Christ, love between spouses becomes like his: total, exclusive, faithful, and fruitful. With the coming of Christ and by his intention, as the apostle proclaims, marriage does not merely return to its original perfection but it is enriched with new content (cf. Eph 5:25-33). Christian marriage is a sacrament in which human love is sanctifying and communicates divine life through the work of Christ; a sacrament in which the spouses signify and embody the love of Christ and his Church, a love that travels the road of the cross, of limitations, forgiveness, and failings in order to arrive at the delight of resurrection. It must be kept in mind that "a valid matrimonial contract cannot exist between baptized people without its being by that very fact a sacrament"(CIC 1055:2). **213**

In the plan of God, Creator and Redeemer, the family discovers both its identity and its mission: to protect, reveal, and communicate love and life through four fundamental responsibilities (cf. FC 17): **214**

a) The mission of the family is to live, grow, and improve as a community of persons characterized by unity and indissolubility. The family is the privileged site for personal fulfillment together, alongside those one loves.

b) To be "sanctuary of life" (CA 39) and serve life, since the right to life is the foundation of all human rights. Such service is not limited to mere procreation, but is real help for transmitting and educating in genuinely human and Christian values.

c) To be the "primary and vital cell of society" (FC 42). By its nature and vocation, the family should foster development and be an advocate for policies that truly favor families.

d) To be a "domestic church" receiving, living, celebrating, and proclaiming God's word; it is a sanctuary where holiness is built up, and from which the Church and the world can be made holy (cf. FC 55). Despite the grave crisis of the family, we note that many Latin American and Caribbean families are full of hope and faithful to the plan of God, Creator and Redeemer. They are struggling to embody fidelity, openness to life, the Christian education of their children, and commitment to the Church and the world.

215   God is the very Lord of life. Life is God's gift. The human being is not, and cannot be, the arbiter or master of life. Families must responsibly accept a child as a most precious and unique gift from God. The conceived unborn child is the poorest, most vulnerable and most defenseless being and must be defended and guarded. Today, it is even more obvious that birth control and abortion are connected both objectively and subjectively. The unitive significance of the conjugal act is sharply cut off from its procreative meaning, thus betraying the very meaning of love.

2.3.2 Challenges Confronting the Family and Life Today

216   • Historical and cultural change has had an impact on the traditional image of the family. Couples living together, divorce, and abortion are increasingly common. What is new is that these family problems have become an ethicopolitical problem, partly has a result of a "secularizing" mindset and of the media.

217   • The fact that marriage and the family have been proposed by God, who invites man and woman, who have been created out of love, to carry out his loving project in fidelity to death, is too often ignored due to the prevailing secularism and psychological immaturity, as well as for socioeconomic and political reasons. All these factors lead to the breakdown of the moral and ethical values of the family itself. The upshot is the painful reality of broken families, couples in irregular unions, the growth of civil matrimony without a sacramental celebration, and unmarried couples living together.

218   • A growing number of families in Latin America and the Caribbean represent a challenge to governments, society, and international agencies by reason of their situation of dire poverty and hunger due to unemployment, the lack of decent housing and of schooling, sanitation, and low pay; and by reason of the abandonment of old people and the growing number of single mothers.

219   • The culture of death is challenging us. As human beings we are saddened, and as Christians we are concerned to be witnessing campaigns against life spreading through Latin America and the Caribbean and disrupting the attitude of our people with a culture of death. Selfishness, fear

of sacrifice and the cross, combined with the hardships of modern life are causing a rejection of the child, who is not welcomed in the family with responsibility and joy, but is regarded as an aggressor. A genuine "demographic terrorism" is used to instill fear in people by exaggerating the degree to which population growth may jeopardize quality of life.

There is a widespread distribution of contraceptives, most of which cause abortions. Large numbers of women are victims of mass sterilization programs. Men are also falling prey to these threats. Our continent is suffering from "contraceptive imperialism, which entails imposing on peoples and cultures any kind of contraception, sterilization, and abortion considered effective with no respect for religious, ethnic, or family traditions of a people or a culture" (*Letter* of the Holy See to the WHO [World Health Organization] Meeting in Bangkok).

The massacre of abortion grows greater every day and is producing millions of victims in our peoples of Latin America. Besides being prenatal euthanasia, such an anti-life attitude leads to the elimination of newly born children and of the old and sick, who are regarded as useless, defective, or a "burden" for society. Other expressions of the culture of death are euthanasia, war, guerrilla warfare, kidnapping, terrorism, and drug trafficking.

- The Christian faithful are confused when they see contradictions and **220** inconsistency on the part of those working in family pastoral work who do not follow the Church's magisterium (*Humanae Vitae; Familiaris Consortio; Reconciliatio et Poenitentia*).

- Latin America and the Caribbean have a growing child population. **221** Children, adolescents, and young people make up more than half the continent's population (55%). This "silent emergency" in Latin America and the Caribbean is a challenge not only from a numerical standpoint, but especially from a human and pastoral standpoint. Indeed, in many cities there is a growing number of "street children," who wander about day and night with no home and no future. In some countries, they have suffered campaigns waged by police and private groups to wipe them out; there are children with no family, no love, no access to education — in other words, children in extreme physical and moral misery, often as the result of family breakdown. We even observe a grotesque buying and selling of boys and girls, a traffic in organs, and even children used for devil worship. From the standpoint of education in their faith, there is a notable neglect of reception of the sacraments and catechesis.

2.3.3 Pastoral Directions

1. Emphasize the priority and centrality of family pastoral work in the **222** diocesan Church. Pastoral agents must be trained for that purpose. The apostolic movements directed at marriage and the family can offer valuable cooperation to local Churches, within a comprehensive plan.

- Family pastoral work cannot be limited to a merely protective stance;

it must be forward-looking, bold, and positive. It must discern with gospel wisdom the challenges that cultural changes pose to the family. It must condemn violations against justice and the dignity of the family. It must stand by families from the poorer segments in the countryside and the cities and promote their solidarity.

• Family pastoral work must take care to train future spouses and to accompany spouses, especially during the first years of their married life. Courses to prepare engaged couples before the marriage ceremony have proven their worth.

223   2. Proclaim that God is the only Lord of life, and that the human being is not, and cannot be, master or arbiter of human life. Condemn and reject any violation by the authorities on behalf of birth control, euthanasia, sterilization, and deliberate abortion. Likewise, condemn and reject the policies of some governments and international agencies that condition economic aid on anti-life programs.

224   Seek, following the example of the Good Shepherd, approaches and ways of carrying out a pastoral work aimed at couples in irregular situations, especially divorced women, and those who have remarried civilly.

225   Strengthen the life of the Church and society on the basis of the family: enrich it with family catechesis, prayer in the home, the eucharist, participation in the sacrament of reconciliation, and knowledge of God's word, in order to be leaven in the Church and society.

226   3. Invite theologians, scholars, and Christian married couples to work together with the hierarchical magisterium in order to clarify the biblical grounds, ethical motivations, and scientific reasons for responsible parenthood, and for deciding freely in accord with a well-formed conscience and with the principles of morality, both with regard to the number of children one can educate and the methods in keeping with a genuine responsible parenthood. The fruit of such research will be the promotion of programs and services to make known natural methods of family planning and to prepare manuals for education about sexuality and love, aimed at children, adolescents, and young people.

• In response to the efforts of certain demographic programs, we must recall the Holy Father's words in his opening address to this Conference: "What is needed is to augment resources and distribute wealth with greater justice so that all may participate equitably in the goods of creation" (OA 15).

227   4. Exercise the Church's prophetic mission by condemning any assault against children whether born or unborn. Make known and urge compliance with the "Convention on the Rights of the Child" along with the observations of the Holy See, as well as the letter of the Holy See, *On the Rights of the Family.* Guide lay people to promote in the various countries legislation to protect the rights of the child and press for compliance. Accompany and truly support parents, educators, catechists, and religious congregations devoted to educating children, with special attention to

growth in the faith. Foster a mystique for working on behalf of children and promoting pastoral work with children, through prophetic and charitable actions that testify to Christ's love for the poorest and most abandoned children.

CHAPTER 3: CHRISTIAN CULTURE

INTRODUCTION

The coming of the Holy Spirit at Pentecost (cf. Acts 2: 1-11) makes **228** manifest the universality of the commission to evangelize: the aim is to reach every culture. It also makes manifest the cultural diversity of the faithful when they hear the apostles speaking, each in his own language.

Culture arises with God's initial command to human beings: to grow and multiply, to fill the earth and subdue it (cf. Gn 1:28-30). Thus, culture means cultivating and expressing the full range of the human in a loving relationship with nature and in the community dimension of peoples.

When through the incarnation Jesus Christ assumes and expresses everything human except sin, the Word of God enters into culture. Jesus Christ is thus the measure of everything human, including culture. He who took flesh in his people's culture, brings to each culture in history the gift of purification and plenitude. All the cultural values and expressions that can be oriented to Christ foster what is genuinely human. What does not go by way of Christ will not be redeemable.

Through our radical adhesion to Christ in baptism, we have been com- **229** mitted to strive so that faith—fully proclaimed, thought, and lived—may become culture. Thus, we may speak of a Christian culture when a people's shared sense of life has been so permeated that the gospel message has been placed "at the basis of its thinking, its fundamental principles of life, its criteria for judgment, and its norms for activity" (OA 24), and from there "is projected into the 'ethos' of a people . . . its institutions and all its structures" (OA 20).

This evangelization of culture, which reaches into its dynamic core, is expressed in the inculturation process, which John Paul II has called the "center, means, and aim of the new evangelization" (*Address to the International Council on Catechesis,* September 26, 1992). Authentic Christian values, discerned and assumed in faith, are necessary in order to incarnate the gospel message and the Church's reflection and practice into that culture.

The Virgin Mary is with the apostles when the Spirit of the risen Jesus enters and transforms those peoples from different cultures. Mary, who is the model for the Church, is also a model for the evangelization of culture. She is the Jewish woman who represents the people of the old covenant with all its cultural reality. However, she opens herself to the newness of the gospel and is present in our lands as common mother, both of the native peoples and of those who have come here. From the outset, she encourages the fresh cultural synthesis that constitutes Latin America and the Caribbean.

INCULTURATION OF THE GOSPEL

230   Since we stand before "a cultural crisis of unsuspected dimensions" (OA 21) in which gospel values and even basic human values are vanishing, the Church is presented with an enormous challenge, that of undertaking a new evangelization. We propose to respond to this challenge with the effort to inculturate the gospel. The gospel must be inculturated in the light of the three great mysteries of salvation: Christmas, which demonstrates the path of the incarnation and prompts evangelizers to share their lives with the evangelized; Easter, which leads through suffering to the purification of sins, so that they may be redeemed; and Pentecost, which by the power of the Spirit enables all to understand the wonders of God in their own language.

The inculturation of the gospel is a process that entails recognizing those gospel values that have been maintained more or less pure in present-day culture and recognizing those new values that are congruent with the message of Christ. The aim of inculturation is to bring society to discover the Christian nature of those values, to esteem them, and to maintain them as values. It also seeks to incorporate gospel values that are not present in the culture, either because they have been obscured or have even disappeared. "Through inculturation, the Church makes the gospel incarnate in different cultures and at the same time introduces peoples, together with their cultures, into her own community" (RM 52). By becoming incarnate in these cultures, faith seeks to correct their errors and prevent syncretism. Inculturating the faith is a task proper to local Churches, under the direction of their pastors and with the participation of the whole people of God. "Properly applied, inculturation must be guided by two principles: compatibility with the gospel and communion with the universal Church" (RM 54).

3.1 CULTURAL VALUES: CHRIST, STANDARD FOR OUR MORAL BEHAVIOR

231   • Created in God's image, we find the standard for our moral behavior in Christ, Word made flesh, and fulfillment of the human being. Natural ethical activity, which is essentially connected to human dignity and the rights that follow from it, is the foundation for a dialogue with nonbelievers.

Through baptism, we are born into a new life and are enabled to approach our model, who is Christ. Christian morality means journeying toward him; that is the way of life proper to the believer, who with the aid of sacramental grace follows Jesus Christ, lives the joy of salvation, and overflows with expressions of charity for the life of the world (cf. Jn 15; OT 16).

• Conscious of the need to continue along this journey, the Christian strives to form his or her own conscience. The development and wealth of peoples is dependent on doing so both individually and collectively, and on the maturity of their attitude, their sense of responsibility, and the purity of their customs (cf. OA 19). Christian morality is only understood within the Church, and it reaches fulfillment in the eucharist. Everything we can offer in the eucharist is life; what cannot be offered is sin.

Pastoral Challenges.

• In Latin America and the Caribbean many people still remain faithful   **232** to Jesus Christ, thank God, even in adverse circumstances. Nevertheless, in our societies there is an obvious growing ethical and moral gap, and more specifically we note a distortion of conscience, a permissive ethics, and a notable decline in the sense of sin. Faith has a declining influence; esteem for religion is on the wane; and God is not acknowledged as supreme good and final judge. The practice of the sacrament of reconciliation is declining. The Church's official moral teaching is presented inadequately.

• Corruption is widespread. Public funds are mismanaged; demagoguery,   **233** populism, and the "political lie" during election campaigns are on the rise; justice is mocked, impunity is becoming commonplace, and the community feels impotent and defenseless against crime. The result is a growing social insensitivity and skepticism when justice is not done, and laws contrary to fundamental human and Christian values are passed. The goods of the earth are not distributed fairly; nature is abused; and the ecosystem is being damaged.

• Birth control campaigns, genetic manipulation, the abominable crime   **234** of abortion, and that of euthanasia all foster an anti-life attitude and actions. Life comes to mean the conquest of the weak by the strong, thereby encouraging actions of hatred and destruction and preventing human fulfillment and growth.

• Thus, it is clear that the dignity of the human person is being increas-   **235** ingly undermined. The culture of death, violence and terrorism, drug addiction and drug traffic are growing. The wholeness of human sexuality is being debased, as men and women and even children are turned into an industry of pornography and prostitution; within the overall atmosphere of permissiveness and sexual promiscuity, the terrible evil of AIDS is spreading, and venereal disease is on the rise.

• What is called the "civil" or "citizen ethics" is being introduced as a   **236** norm of morality. It is based on a minimum consensus of all with the prevailing culture, with no need to respect natural morality and Christian standards. We can observe a "situation morality" that holds that something inherently evil would cease to be so in accordance with the persons, circumstances, or interests that may be at stake. The media often echo all such criteria and disseminate them.

Pastoral Directions.

237   • Work to develop a Christian conscience and restore what has been lost in Christian morality. Become aware once more of sin (of both original sin and personal sins) and of God's grace as strength to enable us to continue to follow our Christian conscience. Awaken in all the experience of the love that the Holy Spirit pours into our hearts as the strength of all Christian morality.

238   • Exercise vigilance so that the media will neither be manipulative nor manipulated into transmitting, under the guise of pluralism, what destroys the Latin American people. Strengthen the unity of the family and its influence in the formation of moral conscience.

239   • Present the moral life as the following of Christ, with the emphasis on practicing the beatitudes and frequently participating in the sacraments. Communicate the moral and social virtues, so as to make us new human beings and creators of a new humankind. This proclamation must be vital and *kerygmatic,* especially where secularism has made greater inroads. Catechesis should present Christian behavior as the genuine following of Christ. Take care to assure that the proper application of criteria of degree in moral matters not diminish the demanding requirements of conversion.

240   • Encourage ongoing formation for bishops and priests, deacons, men and women religious, lay people, and especially pastoral agents, in keeping with the teaching of the magisterium. The liturgy should express more clearly the moral commitments it entails. Popular religiosity should be oriented toward conversion, especially at devotional shrines. Approach to the sacrament of reconciliation should be encouraged and made easier.

241   • With regard to drug problems, encourage preventive action in society and attention and care for drug addicts; courageously condemn the harm that drug addiction and drug traffic wreak on our peoples and the very serious sin entailed in their production, commercialization, and consumption. Point out in particular the responsibility borne by the powerful consumer markets. Encourage national and international solidarity and cooperation in combatting this scourge.

242   • Guide and pastorally accompany those who build society to develop a moral conscience with regard to their tasks and their political activity.

           • Ever be open to dialogue with those who conduct their lives on the paths differing from those of Christian ethics. Commit ourselves truly to achieving the justice and peace of our peoples.

3.2 UNITY AND PLURALITY OF INDIGENOUS, AFRICAN AMERICAN, AND *MESTIZO* CULTURES

Theological Perspectives.

243   • Through the Spirit, God's action is continually at work within all cultures. In the fullness of time, God sent his Son, Jesus Christ, who assumed

the social and cultural conditions of peoples and has truly become one of us "in every way, yet without sin" (Heb 4:15; cf. GS 22).

• The analogy between the incarnation and the Christian presence in the sociocultural and historic context of our peoples leads us to pose the question of inculturation in theological terms. Such inculturation is a process conducted on the basis of the gospel from within each people and community by means of language and symbols that are comprehensible and that the Church regards as appropriate.

• One goal of inculturated evangelization will always be the salvation and integral liberation of a particular people or human group, strengthening its identity and trusting in its specific future. At the same time, it will stand opposed to the powers of death by taking on the perspective of Jesus Christ incarnate, who out of weakness, poverty, and the redeeming cross, saved humankind. The Church defends the genuine human values of all peoples, especially of those who are oppressed, defenseless, and excluded as they confront the overwhelming power of the structures of sin manifested in modern society.

Pastoral Challenges.

• Latin America and the Caribbean constitute a multiethnic and multi-   244
cultural continent on which indigenous, African American, and *mestizo* peoples and those descending from Europeans and Asians live together. Each has its own culture, which provides it with its own social identity in accord with each people's world vision, but they seek unity on the basis of their Catholic identity.

• The indigenous peoples of today cherish very important human values,   245
and as John Paul II says, they hold the "belief that evil is identified with death and good with life" (*Message to Indigenous People,* 2). Those values and convictions derive from "the seeds of the Word," which were already present at work in their ancestors, enabling them to go on to discover the Creator's presence in all his creatures: the sun, the moon, mother earth, and so forth (cf. ibid.).

From its first encounters with these native peoples, the Church sought to accompany them as they struggled for survival out of the unjust situation of people who had been defeated, invaded, and treated as slaves, and it taught them the way of Christ the Savior. Along with enormous suffering, the first evangelization brought major accomplishments and attained valuable pastoral insights. Their fruit has lasted to the present.

• African American cultures in Latin America and the Caribbean are   246
marked by a continual resistance to slavery. These peoples, who number in the millions, also have in their cultures human values that express the presence of God the Creator.

• It is true that during the first four centuries several million Africans were brought as slaves. They were violently torn away from their lands, separated from their families, and sold as items of merchandise. The enslaving of blacks and killing of Indians were the worst sin of the West's colonial expansion. Unfortunately, some baptized people were involved in slavery, racism, and discrimination.

247   • As the *Puebla Conclusions* state forcefully, in those peoples that are the fruit of racial mixing, there has taken shape a particular *mestizo* culture in which popular religiosity, as an inculturated form of Catholicism, is very much alive. Nevertheless, the failure to observe Christian obligations stands side-by-side with admirable examples of Christian living, and ignorance of church teaching stands alongside Catholic experiences rooted in gospel principles.

• The cultural and religious expressions of peasants and people in outlying urban areas reflect a great deal of the continent's Christian legacy and a faith rooted in the values of God's reign.

248   **Pastoral Directions: Inculturated Evangelization.** After having joined the pope in asking forgiveness of our indigenous and African American brothers and sisters "before God's infinite holiness for everything . . . that has been marked with sin, injustice, and violence" (*General Audience* [October 21, 1992], 3), we intend to carry out an inculturated evangelization:

1. *Toward Our Indigenous Brothers and Sisters*

• Offer the gospel of Jesus with the witness of a humble, understanding, and prophetic attitude, esteeming what they have to say through a respectful, frank, and fraternal dialogue; strive to learn their languages.

• Acquire greater critical knowledge of their cultures in order to appreciate them in the light of the gospel.

• Foster an inculturation of the liturgy by appreciating and drawing on those symbols, rituals, and religious expressions of theirs that are compatible with the clear meaning of the faith, while maintaining the value of the universal symbols and in harmony with the Church's general discipline.

• Accompany their theological reflection by respecting their cultural formulations, which help them to provide a reason for their faith and hope.

• Acquire greater knowledge of their world vision, which makes the complex of God-human-world a unity that pervades all human, spiritual, and transcendent relationships.

• Promote within the indigenous peoples their own native cultural values by means of an inculturation of the Church so as to embody God's reign more fully.

249   2. *Toward Our African American Brothers and Sisters.* Conscious of the problem of exclusion and racism weighing down on the black population, the Church in its evangelizing mission wishes to share in their sufferings and to accompany them in their legitimate aspirations for a more just and decent life for all (cf. ibid.).

• Hence, the Church in Latin America and the Caribbean wants to support African American peoples in defending their identity and in acknowledging their own values, and to help them to keep alive those practices and customs of theirs that are compatible with Christian teaching (cf. *Message to African Americans,* 3).

• We likewise commit ourselves to devote special attention to the cause of African American communities in the pastoral field by encouraging the manifestation of the religious expressions proper to their cultures (cf. ibid.).

3. Develop *mestizo* consciousness not only of racial amalgamation *mes-*   **250**
tizaje but also of the cultural amalgamation that is typical of the majority of the people in many of our countries, for it is connected to the inculturation of the gospel.

Human Development of Ethnic Groups. In the interest of genuine human   **251**
development, the Church wants to support the efforts that these people are making to bring national and international law to recognize them as peoples with full rights to land and to their own organizations and ways of life, in order to safeguard their right to live in accordance with their identity, speaking their own language and observing their ancestral customs, and to establish relations with all the peoples of the earth on an equal footing.

Therefore, we take on the following commitments:

• Overcome the mindset and practice of development imposed from outside, and replace it with self-development so that these people may be artisans of their own destiny.

• Contribute effectively to slowing and halting policies that tend to cause indigenous cultures to vanish through forced integration or, at the other extreme, policies that seek to keep indigenous people isolated and excluded from the nation.

• Press for full respect for the human rights of indigenous and African American people, including their legitimate defense of their lands.

• As a specific gesture of solidarity with peasants, indigenous people, and African Americans, support the *Populorum Progressio* Foundation established by the Holy Father.

• Thoroughly reexamine our education systems in order to eliminate once and for all any trace of discrimination in teaching methods, sums invested, or in where they are invested.

• Do everything possible to guarantee to indigenous people and African Americans an education adequate to their particular cultures, beginning with bilingual literacy training.

3.3 NEW CULTURE

3.3.1 Modern Culture

Situation.

• Although Latin America and the Caribbean are multicultural, they are   **252**
deeply marked by Western culture, whose memory, consciousness, and aspirations are ever present in our prevailing common way of life. That is why modern culture has had such a great impact on the way we are, and why its postmodern period now opens other possibilities to us.

• The characteristic features of modern culture are the centrality of the human being; the values of personalization, of the social dimension, and of shared life; the absolutizing of reason, whose triumphs in science, technology, and information processing have satisfied many human needs. These same triumphs of reason have led to an attempt to be autonomous vis-à-vis nature, which is under its domination; autonomous vis-à-vis history, for which human beings now assume responsibility; and even autonomous vis-à-vis God, who is of no concern or who is relegated to personal consciousness, while only the temporal order is regarded as important.

• Postmodernity is the product of the failure of the reductionistic pretension of modern reason. It leads humankind to question some of the gains of modernity, such as trust in unlimited progress, although it also recognizes its positive features, as indeed the Church itself does (cf. GS 57).

• Both modernity, with its positive and negative features and postmodernity, insofar as it is a space open to transcendence, present serious challenges to the evangelization of culture.

Pastoral Challenges.

253   • Cleavage between faith and culture insofar as modern human beings rule out transcendence and as a result of overspecialization, which makes it difficult to see the whole.

• Little awareness of the need for a true inculturation as the way to evangelize culture.

• Lack of correspondence between the values of the people which take their inspiration from Christian principles and social structures that cause injustice, preventing human rights from being exercised.

• The ethical vacuum and the prevailing individualism, which reduce the basis for values to a merely subjective consensus in society.

• The enormous power of the media, which often promote negative values.

• The fact that the Church is scarcely present in the area of the major expressions in art; in philosophical, anthropological, and social thought; and in the realm of education.

• The new urban culture, with its values, expressions, and characteristic structures; with its space at once open and diversified; with its mobility; and its predominantly functional relationships.

Pastoral Directions.

254   • Present Jesus Christ as paradigm for every attitude, personal and social, and as answer to the problems afflicting modern cultures: evil, death, lovelessness.

• Intensify dialogue between faith and science, faith and expressions, faith and institutions, which are major realms of modern culture.

• Exercise care for the signs and cultural language that point to the Christian presence and that make it possible to introduce the originality of the gospel message into the heart of cultures, especially in the realm of the liturgy.

• Develop and train the laity to exercise their threefold function in the world: the prophetic function in the area of the word, thought, and their expression and values; the priestly function, in the world of celebration and sacrament, enriched with expressions, art, and communication; the royal function in the world of social, political, and economic structures.

• Encourage knowledge and discernment of modern culture with a view toward adequate inculturation.

3.3.2 The City

Pastoral Challenges.

• Today, Latin America and the Caribbean are in the midst of a rapid   255
urbanization process. The post-industrial city is not merely a variant form of the traditional human habitat but, indeed, represents the passage from rural culture to urban culture, which is the location and driving force of the new universal civilization (cf. *Puebla Conclusions,* 429). In the city, the very way human beings in a social group, a people, or a nation, cultivate their relationship with themselves, with others, with nature, and with God is changing.

• By the very nature of city, relationships with nature are almost always limited to the process of producing consumer goods. Relationships between persons become largely functional. Relations with God undergo a pronounced crisis because the mediation of nature, which is so important to rural religiosity, is now gone and because modernity itself tends to enclose the human being within the immanence of the world. Relations of urban people with themselves also change because modern culture leads people to prize especially their freedom, their autonomy, scientific, and technological rationality, and, in general, their subjectivity, their human dignity, and their rights. Indeed, the major centers creating modern science and technology are in the city.

• However, our Latin American metropolitan centers are also typically surrounded by belts of poverty and misery. They almost always make up the bulk of their population and are the result of exploitive and excluding economic models. The spread of communication and transportation is leading to the urbanization of the countryside itself.

• Today's city person is different in type from the rural person: he or she trusts in science and technology; is influenced by the media; is energetic and oriented toward what is new; is consumption-oriented, audiovisual, absorbed in the anonymous masses, and uprooted.

Pastoral Directions.

• Carry out a kind of pastoral work inculturated into the city in the areas   256
of catechesis, liturgy, and the way the Church is organized. The Church should inculturate the gospel into the city and in the urban person. Discern the positive and negative features of such persons; grasp their language

and their symbols. The inculturation process encompasses the proclamation, assimilation, and reexpression of the faith.

257   • Reshape the urban parish. The Church in the city must reorganize its pastoral structures. The urban parish must be more open, flexible, and missionary, allowing for transparochial and supraparochial pastoral activity. Indeed, the city structure demands a pastoral approach devised specifically for it. The large cities, where new forms of culture and communication emerge, ought to be privileged sites for mission.

258   • Encourage the training of lay people for urban mission, through biblical and spiritual formation; create ministries conferred on lay people in order to evangelize large cities.

259   • Multiply small communities, ecclesial movements and groups, and Christian base communities. Undertake what has been called the "ministry of buildings" through the activity of committed lay people living in them.

260   • Organize a pastoral activity aimed at particular circles and functions that is differentiated in accord with city spaces. A ministry of welcome to deal with migration. A ministry for marginal groups. Assure that the religious needs of the inhabitants of large cities receive attention during the summer months and vacations. Strive to provide pastoral attention for those who habitually spend their weekends outside the city, where they are unable to fulfill their Sunday obligation.

261   • Encourage the evangelization of influential groups and those who are responsible for the city in the sense of making it a decent habitat for people, and especially in the vast poor neighborhoods.

262   • Promote meetings and courses on the evangelization of large cities on the continental (CELAM), national, and regional levels.

3.4 THE CHURCH'S EDUCATIONAL ACTIVITY

Theological Perspectives.

263   • We reaffirm what we have said at Medellín and Puebla (see *Medellín Conclusions,* "Education"; and *Puebla Conclusions*); with that as a starting point, we indicate some aspects that are important for Catholic education today.

         • Education is the assimilation of culture. Christian education is the assimilation of Christian culture. It is the inculturation of the gospel into culture itself. It takes place on a wide variety of levels: in school and outside; elementary and higher; formal and nonformal. In any case, education is a dynamic lifelong process of the person and of peoples. It gathers the memory of the past, teaches how to live the present, and projects toward the future. Hence, Christian education is absolutely necessary in the new evangelization.

264   • Christian education develops and strengthens in Christians their life of faith and assures that for them living truly means Christ (cf. Phil 1:21). Hence, the "words of eternal life" (Jn 6:68) sound within them, the "new

creation" is brought about in each of them (cf. 2 Cor 5:17), and the Father's plan to sum up all things in Christ is carried out (cf. Eph 1:1-10). Thus, Christian education is based on a true Christian anthropology, which means the opening of human beings to God as Creator and Father, toward others as brothers and sisters, and toward the world as what has been entrusted to them, not to exercise over it a despotic control that destroys nature but in order to develop its potential.

• No teacher educates without knowing why and toward what he or she **265** is educating. In every educational project there is a human project; whether or not that project is of value depends on whether it builds or destroys the one being educated. That is its educational value. When we talk about a Christian education, we are saying that the teacher is educating toward a human project in which Jesus Christ lives. Education covers many aspects that are part of the project of educating a human being; many values are involved, but these values are never alone; they are always organized into an ordered whole, either explicitly or implicitly. If Christ is the foundation and end of that ordering, such an education is summing up everything in Christ and is a true Christian education. Otherwise, education may talk about Christ but it is not Christian.

• The Christian teacher should be regarded as an active member and representative of the Church who evangelizes, catechizes, and educates in a Christian manner. He or she has a defined identity in the church community. His or her role should be recognized in the Church.

• Currently, we find a series of values that are both challenging and **266** ambivalent. Hence, arises the need to confront these new values in education with Christ, who reveals the mystery of the human being. In the new education, there is an effort to make the person grow and mature in accord with the demands of such new values. Moreover, they must be harmonized with what is specific to the Latin American context.

• On the basis of secularistic criteria, we are generally expected to educate a person to be technically oriented, someone who is ready to dominate the world and live in an exchange of goods produced under certain political norms—as few as possible. This situation emphatically challenges us to be conscious of all the values present in it, and to be capable of summing them up in Christ; it challenges us to continue the direction of the incarnation of the Word in our education and to arrive at the project of life for every human being, namely Christ dead and risen.

Pastoral Challenges.

• The situation of education in Latin America challenges us from other **267** angles as well. We are challenged by the exclusion of many people from even basic school education and by the high degree of illiteracy in a number of our countries; by the crisis of the family, the primary educator, and by the divorce between the gospel and culture; by the social and economic differences that make a Catholic education, especially at higher levels, a heavy burden for many people. We are likewise challenged by the informal education received through so many communicators who are not really Christian (e.g., on television).

268 • The Catholic university and the university of Christian inspiration is a great challenge since its task is particularly that of developing a human being as understood in Christian terms. Hence, it must be in a living, ongoing, step-by-step dialogue with humanism and with technological culture in order to know how to teach the true Christian wisdom in which the model of "worker" is joined to that of "sage" and culminates in Jesus Christ. Only thus will it be able to point to solutions to the complex unresolved problems of the emerging culture and the new social configurations, such as the dignity of the human person; the inviolable rights of life; religious freedom; the family as the first site for social commitment; solidarity on its various levels; the commitment proper to a democratic society, the complex economic and social question; the phenomena of the sects; the speed of cultural change.

269 • Another challenge that arises with regard to schools in a number of countries is the thorny problem of relationships between state education and Christian education. Although these relationships have become easier in some countries, in other countries it is still not understood that a Catholic education is an inalienable right of Catholic parents and their children, and the resources necessary for that aid are not made available, or it is simply prohibited.

270 • Other significant challenges are the religious ignorance of young people, nonschool education, and informal education. Another challenge is that of an education apt for different cultures, and particularly indigenous and African American cultures, not only in the sense that it be in keeping with their own way of life but also that it not cut them off from progress, from equal opportunity, and from being able to build national unity.

Pastoral Directions.

271 • Our commitments in the field of education can no doubt be summed up as pastoral work aiming at inculturation: education is the systematic means for evangelizing culture. Therefore, we take a stand for a Christian education based on life and on behalf of life in the individual, family, and community spheres and in the sphere of the ecosystem; education that fosters the dignity of the human person and true solidarity; and education incorporating a process of civil and social formation inspired by the gospel and the Church's social doctrine. We commit ourselves to an evangelizing education.

272 • We support parents in choosing the kind of education they want for their children in keeping with their convictions, and we condemn all intrusions of the civil power restricting this natural right. It ought to guarantee each person's right to religious formation and, therefore, the right to religious teaching in schools at all levels.

273 • We offer encouragement to Christian educators who work in church institutions, those congregations who continue to work in education, and

Catholic teachers working in non-Catholic institutions. We must promote ongoing formation for Catholic educators so that they may be able to grow in their faith and in the ability to communicate it as true wisdom, above all in Catholic education.

• There is a pressing need for a true Christian formation on life, love, and sexuality to correct the distortions of certain information received in schools. Education toward freedom is also a pressing need, since it is one of the fundamental values of the person. Christian education must also be concerned with education for work, particularly in the circumstances of contemporary culture.   274

• The charisms of the religious orders and congregations serving Catholic education in the various local Churches of our continent are of very great help for fulfilling the commission that we have received from the Lord to go and teach all nations (cf. Mt 28: 18-20), especially by evangelizing culture. We call on the religious men and women who have abandoned this extremely important field of Catholic education to return to their task. We also note that the "preferential option for the poor" includes the preferential option for the means to enable people to escape from their poverty, and that one of the privileged means for doing so is Catholic education. The preferential option for the poor is also made manifest when teaching religious continue to carry on their educational work in the many rural areas that are both remote and in great need.   275

• We must also make efforts that Catholic school education on all levels be within the reach of all people, and not be reserved for just a few, even while keeping in mind the economic problems involved. The responsibility of the parish community in the school and in its management should be developed. We ask that the public funds apportioned for Catholic education be guaranteed.   276

• In particular, we believe that on the basis of the apostolic constitution *Ex Corde Ecclesiae,* the Catholic university is called to carry out an important mission of dialogue between the gospel and cultures and of advancing human development in Latin America and the Caribbean.

• Conscious of the worldwide extension of contemporary culture, we will form a critical consciousness toward the media on every level of Catholic education. There is a pressing need to provide effective criteria to prepare the family to use television, press, and radio.   277

• Transform the Catholic school into a community that is a radiating center of evangelization, through students, parents, and teachers. We are striving to strengthen the educational community and, in it, the process of civic and social formation, taking inspiration from the gospel and from the Church's social teaching so that it may respond to the true needs of the people. Thus, organizations of students, educators, parents, and alumni will be strengthened as a method of civil, social, and political education that may make open the way to the democratic formation of persons. We like-   278 wise ask governments to continue to direct their efforts to make education ever more democratic.

3.5 SOCIAL COMMUNICATION AND CULTURE

Theological Perspectives.

279 • Evangelization, the proclamation of the reign, is communication in order that we may live in communion (cf. *Puebla Conclusions,* 1063): "what we have seen and heard we proclaim now to you, so that you too may have fellowship with us; for our fellowship is with the Father and with his Son, Jesus Christ" (1 Jn 1:3). Every person and every human group develop their identity as they meet others (*otherness*). Such communication is the path that must be taken in order to come to communion (*community*). The reason is that the human being has been made image of the Triune God, and in the heart of revelation, we find God's trinitarian mystery as the eternally interpersonal communication, whose Word becomes dialogue, enters into history through the Spirit, and thus initiates a world of new encounters, exchanges, communication, and communion. This communication is important not only in the world but within the Church.

• In the Father's gesture of communication through the Word made flesh, "the word becomes liberating and redemptive for all humankind in the preaching and activity of Jesus. This act of love through which God reveals himself in conjunction with humankind's response of faith brings about a deep dialogue" (Pontifical Council on the Mass Media, pastoral instruction, *Aetatis Novae,* 6). Thus, Christ is the model for the communicator: in him the wholly Other God comes forth to meet us and to await our free response. This encounter of communion with God is always growth. It is the way of holiness.

• Thus, there is a very close relationship among evangelization, human development, and culture, which is based on communication. The Church thereby has specific tasks and challenges in the area of the media. That is what the pope said in his *Opening Address* to this Conference: "It must certainly be one of your priorities to intensify the Church's presence in the world of the media" (OA 25).

• We know that we are in a new culture of the image and that the gospel message must be inculturated into this culture, thus making it expressive of Christ, who is the utmost communication. We understand the importance of the vast number of electronic means that we now have at our disposal for announcing the gospel. We thank God for granting us this new gift in contemporary culture.

Pastoral Challenges.

280 • Technological advances in the area of communication, particularly in television, offer evangelization extensive possibilities for communicating with the most diverse levels and enable society to be interconnected around the globe. That is the positive feature, but in the current context it also

presents very serious challenges, given the secularistic orientation of much programming.

• We are aware of how the communications industry has developed in Latin America and the Caribbean. It reflects the growth of economic and political groups that concentrate ownership of the various media into the hands of a powerful few. They come to manipulate communication, imposing a culture that encourages hedonism and consumerism and tramples our cultures along with their values and identities.

• We see how advertising often introduces false expectations and creates false needs. We also see how television programming in particular is full of violence and pornography, which aggressively make their way into the bosom of the family. We also note that the sects are continually intensifying and expanding their use of the media.

• Moreover, the Church's presence in the media world is still insufficient, and there are not enough workers with proper training to face the challenge. Moreover, the various episcopacies do not have adequate planning for pastoral work in the media.

• Telecommunications and information processing are new challenges to the integration of the Church into this world.

Pastoral Directions.

• Support and energize the efforts of all those who in their use of the **281** media are defending their cultural identity, by taking on the challenge of meeting new and different situations and striving to assure that an authentic dialogue takes place. Connect mass communication with community and group communication. Strive to have our own media and, insofar as possible, a video production unit to serve Latin America and the Caribbean.

• Help to discern and guide communication policies and strategies. Their **282** aim should be to enable persons to encounter one another so that an authentic and responsible freedom of expression may be in effect, to foster people's own cultural values, and to seek Latin American integration.

• Give Catholic media professionals enough support so that they can **283** carry out their mission. Strive for a growing relationship of ecclesial communion with international organizations (e.g., OCIC-AL, UNDA-AL, UCLAP) "whose members can be valuable and competent collaborators of the bishops conferences and of individual bishops" (Pontifical Council on the Media, pastoral instruction, *Aetatis Novae,* 17). The episcopal commissions on the media in each country and DECOS-CELAM and SERTAL should augment and improve their presence in this field.

• Every effort should be made to assure that all pastoral agents working **284** in and with the media be prepared technically, doctrinally, and morally. Likewise, there must also be an education plan aimed at critical perception, especially in homes, and at the ability to utilize the media and their language actively and creatively by employing our people's cultural symbols.

• Catholic universities must be encouraged to provide the highest quality **285** human, academic, and professional media training. The languages and corresponding techniques of communication are to be taught in seminaries and houses of religious formation so as to assure sufficient systematic preparation.

Today, it is absolutely essential to use computers and information science to optimize our resources for evangelization. Progress must be made in installing the Church's information network in the various bishops conferences.

286   • Catholic publishing houses are to act in a coordinated manner within planned comprehensive pastoral activity.

Part III

Jesus Christ,
Life and Hope of Latin America
and the Caribbean

Primary Pastoral Directions

We have come to Santo Domingo from our local Churches. We brought
"the joys and the hopes, the griefs and the anxieties" (GS 1) of our peoples.
Yearnings that our continent have life and hope came with us.

Our meeting with the Holy Father confirmed us in faith, hope, and love
for the Lord and for the Church. The spiritual company of so many brothers
and sisters who prayed for us and offered us their support gave us strength.

Daily celebration of the eucharist, meditation on God's word, and the
work we did together with our trust placed in the Lord enabled us to
experience truly the presence of Jesus in our midst (cf. Mt 18:20) and the
action of the Spirit.

"Jesus Christ, the same yesterday, today, and forever" (Heb 13:8) has
made us feel that he makes us "new creatures," (cf. 2 Cor 5:17); that he
gives us "life . . . abundantly" (Jn 10:10); that he promises us "eternal life"
(Jn 6:54). He is "our hope" (1 Tm 1:1).

We now return to our various fields of ministry. We will proclaim the
gospel of life. We will continue to give a "reason for our hope" (1 Pt 3:15)
to every single person whom the Lord sets on our paths.

As we conclude our reflections, with our hearts grateful to God, we turn
to look over the work we have done in order to identify the main lines of
pastoral work that we found and in order to continue our journey, guided
by the three topics that the Holy Father invited us to study, deepen, and
apply, starting here in this Fourth Conference.

Looking back at our journey, we proclaim with new ardor our faith in
Jesus Christ, Son of the Living God, sole reason for our life, and source of
our mission. He is the Way, the Truth, and the Life. He gives us the life
that we wish to communicate fully to our peoples so that all may have a
spirit of solidarity, reconciliation, and hope.

289   We make this profession of faith under the protection of Our Lady of Guadalupe, patroness of Latin America, who has been with us in this episcopal gathering, and who is ever with us in the mission that the Lord entrusts to us.

290   We renew our intention to further the pastoral guidelines, set by Vatican II, which were applied at the General Conferences of Latin American Bishops at Medellín and Puebla, and bring them up-to-date by means of the pastoral guidelines laid down at this Conference.

291   We regard the three topics that the Holy Father proposed to us as the three major pastoral directions that we assume for our Churches. Within the Santo Domingo guidelines, each local Church and each bishops conference will be able to find the challenges and pastoral directions that best meet its specific needs.

292   In the name of our local Churches in Latin America and the Caribbean, we commit ourselves to working on:

1. A new evangelization of our peoples.
2. A comprehensive development of our Latin American and Caribbean peoples.
3. An inculturated evangelization.

— In this sense, we now highlight those elements that received special emphasis during the conference and were approved, in order to specify the three main pastoral directions and impel them forward.

1. A NEW EVANGELIZATION OF OUR PEOPLES

293   *1.1. The commitment involves everyone and arises out of living communities.* Lay people have a special role to play as the guidelines of the apostolic exhortation *Christifideles Laici* have stated. Among lay people, we once more invite young people to be a force of renewal in the Church and of hope for the world, as the pope has continually pleaded.

In order to raise up priests, permanent deacons, men and women religious, and members of secular institutes to take part in the new evangelization, we will encourage a vigorous vocational work.

294   *1.2. We are all called to holiness* (cf. LG 39-42). In a Church that is a missionary community, we must strive firmly for ongoing education of the faith through catechesis, whose foundation is the Word of God and the teaching authority of the Church, and which enables Catholics to give reasons for their hope at every moment vis-à-vis the sects and the new religious movements.

The celebration of faith in the liturgy, the summit of the Church's life, must be carried out joyfully and in a way that makes possible a more lively and active participation that is committed to the situation of our peoples.

295   *1.3. This is the missionary moment in the Americas.* We heartily and enthusiastically invite all to take part in evangelization, not only within our Churches but beyond our borders. That will be our response to the example

of missionaries who came to the Americas from other lands to communicate their faith to us. It will also be a source of generosity for our young people and a blessing for our Churches.

2. A COMPREHENSIVE HUMAN DEVELOPMENT FOR THE PEOPLES OF LATIN AMERICA AND THE CARIBBEAN

2.1. *We make ours the cry of the poor.* In continuity with Medellín and Puebla, we assume with renewed ardor the gospel preferential option for the poor. This option, which is neither exclusive nor excluding, will, in imitation of Jesus Christ, shed light on all our evangelization activity.   **296**

With that light, we urge the development of a new economic, social, and political order in keeping with the dignity of each and every person, fostering justice and solidarity, and opening horizons of eternity for all of them.

2.2. *We say yes to life and to the family.* Facing very serious assaults on life and the family, which have intensified in recent years, we propose a firm action to defend and promote life and the family, which is the "domestic church" and sanctuary of life, from its conception to the natural end of its temporal stage. All human life is sacred.   **297**

3. AN INCULTURATED EVANGELIZATION

This is the third commitment that we assume in the perspective of new methods and expressions for living the gospel message today.

3.1. *Large cities in Latin America and the Caribbean, with their many problems, have challenged us.* We will devote attention to evangelizing these centers where most of our population now lives. Our care will also extend to rural areas; they already feel the impact of cultural changes.   **298**

3.2. *We want to come close to indigenous and African American peoples* so that becoming incarnate in their cultures, the gospel may manifest all its vitality and they may enter into the dialogue of communion with other Christian communities for the sake of mutual enrichment.   **299**

3.3. *We will likewise seek to stimulate an effective educational activity* and a steadfast effort at modern communication.   **300**

We place ourselves under the impulse of the Holy Spirit, who has been leading the Church in love since Pentecost. He granted us the grace of Vatican Council II and our General Conferences in Rio de Janeiro, Medellín, and Puebla.   **301**

We are certain that we will enjoy the help of the Spirit so that, as we leave Santo Domingo, we will continue even more united among ourselves, and under the guidance of the Holy Father, successor to Peter, and despite our limitations, we will be able to project enthusiastically the proclamation of Jesus Christ and his reign over Latin America and the Caribbean.

The Church in Latin America and the Caribbean proclaims its faith: **302**

"JESUS CHRIST: YESTERDAY, TODAY, AND FOREVER" (cf. Heb. 13:8)

Our local Churches, united in hope and love,
under the protection of Our Lady of Guadalupe,
in communion with the Holy Father
and in continuity with the pastoral directions given
at the general conferences held at Medellín and Puebla
commit themselves to work toward:

1. A New Evangelization of Our Peoples
    — To which *all* are called.
    — With emphasis on *encouraging vocations* with particular involvement by *lay people,* and among them, by *young people.*
    — Through ongoing education in the faith and its celebration: *catechesis* and *liturgy.*
    — Also beyond our borders: *missionary Latin America.*

2. A Comprehensive Development of the People of Latin America and the Caribbean
    — Out of a renewed gospel preferential option for the *poor.*
    — At the service of *life* and the *family.*

3. An Inculturated Evangelization
    — That can permeate environments characterized by *urban culture.*
    — That can take flesh in *indigenous and African American cultures.*
    — With an effective *educational activity* and *modern communications.*

303   **PRAYER**

Lord Jesus Christ, Son of the Living God,
Good Shepherd, and our Brother.
Our only option is for You.

United in love and hope
under the protection of our Lady of Guadalupe,
Star of Evangelization, we pray for your Spirit.

Grant us the grace
so that, in continuity with Medellín and Puebla,
we may heartily carry out a new evangelization
to which we are all called
with special involvement by lay people,
and particularly youth,
committing ourselves to an ongoing education of
    faith,

celebrating your praise,
and proclaiming you beyond our own borders
in a firmly missionary Church.
Increase our vocations
so that there may be laborers for your harvest.

Encourage us to be committed
to promote a comprehensive development
of the Latin American and Caribbean people
out of a gospel-inspired and renewed
preferential option for the poor
and at the service of life and the family.

Help us to work
toward an inculturated evangelization
that may permeate the *milieux* of our cities
and may take flesh in indigenous and African Amer-
    ican cultures
through an effective educational activity
and modern communications.

Amen.

Appendix I

John Paul II's Message to Indigenous People

Beloved Indigenous Brothers and Sisters of the American Continent,

1. In commemorating the Fifth Centenary of the Beginning of the Evangelization of the New World, there is a special place in the Pope's heart and affection for the descendants of the men and women who populated this Continent when the cross of Christ was planted there on October 12, 1492.

From the Dominican Republic, where I had the joy of meeting some of your representatives, I send my message of peace and love to all the indigenous ethnic groups and their members, from the Alaskan peninsula to Tierra del Fuego. You are the heirs of the peoples — Tupi-Guaraní, Aymara, Maya, Quechua, Chibcha, Nahualt, Mixtecó, Araucano, Yanomani, Guajiro, Inuit, Apaches, and so many others — who were known for their nobility of spirit, whose autochthonous cultural values stood out, such as the Aztec, Inca, and Mayan civilizations, and who can be proud of the fact that they have a view of life that recognizes the sacredness of the world and of the human person. Simplicity, humility, love of freedom, hospitality, solidarity, attachment to the family, a closeness to the earth, and a sense of contemplation are some of the many values that America's indigenous memory has kept to this very day and which are a contribution that can be found in the Latin American soul.

2. Five hundred years ago the Gospel of Jesus Christ came to your peoples. Even before that, however, even though no one suspected it, the living and true God was present, enlightening your paths. The Apostle John tells us that the Word, the Son of God, is "the true Light which enlightens everyone who comes into this world" (Jn 1:9). Indeed, the "seeds of the Word" were already present and enlightening the hearts of your ancestors that they might discover the imprint of God the Creator in all his creatures: sun, moon, mother earth, volcanoes and forests, lakes and rivers.

However, in the light of the Good News, they discovered that all the wonders of creation were but a pale reflection of their Author and that the human person, because he is the image and likeness of the Creator, is much higher than the material world and is called to an eternal, transcendent

156

destiny. Jesus of Nazareth, the Son of God made man, freed us from sin by his death and resurrection, making us God's adoptive children and opening up for us the path to life without end. The message of Jesus Christ made them see that all people are brothers and sisters because they have a common Father: God. And all are called to form part of the one Church which the Lord founded with his blood (cf. Acts 20:28).

In the light of Christian revelation, the ancient values of your ancestors, such as hospitality, solidarity, a spirit of generosity, reached their fullness in the great commandment of love, which must be the Christian's supreme law. The conviction that evil is identified with death and good with life opened up to them the heart of Jesus, who is "the Way, the Truth, and the Life" (Jn 14:6).

All of this, which the Fathers of the Church call the "seeds of the Word," were purified, deepened, and completed by the Christian message which proclaims universal brotherhood and defends justice. Jesus said that those who thirst for justice are blessed (cf. Mt 5:6). What motive other than preaching the gospel ideals impelled so many missionaries to denounce the abuses committed against the *Indios* with the arrival of the *conquistadors*? To demonstrate this, we have the apostolic activity and the writings of intrepid Spanish evangelists like Bartolomé de Las Casas, Fray Antonio de Montesinos, Vasco de Quiroga, Juan del Valle, Julián Garcés, José de Anchieta, Manuel de Nóbrega, and so many other men and women who generously devoted their lives to the natives. The Church has always been at the side of the indigenous people through her religious priests and bishops; in this Fifth Centenary, how could she possibly forget the enormous suffering inflicted on the peoples of this Continent during the age of conquest and colonization! In all truth, there must be a recognition of the abuses committed due to a lack of love on the part of some individuals who did not see their indigenous brothers and sisters as children of God their Father.

3. In this commemoration of the Fifth Centenary, I want to repeat what I said during my first pastoral visit to Latin America: "The Pope and the Church are with you and love you; they love your persons, your culture, your traditions; they admire your marvelous past, they encourage you in the present, and hope so much for the future" (*Address at Cuilapan,* January 29, 1979 [English trans., see *L'Osservatore Romano,* February 12, 1979]). Therefore, I want to become the echo and spokesman of your deepest longing.

I know you want to be respected as persons and citizens. The Church, on her part, makes her own your legitimate aspiration, since your dignity is no less than that of any other person or race. Every man and woman has been created in the image and likeness of God (cf. Gn 1:26-27). Jesus, who always showed his preference for the poor and abandoned, tells us that whatever we do or fail to do "for one of these least brothers of mine," we do for him (cf. Mt 25:40). No one who claims to be a Christian can reject or discriminate against anyone because of race or culture. The Apostle Paul admonishes us to have respect: "For in one Spirit we were all baptized into one body, whether Jews or Greeks, slaves or free persons" (1 Cor 12:13).

Faith, dear brothers and sisters, overcomes the differences between people. The faith and baptism give life to a new people: the people of the children of God. Without a doubt, although it overcomes differences, faith does not destroy them but respects them. The unity of all of us in Christ does not signify, from the human point-of-view, uniformity. On the contrary, the ecclesial communities feel enriched by welcoming the manifold diversity and variety of all their members.

4. Therefore, the Church encourages indigenous peoples to maintain and promote with legitimate pride the culture of their peoples: their healthy traditions and customs, their own language and values. In defending your identity, you are not only exercising your right; you are also fulfilling your duty to hand on your culture to future generations, thus enriching the whole of society. This cultural dimension, with its effects on evangelization, will be one of the priorities of the Fourth General Conference of the Latin American Episcopate, which I had the joy of inaugurating as the most important act of this visit on the occasion of the Fifth Centenary.

Protection of and respect for cultures, making good use of all that is positive in them, doubtlessly does not mean that the Church is renouncing her mission of elevating customs, rejecting everything that is in opposition to or contradicts gospel morality. "The Church's mission," the *Puebla Conclusions* states, "is to bear witness to 'the true God and one Lord.' So there is nothing insulting in the fact that evangelization invites peoples to abandon false conceptions of God, unnatural patterns of conduct, and aberrant manipulations of some people by others" (405-406).

A central element of indigenous cultures is their attachment and nearness to mother earth. You love the land and want to keep in contact with nature. I join my voice to that of those who are asking for the adoption of strategies and means to protect and preserve nature, which God has created. Due respect for the environment must always be held above purely economic interests or the abusive exploitation of the resources of land and sea.

5. Among the problems that afflict many indigenous communities are those related to land ownership. I know that the Church's pastors, based on the demands of the gospel and in harmony with her social magisterium, have consistently supported your legitimate rights, promoting proper agrarian reform and urging everyone to solidarity as the sure path to justice. I also know the difficulty you have in regard to topics such as social security, the right of association, the empowerment of farmers, participation in the national life, the integral formation of your children, education, health care, housing, and so many other problems that concern you. In this regard, I am reminded of the words that I addressed several years ago to the *Indios*

during that memorable meeting in Quetzaltenango: "The Church knows, beloved sons and daughters, the social discrimination that you suffer, the injustices that you bear, the serious difficulties you have in defending your lands and your rights, the frequent lack of respect for your customs and traditions. For this reason, in carrying out her task of evangelization, the Church wants to stay close to you and to raise her voice of condemnation when your dignity as human beings and children of God is violated; she wishes to accompany you peacefully, as the gospel demands, but with resolve and energy, in achieving the recognition and the promotion of your dignity and your rights as persons" (*Address at Quetzaltenango,* March 7, 1983 [English trans., see *L'Osservatore Romano,* May 9, 1983]).

Within the context of the religious mission that is hers, the Church will spare no effort in continuing to encourage all those initiatives aimed at promoting the common good and integral development of your communities, in addition to fostering legislation that respects and adequately protects the authentic values and rights of the indigenous peoples. A proof of this determined desire for cooperation and assistance can be seen in the Holy See's recent establishment of the *Populorum Progressio* Foundation, which has a fund to help the poorest indigenous groups and rural populations of Latin America. I encourage you, then, to make a renewed commitment to be actively involved in your own spiritual and human growth through dignified and constant labor, fidelity to the best of your traditions, and the practice of virtue. For this, you can count on the genuine values of your culture, refined over time by the generations who have preceded you in this blessed land. Most of all, however, you can count on the greatest wealth which you have received by God's grace, your Catholic faith. Following the teaching of the gospel, you will succeed in making your people, faithful to their legitimate traditions, progress materially as well as spiritually. Enlightened by faith in Jesus Christ, you will recognize other people as your brothers and sisters over and above any difference in race or culture. Faith will enlarge your hearts so that you can accept all your fellow citizens. This same faith will lead others to love you, to respect your characteristics, and to join with you in building a future in which everyone will take an active and responsible part, as is fitting to Christian dignity.

6. Concerning your proper place in the Church, I urge everyone to promote those pastoral initiatives that foster the indigenous communities' greater integration and participation. For this, renewed effort will have to be made in whatever is related to the inculturation of the gospel since "a faith which does not become culture is a faith which has not been fully received nor thoroughly thought through nor faithfully lived out" (*Address to the World of Culture,* Lima, May 15, 1988 [English trans., see *L'Osservatore Romano,* June 20, 1988]). Ultimately, it is a question of indigenous Catholics becoming the agents of their own development and evangelization in all areas, including the various ministries. What a great joy it will be to see the day when your communities can be served by missionaries, priests, and

bishops who have come from your own families and can guide you in adoring God "in spirit and truth" (Jn 4:23)!

The message that I entrust to you in the American land today, commemorating five centuries of the gospel's presence among you, is intended to be a call to hope. The Church, which has been with you in your journey throughout these 500 years, will do everything in her power to help the descendants of the ancient peoples of America to occupy their rightful place in society and the ecclesial communities. I am aware of the serious problems and difficulties you face. However, be sure that you will never lack God's help and the protection of his most holy Mother, as was promised once on Tepeyac hill to the *Indio* Juan Diego, an illustrious son of your own blood, whom I had the joy of raising to the honors of the altar: "Listen and understand, my littlest son, that nothing should frighten or bother you; do not let your heart be troubled, do not fear this infirmity, nor any other infirmity or anxiety. Am I not here, your mother? Are you not in my shadow? Am I not your protection? Are you not perhaps in my lap?" (*Nican Mopohua*).

May Our Lady of Guadalupe protect all of you. I cordially bless you in the name of the Father, and of the Son, and of the Holy Spirit. Amen.

Given at Santo Domingo, October 12, 1992,
the Fifth Centenary of the Evangelization of America.

Appendix II

John Paul II's Message to African Americans

Dearly Beloved African American Brothers and Sisters,

1. The Fifth Centenary of the Evangelization of the New World is an appropriate occasion to address my message of encouragement to you from the city of Santo Domingo. May it increase your hope and sustain your Christian commitment, renewing the vitality of your communities to which, as Successor of Peter, I send an intimate and affectionate greeting in the words of the Apostle Paul: "We wish you the favor and peace of God our Father, and of the Lord Jesus Christ" (Gal 1:3).

The evangelization of America is a reason for giving heartfelt thanks to God who, in his infinite mercy, wanted the message of salvation to reach the inhabitants of this blessed land, made fruitful by the cross of Christ, which has left an imprint on the life and history of his people and has produced such abundant fruits of holiness and virtue throughout the span of these five centuries.

The date of October 12, 1492 marks the initial encounter of races and cultures that feature in the history of these 500 years, during which the penetrating Christian gaze enables us to discover God's loving intervention, in spite of human shortcomings and faithlessness. In fact, in the course of history, there is a mysterious confluence of sin and grace, but in the long run, grace triumphs over the power of sin. As Saint Paul tells us: "Despite the increase of sin, grace has far surpassed it" (Rom 5:20).

2. In these celebrations of the Fifth Centenary, I could not fail to bring my message of closeness and warm affection to the African American peoples who are an important part of the population of the whole Continent; they enrich the Church and society in so many countries with their human and Christian values, as well as with their culture. In this context, the words of Simón Bolívar come to mind. He declared that "America is the result of the union of Europe and Africa with aborigine elements. That is why there is no room there for racial prejudice, and if it were to appear, America would return to a state of primitive chaos."

Everyone is aware of the serious injustice committed against those black peoples of the African continent who were violently torn from their land, their culture, and their traditions, and shipped to America as slaves. During my recent apostolic visit to Senegal, I did not want to omit a visit to the Island of Gorée, where this ignominious trade began; I wanted to show the Church's firm repudiation of it with words that I should now like to recall: "The visit to the 'slave house' recalls to mind that enslavement of black people which in 1462 Pius II, writing to a missionary bishop who was leaving for Guinea, described as an 'enormous crime,' the *'magnum scelus.'* Throughout a whole period of the history of the African continent, black men and women and children were brought to this cramped space, uprooted from their land and separated from their loved ones to be sold as goods. They came from all different countries and, parting in chains for new lands, they retained as the last image of their native Africa Gorée's basalt rock cliffs. We could say that this island is fixed in the memory and heart of all the black diaspora. These men, women and children were the victims of a disgraceful trade in which people who were baptized, but who did not live their faith, took part. How can we forget the enormous suffering inflicted, the violation of the most basic human rights, on those people deported from the African Continent? How can we forget the human lives destroyed by slavery? In all truth and humility this sin of man against man, this sin of man against God, must be confessed" (*Speech on the Island of Gorée,* February 22, 1992).

3. Looking at the current situation in the New World, we see vigorous and thriving African American communities which, without forgetting their past history, contribute the wealth of their cultures to the wide variety of cultures on the Continent. With a tenacity not free from sacrifice they contribute to the common good, becoming integrated in the social whole but preserving their own identity, traditions, and customs. This fidelity to their own being and spiritual heritage is something that the Church not only respects but encourages and desires to strengthen; since human beings — all human beings — are created in the image and likeness of God (cf. Gn 1:26-27), any genuinely human reality is an expression of this image, regenerated by Christ through his redemptive sacrifice.

By means of Christ's redemption, dear African American brothers and sisters, all humanity has passed from the shadow to light, from being "not my people" to being "children of the living God" (Hos 2:1). As "God's chosen ones" we form one body, that is, the Church (cf. Col 3:12-15), in which, in the words of Saint Paul, "there is no Greek or Jew here, circumcised or uncircumcised, foreigner, Scythian, slave or freeman. Rather, Christ is everything in all of you" (Col 3:11). Indeed, faith overcomes the differences between people and gives life to a new people, the people of the children of God. Without exception, while overcoming the differences in the common condition of Christians, faith does not destroy them but respects and dignifies them.

This is why, in commemorating this Fifth Centenary, I urge you to defend your identity, to be conscious of your values and to make them bear fruit.

However, as pastor of the Church, I urge you above all to be aware of the great treasure that you have received through God's grace, your Catholic faith. In the light of Christ, you will manage to help your communities to grow and progress spiritually as well as materially, thus spreading the gifts that God has granted you. Illuminated by Christian faith, you will look upon other human beings, regardless of any difference of race or culture, as your brothers and sisters, children of the same Father.

4. The Church's solicitude for you and your communities in view of the new evangelization, human development, and Christian culture will be highlighted at the Fourth General Conference of the Latin American Episcopate, which I had the pleasure of inaugurating yesterday. Without forgetting that many gospel values have penetrated and enriched the culture, mentality, and life of African Americans, there is a desire to increase pastoral attention and to encourage the specific elements of the ecclesial communities in their own expression.

Evangelization does not destroy your values but is incarnated in them; it consolidates and strengthens them. It causes the growth of the seeds scattered by the "Word of God who was in the world as 'the true light that enlightens every man' (Jn 1:9), before becoming flesh to save and gather up all things in himself" (*Gaudium et Spes,* 57). Faithful to the universality of her mission, the Church proclaims Jesus Christ and invites people of all races and conditions to accept his message. As the Latin American Bishops declared at the General Conference of Puebla de los Angeles, "the Church's mission is to bear witness to 'the true God and the one Lord.' So evangelization invites people to abandon false conceptions of God, unnatural patterns of conduct, and aberrant manipulations of some people by others" and cannot be seen as a mere accident (406). Indeed, with evangelization, "the Good News of Christ continually renews the life and culture of fallen man; it combats and removes the error and evil that flow from the ever-present attraction of sin; it never ceases to purify and elevate the morality of peoples. It takes the spiritual qualities and endowments of every age and nation, and with supernatural riches it causes them to blossom, as it were, from within; it fortifies, completes, and restores them in Christ" (*Gaudium et Spes,* 58).

5. However, the life of many African Americans in various countries is not without hardships and difficulty. Well aware of this, the Church shares your suffering and accompanies you and supports your legitimate aspirations for a more just and dignified life for everyone. In this regard, I cannot refrain from expressing my heartfelt gratitude and from encouraging the apostolic activities of so many priests and religious who are exercising their ministry with the poorest and the most destitute. I ask God that your Christian communities may give rise to many vocations to the priesthood and the religious life so that the African Americans of the Continent may be able to rely on ministers from their own families.

While I entrust you to the motherly protection of the blessed Virgin to whom devotion is so widespread in the life and Christian practices of African American Catholics, I bless you in the name of the Father, and of the Son, and of the Holy Spirit. Amen.

Given at Santo Domingo, October 12, 1992,
the Fifth Centenary of the Evangelization of America.

Part III

BEYOND SANTO DOMINGO:

COMMENTARIES

AND

REFLECTIONS

The Winds in Santo Domingo and the Evangelization of Culture

Jon Sobrino, S.J.

SANTO DOMINGO AS AN EVENT

In this article I shall reflect on Santo Domingo as an event, with the potential to evangelize culture. This does not negate the need to analyze it from other perspectives, and especially to analyze the text that the bishops produced there. But I shall focus here on the Santo Domingo event because I believe that as an event it has its own meaning and its own capacity to shape the reality of our world in one way or another. Before that, however, let me reflect on the title and purpose of this article.

First, Santo Domingo as an event was made up of many elements. The most important of these were the tasks of preparation, the differing degrees of participation by all the members of the Latin American church, the texts produced during that period, the measures and reactions of the Vatican, and of course what happened in Santo Domingo: the presence and messages of the pope, the presence of the bishops, their personal declarations and positions, why some of them were absent, the debates, tensions, and agreements reached in the hall, the celebrations, the various versions of the text, the final text, its interpretation and reception . . .

All these elements converge on a text, but they are more than the written text; we might call them a text *in actu*, which can have even more impact than the one approved by the pope. This impact comes from what was said and done throughout the process, from what was not said and done, and from the way it was said and done. We must keep all that in mind in speaking of Santo Domingo, although one element may have more relevance than another, in practice or in principle. And all these elements — not only the text — are transmitted to the church and society through what I call "the winds" that have moved the process and have been set in motion by it. In the title of these reflections I am emphasizing that these "winds" will inspire or fail to inspire ideals, will encourage or discourage practices, and will shape collective consciousness, more than the texts of Santo Domingo will.

This is nothing new; it has always been that way. Important events always

generate a text and a spirit — "winds," literally speaking — and both the text
and the spirit influence history. Each does so in its own way, but I think
that when the events are relatively recent, the spirit has more influence on
the church and society than the text itself. To put it more graphically, after
the metaphor of the winds: the music lasts longer than the words, except
of course in the minds of the experts, analysts, and transmitters of the
words.

For example, few people today remember the texts of Vatican II, but its
refreshing breeze still lingers. In a disincarnated church, closed in on itself,
authoritarian, condemning almost everything outside itself, tormented and
tormenting by its sin-obsessed vision, a miracle was produced: the church
opened doors and windows, replacing fear with hope, imposition with dialogue, dogmatism with honesty. Obviously the council texts must be analyzed. We can endlessly debate their authentic interpretation, as people
are doing today in some places. But as important as the texts are, what
seems more important today is the council's spirit of honesty, dialogue,
freedom, hope, compassion, of returning to Jesus. That, I think, is the issue
in the church today, even though it is posed in terms of textual interpretation. And if the texts are still meaningful and relevant today, it is because
in their totality, although some are better than others, they are imbued
with that spirit.

The same can be said of Medellín. Again, few people today know its
texts. Moreover, some who know them say that Puebla and even Santo
Domingo have produced better texts than Medellín. And in a way they are
right. But I do not believe that the spirit of Medellín has been surpassed,
and it is that spirit that — against wind and tides, to follow the metaphor —
preserves what is fundamental: that the church must go to the poor of this
world, incarnate itself in them, defend them and take risks for them,
denounce their oppressors. In that way the church becomes the church of
Jesus; Christians become followers of Jesus, believers in the God of Jesus.

Medellín is still — despite its "outdated" texts — the unsurpassed symbol
of the new evangelization. Its spirit — and not this or that text — has produced the most radical change in the history of the Latin American church,
changing it from an evangelically watered-down and historically imported
church to a Christian and Latin American church.

My second preliminary reflection is also suggested and even demanded
by the central theme of Santo Domingo: the new evangelization, and more
specifically, the evangelization of cultures. The latter can be understood in
several ways: as the inculturation of faith in diverse cultures, or as the
shaping of any given culture according to Christian values and formulations.
But here I shall approach the evangelization of culture from a different
perspective.

To put it simply, we can ask whether the air we breathe is purified or
contaminated. We can ask if our atmosphere is not so corrupted by lies
and deceit, cruelty and injustice, *hubris* and arrogance, that culture — from

the beginning, structurally—leads us toward evil rather than good. We can ask if pollution is destroying the ecology, not only of the body but of the spirit. If so, to evangelize culture—by whatever Christian methodology—also means introducing honesty, mercy, compassion, justice, dignity into this atmosphere.

Important historical events must also be analyzed from this perspective. So we must ask whether Santo Domingo, as an event, has evangelized our world; whether it has helped to purify or contaminate the atmosphere. In replying we must also be clear that, like any evangelization, this one does not start with a clean slate. Like Jesus, we must proclaim good news in the presence of and against evil realities; we must proclaim the kingdom of God in the presence of and against the antikingdom of the idols. Therefore in analyzing the Santo Domingo event we must see whether or not that event has evangelized the culture, the air we breathe; and whether with this or that action it has confronted the powerful. And let us remember: this may be expressed in texts, but it also goes beyond them.

From this perspective we shall raise the following question as objectively as possible: In what ways and in what degree has Santo Domingo evangelized, or failed to evangelize, the world we live in? How has it contributed, or failed to contribute, to putting in practice the formulations of faith that it requires and the texts that it offers?

SANTO DOMINGO AS AN EVANGELIZING EVENT

Latin American Identity and Roman Imposition

In the preparatory document entitled *Secunda Relatio*, drafted by the Latin American bishops in their own dioceses, we have this splendid text, which so well summarizes the newness, the identity, and the best aspects of the Latin American church since the Second Vatican Council:

On March 24, 1980, the whole church and world opinion were shaken by the horrible assassination of the archbishop of El Salvador, Oscar Arnulfo Romero, who was shot down in the act of celebrating mass, a martyr of the episcopal ministry because of his prophetic witness.

Almost ten years later, in the same city of San Salvador, the night of November 16, 1989, six Jesuit Fathers at the Central American University, together with two household employees, were cravenly massacred in their residence by soldiers under cover of a curfew. This news again shocked the world; they died for their priestly and religious commitment to justice and respect for human rights, and for their ministerial option for youth and the poor.

These events and many others show that our church in Latin America, in recent decades, has become a church of martyrs and the persecuted. In the galaxy of assassinated martyrs, together with bishops, priests, seminarians, and religious, the great majority are lay pastoral workers, peasants and laborers; many others have been slandered, kidnapped, tortured, exiled.

The historical novelty of this persecution is in its context, because it is carried out in the western Christian world by those who call themselves defenders of this culture and even of Christian principles. This is because the diverse oppressive idolatries of the continent, denounced in Puebla, have perceived a great threat from the church beginning with Medellín and Puebla, and have tried to counteract it in diverse ways: by spreading and financing sects that advocate a spiritualistic and uncommitted religiosity, by offering a liberal individualistic Christianity, and by direct attack and persecution.

In this way the church in the Latin American reality, faithful to its faith in the God of life and to its mission of salvation and liberation, gives testimony in persecution and martyrdom.

There is not even a pallid reflection of this eloquent text in the final document. I shall come back to it later, but here I should ask the reason for such a notable omission. In my opinion—quite apart from the details—the reason is in the imposition of Rome over a Latin American church that was developing its own evangelical identity. And that is where I want to start this reflection.

There is authoritarianism in every society, and there is centralism in the world as a whole, with the corresponding submissiveness to the superpowers. Other people in turn advocate dialogues, truly "democratic" attitudes, which is a political way of describing the fraternal relationships that the gospel demands. This happened *in actu*—more than in theoretical discussion—in Santo Domingo, even more acutely than in Medellín and Puebla. Despite the denials and euphemisms, there was not only diversity and pluralism but a strong and undisguised tension between the Vatican, with some bishops supporting its policy, and a solid majority of the Latin American bishops.

This specific tension goes beyond ideological and theological positions; it was expressed in the clear imposition of the Vatican over the conference, which did not happen at Medellín and Puebla. The Vatican selected the three presidents of the assembly, well known for their conservative tendency; it controlled the editing commission; it replaced the traditional methodology of seeing-judging-acting with that of judging-seeing-acting (I shall come back to this, because a lot more is at issue than a simple change of word order); it blocked the use of the excellent text of the *Secunda Relatio* and even the more moderate *Documento de Trabajo* as a real basis for the debate. Moreover, at important and symbolically meaningful moments there was a strong tension between the president and the assembly. The tension appeared, for instance, in the Mass to ask for forgiveness (which the two first presidents did not attend); and in the request for a letter of congratulation to Rigoberta Menchú on the occasion of her Nobel laureate, which was rejected by the presidency out of fear that such a letter from the assembly might be used for ideological purposes.

These and many other things show the undisguisable tension between the Vatican and the Latin American church. The tension is not new; it was present in the Vatican instructions of 1984 and 1986 about the theology of liberation, in the Vatican intervention regarding the Conference of Latin American Religions, and generally in Vatican policy on the naming of bishops, so that the generation of bishops entering the new century will be very different from that of Medellín.

Santo Domingo has not been an exception. The majority of Latin American bishops, as a group, did not seem to consider servility a virtue — although they accept responsible obedience; nor did they let themselves be manipulated as easily as the presidency would have liked, as was clear in many of the debates and votes inside the hall, and some declarations outside. But finally they had to accept the Vatican demands. In their method, their key commissions, and their basic theological orientation, the majority had to accede to Vatican pressure.

This ecclesial authoritarianism or centralism does not do the church any good. From an intraecclesial viewpoint it does not reflect but greatly obstructs, *in actu*, the role of the *communio* as the maximum expression of the ecclesial mystery — despite so many recent Vatican declarations in support of that role. This procedure reflects neither the community nor the freedom of God's sons and daughters. And as far as the Santo Domingo assembly is concerned, the Vatican imposition was not only evident from the beginning, but determined the direction of the assembly; it caused innumerable energies to be wasted, which would have been better used in drafting a good text. What is more important, it transmitted a sad message to the local churches and even more to the periphery: a fear of liberty and creativity, of seeing reality and even God from a different and peripheral viewpoint, of being themselves.

From the viewpoint of the evangelization of culture, on the one hand we must be encouraged by the firm resistance of the bishops of the periphery, to the imposition of the center. But on the other hand, the atmosphere of imposition and the real imposition that prevailed in Santo Domingo have meant a lost opportunity to evangelize a world that has much to gain from authoritarianism and centralism. A lost opportunity, for example, to say to the powers of the North, to the United Nations and other international forums, that they should hear, respect, and encourage the voice of the periphery and not — as usually happens — impose their will on it.

I have begun at this point out of realistic honesty; also because this tension between Roman imposition and Latin American creativity led the conference not only toward ambivalence — the theoretical presence of two values, hierarchy and base — but really toward ambiguity, because at least for now it has put a full stop to the whole process that surrounded Santo Domingo. It also shows the need for decisiveness and boldness to put the best of the text into practice, without waiting for favorable winds from the Vatican.

But our last reflection is also true and positive. There was imposition, many hours were wasted in debates and quarrels, because there is identity in the Latin American church; Medellín is not dead. That church no longer enjoys a favorable wind, but it is there. Administrative measures may be used to neutralize it, but that identity still supports the church's pastoral practice, theology, evangelization, and faith. Sadly it must still appear *sub specie contrarii*, in resistance to imposition, but it has appeared and it can be put to work.

Asking Seriously for Forgiveness

History (the quincentenary) and geography (Santo Domingo, the ancient isle of Hispaniola) demanded a word from the church about what happened then and has happened in these five centuries. In that context it was necessary to take a position on whether or not to ask forgiveness of the surviving indigenous peoples; whole races and peoples, religions and cultures, became extinct or were annihilated by the conquerors. And of the Africans who were brought infamously, as merchandise, in one of the greatest and cruelest aberrations known to history.

Beyond all doubt, even without dwelling on the horror stories, there was an immense sin of lèse humanité, which evolved into original and originating sin. Asking forgiveness, which is so indispensable in order to evangelize and to purify the air contaminated by denial, arrogance, and disrespect for the other, is something never done by governments, nor by armies, nor by transnational corporations; yet in some ways the church has done it.

Certainly the church has asked forgiveness in ambiguous ways. Some bishops — those who live with indigenous and black peoples, who still bear the mark of centuries of oppression, indignity, and suffering — have done so sincerely. Others less sincerely; the cardinal archbishop of Santo Domingo, president of CELAM and second vice-president of the assembly, did not permit the Mass of forgiveness to be celebrated in his cathedral. We must also note that although it was quite clear what sins were to be forgiven, it was not always so clear who were the sinners of five centuries ago: the conquerors alone, or the clergy as well. There was no cause for triumphalism.

Even so, it was important that John Paul II asked forgiveness in Santo Domingo and did so again on his return to Rome, that the bishops did so in a eucharist and inserted it in some parts of the text. In the world of the North, sinful and hypocritical, never expecting to ask forgiveness of anyone — not for the violent death generated in Vietnam, Afghanistan, or Iraq, in El Salvador, Guatemala, Grenada, or Panama, nor for the slow death of the Southern half of the planet — asking forgiveness is healthy and purifies the air we breathe.

So the forgiveness of Santo Domingo was good, but it is also necessary — in order to evangelize cultures — for everyone, the pope, the bishops, priests, religious, to treat it with real conviction rather than evasively, with a purpose of change and a spirit of healing toward the blacks and Indians, just as Bishop Leonidas Proaño had asked on his deathbed: that the church repair all the damage it has done to the Indians. The church must also ask forgiveness in all honesty not only for the past, but in and for the present; otherwise it will have no credibility when it asks forgiveness for the past. And forgiveness must be asked with a real disposition to be forgiven, which although it seems paradoxical is the hardest part, since in the famous words of Karl Rahner, "only the forgiven one knows himself as a sinner." But that is also the most Christian part, because then forgiveness becomes a gift and a grace, an undeserved and unexpected gift of acceptance by the victims, the aggrieved.

To introduce in this world the humility and honesty of asking forgiveness, and the willingness to receive it as a grace, is no small thing for the church to do. In this way it can evangelize a culture of hypocrisy and arrogance. Santo Domingo timidly opened a path in this direction, which the church must follow and offer to everyone.

The Sin of the World and the Sin of the Church

According to a certain thesis in the Western world, although there are serious problems, the world is going well, or at least it is improving. With the fall of the Eastern bloc and of many military regimes, with gradual democratization even though it is often only formalistic, and with the imposition — without opposition — of economic neoliberalism, we have come to the "end of history." And this is repeated even though daily experience — and a technical report from the United Nations — shows that at least in the short term things are getting worse in the world as a whole, and the endless promises of early improvement are not credible for the majority of people.

In this context Santo Domingo, following Medellín and Puebla, has done two important things: it has shown a fundamental honesty with regard to the truth of reality and its ethical demands. In the first case it has again denounced the atrocious situation of misery and injustice, and has criticized economic neoliberalism not only as an inhuman and insufficient way of solving the problem, but as a contributing cause of misery. Many bishops outside the hall, and the text itself, make that point. Things are bad and getting worse, they say: "growing impoverishment"; "the statistics eloquently show that in the last decade poverty has grown in both absolute and relative numbers"; "neoliberal policies deepen even more the negative consequences." To put all that in the tradition of Puebla, "we must lengthen the list of suffering faces."

We do not know how much note the world will take of Santo Domingo on this point; as I have already said, the same world that applauded John Paul II for his contribution to the fall of the Eastern bloc, ignored him when he denounced the war in Iraq. The same thing may happen now with Santo Domingo, which may well be ignored in that fundamental denunciation of the sin of institutionalized injustice. But it is already an evangelization of a culture of indifference and injustice, that Santo Domingo has again spoken the truth and has not sought to cooperate with the denial and institutionalized lie that the world is now on the right path—now that real socialism has disappeared—as long as it obeys the North.

In the second case, regarding the ethical demands of reality, Santo Domingo has again affirmed the option for the poor; a preferential option based on the word of God and not on ideologies, but an option in any case, and in the words of John Paul II, a "firm and irrevocable" option that shows "the measure of our following Christ." That is also why the bishops, in a utopian way and without contributing much from a technical viewpoint, have offered as an alternative to neoliberalism an "economy of solidarity"; that is, an economy that focuses directly on the possibility of life for the majorities—and not only as a potentially positive by-product of neoliberalism, which always directly favors the most powerful.

Beyond doubt, the denunciation of unjust poverty and the option for the poor are evangelizing acts in our world. The very words "justice" and "injustice" are disappearing from the world's official vocabulary, as if they had nothing to do with the problems and their solution. And the option for the poor sounds like a macabre euphemism, when almost none of the nations are complying with the goal of contributing 0.7 percent to assist the underdeveloped countries. Nevertheless, here again the church has no cause for triumphalism.

Although some bishops—for instance, those associated with Cardinal Arns—have personally and vigorously communicated these denunciations and unmaskings, the texts do not have the pathos of those from Medellín and Puebla. This may be because it is no longer new, but also because there is no evidence here of the earlier texts' decisiveness in struggling for justice and taking the risk of denunciation. Strictly speaking, the texts describe the tragedy in which we are living, but they are not texts of denunciation, let alone of unmasking or confrontation with those responsible for the tragedy they describe. That is still very much needed, even though the world seeks to reduce the level of confrontation. To give just one example: the Atlacatl battalion, sadly known for the massacre at El Mozote and the assassination of the Jesuits, still proudly proclaims its motto "For the fatherland and with God." In the face of such things it is not enough to denounce the reality; we must enter into confrontation with those who have made it a tragic reality.

Moreover, however bold the texts may be, no one can fail to notice the disappearance — with apparent intentionality on the part of the Vatican — of the generation of bishops who put those words into practice and engaged in serious confrontation with the public powers. A few remain, of course, but the governments, armies, and oligarchies know very well that every year there are fewer bishops like Dom Sergio, like Bishop Romero, like Proaño, like Dom Helder. Therefore words about injustice and option, almost identical to the earlier texts, carry less meaning now than they did before. U.S. vice-president Nelson Rockefeller immediately rose up against Medellín, and the advisers of Ronald Reagan against Puebla. So far we have not heard of any worldly powers feeling threatened or affected by Santo Domingo. If so would they rise up against it, or now that the Eastern bloc has fallen, would they consider criticism from religious sectors irrelevant?

We should add that while denouncing the sin of injustice and opting for the poor are ways of evangelizing culture, it is not evangelizing to ignore sin within the church itself, to ignore the church's contribution to the sin of the world, by its action and especially by omission. This is a very old problem, we know, but it bears repeating. The bishops at Santo Domingo too, not to mention those in the Vatican, seem to view the world's problems — injustice, dictatorships, corruption, deceit — as coming from outside. As if the source of today's problems were communists, dictatorships, even capitalists (as in the past it was rationalists, Protestants, unbelievers and pagans), and they would all have been taken care of if people had listened to the church. This is not only groundless triumphalism, but an unevangelizing attitude; the church loses credibility if it only denounces outside problems without at the same time, in sincerity and humility, recognizing those within.

This recognition of the sin within was not even minimally evident at Santo Domingo. The church sees sin much more clearly outside than within itself. When it looks inward it sees sins, weaknesses, or dangers more in the laity than in the clergy and religious, and more in these than in the hierarchy, which in principle seems to be immune to all human limitations.

Of course I am not advocating either an impossible ecclesial angelism, or a paralyzing masochism. But we must be aware that here again, an opportunity to evangelize culture is being lost. In a hypocritical world that refuses to ask forgiveness for the oppression to which it has subjected two-thirds of the planet, that even treats the plunder and destruction of other peoples as historic grandeur, it would be very evangelizing — more than any words — if the church also simply recognized its own limitations and sins.

Recognizing the "Other"

The greatest theoretical contribution of Santo Domingo was a clearer approach to and recognition of the "other" than has been made in earlier church documents; specifically its recognition of women, indigenous peoples, and blacks. If it is hard to achieve recognition of the "poor," recognizing the "other" can be even harder, although they are often the same person or group. The "poor" expresses and is a terrible ethical and theologal demand, of course, but the "other" touches the very roots of liturgy and the mediation of faith, dogma, theology, church doctrine, and the like. The "other" leads us not only to what is different, but to the unknown.

The bishops focused on the other for several reasons. Honesty and responsibility required them to say something serious about indigenous and black peoples during the quincentenary year. A few bishops rose to say that they could not return to their dioceses without a serious text on this matter. It was also clear with regard to women that the church could not go on as it is, nor could it turn its back on these issues or trivialize them with simplistic approaches. Indeed the most vigorous texts were written on these subjects, if only because they were new to the church.

The practical value of these texts will be measured by whether or not they are put to work, whether the bishops and pastoral workers become truly inculturated in these "other" cultures, become open to them, give and receive from them, and whether the Vatican encourages or at least refrains from blocking that action. In a word, whether or not the church overcomes — by opposing — the secular habits of colonialism, paternalism, masculinism, and clericalism.

Things get harder if we add what the church must learn to what it must overcome, for it will have to learn what it thinks it already knows. If today there is great controversy over the ordination of women, even in the apparent absence of insuperable dogmatic problems, and if for now it is being presented as an insoluble problem, then what will happen with a liturgy, an ethic, a dogmatic system based on the "other" — on the unknown, which by definition cannot be resolved with previously accepted concepts and practices?

In fact the "other" is a way of understanding what we call "alterity" in the mystery of God. To face the other, to let the other be other, is a way of facing the mystery of God. And that is as hard today as it has always been. But that — and not a mere liturgical folklorism, as Dom Pedro Casaldáliga has warned — is what is at issue when we accept the reality of women, indigenous peoples, blacks, mestizos, the "other."

So important and difficult advances have been made. In terms of the evangelization of culture, with regard to women it must be said that the world has evangelized the church rather than the other way round. The church must learn this from the world and give it thanks. With regard to indigenous and black peoples, the church — if it really accepts, values, and embraces them — will be evangelizing a culture that even today — despite universal democratic declarations of equality — ignores, oppresses, and disrespects the other, tries to isolate the other geographically and anthropologically; a culture where lately, in several Northern countries, grave and alarming signs of xenophobia are reemerging.

So it is good that Santo Domingo has spoken about the "other," but the church must now defend the other in its real pastoral practice, and take the necessary risks to do so.

Theological Regression

Theologically there have been steps backward, fundamentally in terms of theological procedure or method. Historical reality is no longer seen as a sign of the times in a strictly theologal sense—that is, as the place where God may speak and be present as God. This is an important regression from Vatican II, which enunciated the reality and importance of the signs of the times for the mission of the church; and from Medellín and Puebla, where the signs were scrutinized *in actu* and became the basis of theological reflection.

As I said earlier, in Santo Domingo the presidency imposed the principle of judging-seeing-acting: theology comes first, followed by observation of the world, and then by the application of theology to the world. This means "judging" from God's viewpoint what has not yet been "seen." With regard to the biblical citations, it means seeing God in those texts from the past without having seen God in present reality.

Beyond doubt the relationship between seeing and judging, between reality and theology, is dialectical. Therefore we cannot assume that seeing leads mechanically to correct judgment, that pure experience leads mechanically to theology. But within the necessary hermeneutic circle, we must maintain what is fundamental to all Christian theology, based on a God who has become history: there can be no theology without a prior historical reality, and God cannot be found in texts from the past without discerning God's reality in the present.

What is said here in abstract terms has grave, serious repercussions in the theology of Santo Domingo. One is that its christology, which is considered the backbone of the whole document, is not based on Jesus of Nazareth but on an abstract Christ, as required by the logic described above: Jesus is judged as the Christ, without looking first at the reality of that Christ in Jesus. Thus the historical Jesus disappears, who was present in Medellín, in *Evangelii Nuntiandi*, and in Puebla, perhaps more in their dynamism than in their concrete texts; who is certainly present in the most committed communities from which have come the most martyrs; and who of course is present in the theology of liberation. In Santo Domingo, the choice was made to begin by proclaiming the Christ of faith rather than seeing the Jesus of Nazareth.

Another consequence of this method is that ironically, the best texts of the document are not the theological ones, in which the bishops should be expert, but the historical ones. Indeed the most strictly theological texts, at the beginning of each chapter, are notoriously unread and uninspiring. Certainly they cite passages from scripture, councils, and popes; these may possess magisterial authority and some of them are inspired, but they are not inspiring.

To put it more radically, "that God has loved us" is a central text that expresses an essential and comforting truth of faith. But if this text is not put in the context of concrete reality, it can sound like something purely spiritualistic, routine, unable to mobilize spiritual forces. If it appears at the climax of a story about the victims of this world, their martyrial love and hope, then the same text expresses God's solidarity and tenderness toward them; then the text becomes good news.

The theological method I have analyzed here is of direct concern only to the church, and at most, to scholars. But I think it also has evangelizing potential in our own context, because our world frequently uses ideological a prioris without comparing them to reality. "Truth" and "solutions" are often decided in advance, regardless of what happens in the world. Thus, some say democracy is truth. Neoliberalism, the need for armies, modernism and postmodernism are true (although by definition the last of these cannot be called absolute truth).

In the search for parallels between this phenomenon and the faith of the church, it will doubtless be argued that the truth of ideologies or human institutions cannot be compared with the truth of faith; it will be said that the faith contains truth apart from whatever happens in the world. But without going into that theoretical discussion, pastorally at least it is very important that what we might call the generic truth of faith become concrete truth, and thus active and relevant truth; that happens when truth is compared with reality.

The pastoral relevance of faith is at stake in its ability to be illuminated (verified and entruthed, so to speak) by historical reality. And if this applies to faith, it applies a fortiori to theology. What I am trying to say is that a way of living and understanding faith and theology, opening them to reality, comparing and enriching them with reality—which at least logically implies beginning by "seeing" reality—is also a way of evangelizing culture. It is a way of overcoming a prioris and dogmatisms, which we now see so clearly in the dubious methods of Christendom and in failed dogmatic Marxisms, but which must also be overcome in neoliberalisms, modernisms, pragmatisms, and postmodernisms, which always tend to impose themselves dogmatically.

What today's world needs most is to "see" reality without manipulating it, and even more to "hear" it. Karl Rahner said that "reality wants to say something," and in Medellín and Puebla, that something becomes a heart-rending cry. Would that the church of Jesus might help the world in this difficult task. Certainly if the silenced and still maligned theology of liberation has contributed anything to our world, it has been mainly through its honesty in looking at reality, hearing and trying to respond to the cries.

Silence on the Martyrs

The most dreadful consequence of not beginning by "seeing" reality is silence on the martyrs. It is true that at prayer meetings the bishops remembered Archbishop Romero and other Latin American martyrs, but that will not make up for the incredible silence of the text. That silence is not overcome with a line at the end of the chapter dedicated to the memory of five-hundred years of evangelization, recognizing "those who have witnessed by giving their blood for the love of Jesus." From the extreme parsimony of the text, from the ambiguity of the historical context—does it include today's martyrs?—and from the absence of historical and theological analysis of such a fundamental fact, that sentence seems to have been added more as an escape from a thorny situation than as an expression of deep conviction about the centrality of martyrdom.

However they try to explain it—the danger of manipulation, the cautiousness required by canon law, the conflicts it might cause the church—no one understands, especially in countries like El Salvador and Guatemala, why the martyrs were not only not highly valued but not even mentioned. In Latin America, martyrdom is not anecdotal or exceptional, but a massive and indisguisable reality: it is the new thing, the grace, the credential and seal of the most genuine evangelization that has occurred between Medellín and Santo Domingo. This silence is therefore absolutely incomprehensible, highly suspicious, and above all, terribly impoverishing.

To ignore the martyrs really means ignoring the signs of the times, both because they describe what best characterizes the era—massive martyrdom is the most unique and characteristic aspect of the recent history of the church in Latin America—and because by their quality, they express God's presence in our midst. It also means denying ourselves an irreplaceable hermeneutic principle by which to understand Jesus, because today's martyrs—unlike most of those in past history—have died like Jesus, for the same reason that Jesus died, because structurally, they lived like Jesus. It also means ignoring the historical and theologal origin of the church itself, born out of the martyrdom of Jesus, to pursue the life of Jesus in the hope of resurrection—which is to say, that God has done justice to Jesus the martyr. It means denying ourselves the church's principal reason for credibility, important both for proclaiming the mystery of God to unbelievers and for strengthening doubters in their faith, and so decisive for telling the poor that God loves them. Finally, it means thanklessness toward the martyrs themselves, a denial of comfort to their families, a rejection of those who still give light and courage to their communities.

We have already seen that the *Secunda Relatio*, in the long text cited earlier, moves precisely in the opposite direction. That shows the strength of the tension with the Vatican and the divisions within the Latin American church, since not even an echo of this splendid text remains in the final document. But it also shows that some groups of bishops—and many communities with them—when they reflect on the martyrs in the bloody reality of their countries, see them as witnesses to faith and love, without whom that faith and love cannot be lived.

The text cited above, in a way both obvious and surprising, recalls the martyrs and makes them central. It also develops an important theology about the reasons for martyrdom and why the martyrs are central. This text, and of course the reality behind it—the fact of martyrial love and the grateful recognition of it by Christians—*is* good news, it *is* evangelization for the poor of this world. Even though it may scandalize the powerful. In El Salvador some people are still fearful of Archbishop Romero and Fr. Ellacuría. And even though—as foretold in the Gospel of John—those who killed Archbishop Romero, and the Atlacatl battalion that assassinated the Jesuits, the two women and many others, may use and abuse the name of God and call themselves Catholics as always.

We could endlessly discuss what the "new" evangelization means, but the answer must have one essential and obvious ingredient: it means recovering—in a new way if need be—the good news that Jesus of Nazareth brought and was in his own life. The martyrs have done that more than anyone else. It is they who in our days are proclaiming the kingdom of God to the poor, who proclaim that life, community, and dignity are possible, who confront the idols that make victims of the poor, and who tell the poor that God loves them. It is they who in our days re-create the gospel that Paul preached: Jesus the martyr, crucified and resurrected. For that reason too, it is simply incredible that Santo Domingo did not mention the martyrs, the best that the Latin American church has produced, the best that we have.

PRINCIPLES FOR PUTTING THE SANTO DOMINGO EVENT TO WORK

As we have seen, many different winds were blowing in Santo Domingo, some better than others. As a whole, with all that we have judged positive and negative, Santo Domingo is a faithful reflection of the situation of the church universal and the Latin American church. In the church universal there is a sustained inward-turning movement, originating in the center with plenty of supporters at the periphery, some acting in good conscience, others more militantly. In the Latin American church there is still a serious struggle between maintaining and devaluing the spirit of Medellín.

As a whole, Santo Domingo is certainly no cause for rejoicing, as the bishops themselves have pointed out. Neither should it lead to paralyzing despair, because evangelical and Latin American winds were also present there, although almost never as forcefully as they should have been. In my opinion, the most negative aspect of Santo Domingo is the sadness of a lost opportunity to pursue ecclesial tasks and, above all, to listen to the cries of reality much more closely and to evangelize culture more decisively.

But we must put Santo Domingo to work, because the event is worthy of it and because the poor of the continent expect and need it. To do so we must look for principles that will illuminate the task and motivate us for it, and these are probably to be found more outside than inside the meeting itself. For that reason we must also speak more of principles for putting Santo Domingo to work, than of principles for interpreting Santo Domingo itself.

The latter is really difficult because the differences and tensions were so great that it seems impossible to find an adequate way of unifying the event and the text. Certainly there were also divisions and tensions in Puebla, but the "preferential option for the poor" soon became in fact — and showed a real possibility of becoming also in principle — an interpretive focus for the whole text. But in Santo Domingo there is no self-evident principle to unify the whole. The Vatican has suggested that the interpretive principle is christology, but it was too abstract to carry out that function.

So if not within the event itself, we must find outside it the principles to unify such an uneven event, or at least to put to work the best of the event and the text. They would seem to be as follows:

1. To put Santo Domingo to work effectively, we must take seriously what was also affirmed there: that it must be considered in continuity with Medellín and Puebla. This does not primarily mean collating the texts or even making a synopsis of the three conferences, although that would certainly be useful and advantageous. What it should mean, I believe, is rather to recognize that the Latin American church must go on living by the spirit of Medellín, not out of choice, but because there is not yet anything better. This does not mean of course that the church has no new agendas, but rather that it is very dangerous to emphasize the need for newness, when for the most part that newness has been a reality in the church since Medellín.

Specifically, when Santo Domingo insists on the evangelization of cultures — and would that the church might do so — and the need to approach indigenous and black culture as a challenge to the church, it must not forget that Medellín already proclaimed that fundamental need to demand the incarnation of the church in historical reality. The two things are not exactly the same, but neither are they unrelated; Medellín still shows above all that real movement toward incarnation among the poor is the fundamental way to evangelize Latin American culture, on the one hand, and to inculturate the church, on the other.

Something similar must be said about the "new evangelization." This began in Medellín, which coined the expression before John Paul II popularized it, and the newness that we seek today pales by comparison with that of Medellín. Today we seek to renew the expression, methods, and energy of evangelization, but curiously, no one is asking what evangelization is. That is just what Medellín did: it was not so much concerned with the newness of the things that surround and accompany evangelization, but simply and directly asked what it means to evangelize. Puebla also took the decisive step, still unmatched in today's new evangelization, by affirming that we must not only evangelize but let ourselves be evangelized — with gratitude, humility, and joy — by the poor.

2. Although this article has focused more on the event than on the texts

of Santo Domingo, a word is also needed about the texts and how they can be put to work. Many people, including bishops, have recognized that many of the texts are weak, especially in the first half of the document. I have already noted some of the better ones, especially for the new aspects they introduce.

In my opinion, to put them to work requires making a selection, which is not at all manipulative but a simple matter of common sense. History itself will select among them, as it did with Medellín and Puebla, quite apart from intentions, propaganda campaigns, or even manipulation. But in addition to selecting the texts that are most useful for the communities, we must also put them in their real context; they must be evaluated and related to the concrete tasks they propose and require, and this must have the institutional support of the bishops who approved the texts.

If the newness in the texts is really put to work, then Santo Domingo may even represent—as some people say—a step forward for the Latin American church. But this must be clearly understood. Santo Domingo does represent an obvious advance in the agenda of the church, which can no longer ignore the problems of women, indigenous and black peoples, the ecology ... and this agenda is reflected in some of the texts. But to make it a real advance, a specific ecclesial context must be added: that is, the decision to support it, to put it to work, and to defend it when society reacts with persecution—as will certainly happen if the church decides to defend indigenous and black peoples.

3. Finally, when we ask what was really at issue in Santo Domingo, what caused debates, tensions, and Vatican interventions, and what in my opinion will be its orienting principle for the future, I believe it is the identity of the Latin American church. At bottom Santo Domingo was—and is—a struggle over what it means to be church, to be Christian, and to be a believer in Latin America.

What was really at issue in Santo Domingo is the new identity of the Latin American church. The problem can be covered over in many ways, by alluding to problems of communion with Rome, dangers or exaggerations in orthodoxy and the liturgy, the theology of liberation, and so forth. But in fact neither the bishops, nor the theologians, nor the bases have serious problems with ecclesial communion nor with loyal obedience. The real issue is different; it is the new aspect that has been emerging since Medellín, and it can be summarized in the following three things:

First: for the first time in centuries, the Latin American church is becoming itself. In the historical process of the past thirty years, the church has become increasingly Latin American and Christian. The Latin American reality has led the church to understand the gospel and put it in practice more effectively, and that has led to a better understanding and action on historical reality. The greatest newness of our time is that for the first time, to be Christian and to be Latin American do not contradict but enrich each other. That in turn has meant great creativity and also great conflict, and that is what some bishops fear, here and in the Vatican. Thus the first thing at issue has been the Latin Americanization of the church and the struggle to maintain or dilute that Latin Americanization.

Second, and related to the first: for the first time in centuries the Latin American church has been socially relevant in a way consistent with the gospel. It has not primarily preached itself, defended itself as an institution, or sought to defend old privileges. Rather, like Jesus, it has kept its eyes on the world of sin and has sought to transform that world into the utopia of the kingdom of God. And this too has been at issue in Santo Domingo: whether the church should look at itself or at this world of sin and hope. That is why we have given decisive importance to the analysis of martyrdom in the Latin American church, which was present in the *Secunda Relatio* and absent in Santo Domingo, because martyrdom is the most unequivocal proof of taking the real world seriously, bearing its sin in order to bring the crucified ones down from the cross.

Third: evangelization has been addressed to the church, of course, but now also to the world—by trying not only to "Christianize" it on the surface, but to humanize it, introduce in it the most human values, which are also the most divine values, expressed by Jesus in his own life: honesty, freedom, community, openness to the other. In this way the church is transforming our reality into the kingdom of God, through the evangelization of culture. But to do so the church must be—as it has often been—a society of contrast: it must introduce truth, humility and compassion, in and against a world of lies, arrogance, apathy and cruelty.

In this article I have used the metaphor of wind to orient our reflection. Following that metaphor I can end by saying that Santo Domingo was no gale, like the "rush of a violent wind" at Pentecost. All things considered, we live in a church where the windows opened by the council are being closed again, and the air is getting stale. But in Santo Domingo, and especially in the everyday life of the Latin American churches, the breeze from Medellín, symbolized in the *Secunda Relatio*, is still blowing. And at many moments of commitment and hope, especially moments of martyrdom, that breeze is becoming a gale. And in any case, many people are going forward against wind and tides.

If we say that it is up to the Latin American church to put the best of the Santo Domingo event and texts to work, it is not merely to end on a conventional note or to make a virtue of necessity. As I have tried to show, many different winds were blowing there, some of them favorable. If Christians are still moving forward toward the new identity of the church in the spirit of Medellín, in the face of so many political, economic, cultural, military, religious, sometimes even ecclesial powers, it is because the Spirit of Jesus and the Spirit of God are still at work. And we can move forward with that Spirit.

Translated by Margaret D. Wilde

Santo Domingo through Protestant Eyes

Guillermo Cook

Why should a conference of Roman Catholic bishops concern Protestants in Latin America? If this appears to be begging the question, the answer — that we Protestants live in a region that was colonized by Catholics and still remains culturally Catholic — leaves many of my fellow Protestants (or *evangélicos* as we prefer to be called) unconvinced. Despite Vatican II and Medellín, most Latin American Protestants remain suspicious of the Roman Catholic church. Decades of hostility — and in some countries open persecution of Protestants (almost sixty years ago, my own father was stoned in a Bolivian village by a priest-led mob. I remember; I was there) — have left their toll. As recently as 1990 incidents of anti-Protestant violence that erupted in suburban Mexico City have only hardened anti-Catholic sentiment, in that country at least.[1]

All of the above notwithstanding, Catholicism is very much part of the self-identity of Latin American *evangélicos*. I believe it was Zwinglio Dias, a Brazilian Protestant theologian, who observed a decade or so ago that the self-understanding of Protestants in Latin America was too much dependent upon the overwhelming Catholic presence. Conservative Evangelicals (the vast majority) defined themselves more in terms of their rejection of Catholicism than of their own Reformed heritage. Meanwhile, he commented, "progressive" Protestants like himself established their identity by assimilating Catholic liberation theology with insufficient reference to their own Reformed theology. What was needed, he concluded, was a Latin American Reformed self-awareness that could stand on its own feet.[2]

The picture is somewhat different today. Over the past decade Protestant "liberationists" have been rediscovering their own confessional roots. And as the evangelical mainstream in Latin America becomes more sure of its own identity, it seems to feel less threatened by Catholicism in its several forms. And could it be that Protestant vitality and the Catholic renewal movements that seem to be so troubling to Rome are different manifestations of a surprising reformational self-awareness in Latin American Christianity?[3]

The above statement probably reveals my own personal bias. I am approaching the subject both hampered and helped by my cultural and religious baggage. I am an Evangelical Protestant, an ecumenically sensitive

Christian, and above all, someone who has learned from the poor in Protestant as well as Catholic grassroots communities. Although I did not attend the Santo Domingo Conference of Catholic Bishops (nor Medellín and Puebla for that matter), I have studied the documents and have been privileged to read a number of reports and evaluations by Catholic and secular observers (Protestant observers were ignored).

LEARNING TO READ A CATHOLIC DOCUMENT

Before digesting the Santo Domingo document I returned to Robert McAfee Brown's "brief but important lesson on how to read Catholic documents."[4] Like the Puebla document, Santo Domingo to a Protestant seems somewhat "rambling, repetitious, and occasionally contradictory. Sometimes it rises to eloquent heights, on other pages it resembles an accumulation of trivia."[5] But Santo Domingo could have been far worse, if the process before and during CELAM IV is any measure.[6] The very traditional Consultation Document (1991) was abandoned after the overwhelmingly negative reactions of the national episcopal conferences. A more Latin American *Second Relation* was produced by new CELAM leadership; then the *Working Document* was held up in Rome until the eve of the conference, only to be shelved by the Vatican-approved conference coordinators, who also imposed a top-down agenda and debate procedure. It seemed for a while, according to some observers, "that Santo Domingo was going to end up being a Conference *for* bishops and not *of* bishops."[7] CELAM IV was, apparently, long on theoretical exposition and short on collegial discussion and analysis. The *Final Document* was written in the midst of controversy and haste—there were, by some estimates, as many as ten thousand proposals and amendments![8] The time-tested give and take—I won't vote against your statement if you don't oppose mine—eventually produced something better than was feared, though somewhat less than many had hoped for. In the end, "participants of the Santo Domingo event compared it to the work of diamond miners. A huge mountain of rock and lots of work, to retrieve possible diamonds. . . . It can be worth the trouble."[9] The same metaphor applies to reading the Santo Domingo *Final Document.*

WHAT PROTESTANTS CAN LEARN FROM SANTO DOMINGO

Before looking more closely at some of the issues that Santo Domingo raises for Latin American Protestants, I would like to note some points that have impressed me about the Santo Domingo *Final Document.*

The Spirit of God Acts through Our Human Limitations

Cardinal Arns is said to have reported back to his São Paulo archdiocese that "it was worth it! Nothing extraordinary. The Spirit of God liberated us to be free."[10] Church conferences and their resultant documents are not isolated events, neither are they ends in themselves. Santo Domingo followed in the footsteps of Vatican II, Medellín, and Puebla. Each of these major assemblies contributed to what the Latin American Catholic church is today, warts and all. Only time will affirm or deny the validity of the following assessment:

> It could be said that Medellín turned out a text greater than its participants. The Puebla document was similar to the assembly which produced it; and the Santo Domingo document turned out to be inferior to its authors and to the Church that they represent.[11]

Protestants who, in theory at least, avow their belief in *sola Scriptura*, find it hard to relate to the Catholic belief in the authority of church tradition and the magisterium (49). However, whatever we may say, we do have our own sacred traditions and magisteria, which, in practice, at least, acquire equal status with Holy Writ. We repeat the creeds; we have doctrinal litmus tests that we must sign, and "covenants" and "declarations" to which we are expected to adhere. We may also have our own versions of theological, political, and ecclesiastical infallibility when scripture is interpreted for us. We are concerned with doctrinal, ideological, and ecclesiastical conformity and uniformity. This is reflected in many of our conclaves and in the documents that they produce. In sum, we may be more inclined than some Catholics to reject people and ideas with which we disagree. Even Pentecostals can learn from the Cardinal Arns' admission of human fallibility ("nothing extraordinary") and divine initiative ("the Spirit of God liberated us to be free").

Two lines of thought competed to define the meaning and implications of the three-part theme of the conference — "New evangelization, human development, Christian culture." One emphasis was more traditional and vertical, the other more contextual and horizontal. Both emphases may have something to teach Latin American Protestants.

"Only an Evangelized Church Can Evangelize" (35)

Reevangelization requires prior conversion and recognition of sin. The Latin American Catholic church recognized its fallibility and confessed its corporate sins. From the beginning, the Santo Domingo *Final Document* recognizes our fallen humanity, which is "the source of the individual and collective evils that grieve us in Latin America." The bishops go on to itemize the evils: terrorism, drugs, dire poverty, oppression, injustice, and several others (9). Indirectly admitting Catholic complicity in these evils, the document admits that "many baptized Latin Americans have not personally accepted Jesus Christ through an initial conversion" (32) nor do they "steer their lives by the gospel" (130). Going even further, the bishops recognize that they may be part of the problem. "In many Catholics—ourselves or some of our pastoral agents sometimes included—faith and life are out of joint" (44). This is one of the causes of the exodus of the faithful, because "lack of doctrinal formation and a shallow lack of faith makes many Catholics an easy target for the secularism, hedonism, and consumerism invading modern culture" (44). In the end, the bishops recognized before Latin America and heaven their limitations as pastor-evangelists. "We ask forgiveness for our frailties, and we implore the grace of the Lord so that we may be more effective in carrying out the mission that we have received" (124).

Protestants cannot afford to feel smug about these Catholic admissions. The situations that they reflect may increasingly apply to *evangélicos* in Latin America. How willing are we to recognize our complicity in the social evils of the region? We are excited about our numerical growth, but does this mean that every Protestant truly understands the meaning of conversion? Indeed, do we all steer our lives by the gospel? Are we, our leaders in particular, as willing to admit that we are part of the problem in Latin America as we are to claim that we have the solution? While Protestants grow numerically, they also tend to lose their spiritual vitality. For us also, faith and life may be out of joint. This and deficient doctrinal formation may be the reason why some Protestants move on to the sects (Jehovah's Witnesses, etc.) and even return to the Catholic church.[12] Our questions regarding Catholic doctrine, sacramentalism, and polity, however valid, do not exempt Latin American Protestants from the need to turn to the Lord for forgiveness for our own failures, and to implore God's grace for help in fulfilling divine mission in the world. This was, indeed, the tenor of the final document of the Third Latin American Congress on Evangelization (CLADE III). The one thousand Evangelical Protestants who were present did not "excuse the evangelical church for its historical errors and for the deformations of the gospel as it was introduced and established on this continent."[13]

"The Evangelizing Potential of the Poor"

Santo Domingo reaffirmed the Catholic church's commitment "to a gospel-based and preferential option for the poor ... firm and irrevocable ... not exclusive or excluding" (178; see Inaugural Address, 16,18). Mainstream Protestantism in Latin America has yet to learn that "discovering the face of the Lord in the suffering of the poor (Mt. 25:31–46) challenges all Christians to *a deep, personal, and ecclesial conversion*" (178). Until fairly recently, evangelism as personal conversion and evangelization as social transformation stood in opposition to each other in Latin American Protestantism. Conservatives tended to insist upon the former and ecumenical Protestants to affirm the latter.

Despite this, a more holistic or integral understanding of evangelization is beginning to prevail.[14] In August 1992, the Third Latin American Congress on Evangelization (CLADE III) was convened in Quito, Ecuador. More than a thousand Protestants attended, all with equal voice—laity and clergy, women and men, young and old, native American, blacks, and mestizos, conservatives and progressives from historical, independent, and Pentecostal churches. They worshiped and reflected together with a very open agenda. The CLADE III document is the most recent expression of a new social awareness among Latin American Evangelicals:

> The church must affirm and promote the life denied by all sin, by unjust structures, and by avaricious interest groups. Within its community the different forms of discriminations predominant in society on the basis of sex, educational level, age, nationality, and race must be ended. The church fulfills its mission as it follows Jesus' example and takes seriously God's question to Cain, "Where is your brother?" We recognize that the Latin American church generally has not assumed this responsibility faithfully. It has confused the world, into which it was sent to serve, with worldliness and sin, and has isolated itself from social and political processes. In some cases it even justified violent dictatorial regimes.[15]

A MISSIOLOGICAL CRITIQUE OF SANTO DOMINGO

In my Latin American Protestant tradition, we base our criticism of Roman Catholicism on the great Reformation themes of *solo Christo* (vs. the mediation of Mary, saints, and priesthood), *sola gratia* (vs. sacramentalism), *sola fides* (vs. papal authority), and *sola Scriptura* (vs. Word of God, weight of tradition, and interpretation by magisterium). These issues stand out in Latin America where both traditional or medieval Catholicism and fundamentalist Protestantism remain strong. At the same time we must recognize that most Latin American Protestants are as ignorant of the differences among Catholics on these issues as most Catholics are of the complexities of Protestantism in Latin America.

In his inaugural address the pope called upon the assembled bishops to focus upon: "three doctrinal and pastoral elements . . . three axes of the new evangelization." He urged them to face the challenges of evangelization with "a deep and solid Christology . . . a healthy anthropology, and . . . a clear and correct ecclesiological vision."[16] The documents of Santo Domingo should be measured by the same yardstick.

"A Profound and Solid Christology"

Structurally at least, the Santo Domingo document appears to be christological. It does adhere to a christological outline: (part one) "Jesus Christ, Gospel of the Father"; (part two) "Evangelizer Living in His Church"; (part three) "Life and Hope of Latin America and the Caribbean." And the scripture theme of the conference was "Jesus Christ . . . the same yesterday, today, and forever, Heb. 13:8" (Inaugural Address, 8). But what kind of christology does the *Final Document* reveal?:

> There is no insistence that Jesus is the Son of God and of woman. A decidedly trinitarian perspective does not appear. On the contrary, one could be left with the impression of a species of monistic christology. It speaks of Jesus, who he is, and not so much of what he announced. Thus the reference to the kingdom is too limited. The Christ-man also disappears. The initial profession of faith, in itself very valid, and novel in fact, appears rather more than a study text than something experienced.[17]

The choice of scripture theme is significant. Heb. 13:8 is a mainstay also for Protestants in times of uncertainty and threat. Whatever may happen in society and in the church, we are assured that Christ will not change. He will remain faithful. The textual context is interesting. The Epistle to the Hebrews is couched in sacramental language; and the immediate text, out of context, could be used to affirm magisterial authority ("Remember your leaders, who spoke the word of God to you. Consider the outcome of their way of life and imitate their faith," v. 7). It certainly warns against doctrinal deviation ("Do not be carried away by all kinds of strange teachings," v. 9), as the pope was at pains to point out (Address, 8).

What I am about to say applies just as much to authoritarian Protestantism as it does to hegemonic Catholicism. Our christology always impinges upon our understanding of kingdom, church, and society. When the truth about Christ is static and one-dimensional, as that of Santo Domingo tends to be, it will defend a self-serving and authoritarian ecclesiology and a paternalistic anthropology. Such a view is far from the intention of the biblical writer. Both the human and the divine natures of our Savior are intertwined in the name "Jesus Christ." His "sameness" refers as much to his earthly ministry as it does to his exalted status. Both are present "yesterday, today, and forever." He is as close to the poor in body and spirit today as he was when he walked in Palestine (*Final Document*: 4, 33, 111, 159, 243, 204). He is as opposed to religious domination as when he was crucified on a cross (Mk. 8:31–33). And he always will be. Instead of stasis and conformity, the scripture passage calls for movement and imitation of the pilgrim faith in Jesus Christ of the apostles and elders (v. 7b). He did not fail them then and remains ever ready to walk with his people along the way (vv. 5, 6; see Lk. 24:13–25). The imposition of divine grace through ceremonial rites or culturally relative religious practices (in themselves valueless, v. 9) is what the author of Hebrews calls a "strange teaching." For there is "another altar" (v. 10). We are asked to follow Jesus "outside the gate" and to bear his disgrace. "For here we do not have an enduring city" (static continuity) but look forward as pilgrims (1Pe. 1:17; 2:11) to a totally new order—"the city that is to come" (vv. 12, 14; see Isa. 65:20–25; Rev. 21:1–5). It is from "outside the gate" and to those who gladly bear Christ's disgrace on behalf of others that Hebrews calls for obedience to constituted authority (v. 17).

"A Clear and Correct Ecclesiological Vision"

A clear vision of the church flows from a "solid christology." But the dominant ecclesiology of Santo Domingo favors strongly the hierarchy, not the totality of the people of God. Witness the papal statement at Santo Domingo: "Looking toward Jesus the leader and perfecter of faith" (Heb. 12:2) we follow the path traced by the Second Vatican Council (Address, 1). "Evangelization" and "conversion" continue to be monopolies of Rome. The Santo Domingo document insists that "new evangelization" is not the same as "reevangelization," because Latin America had already been evangelized and many of the original values remain (24). "New evangelization demands that the church undergo a pastoral conversion. *Such a conversion must be in keeping with the council* [emphasis mine] (30)." In contrast to *Evangelii Nuntiandi* (EN), the document does not provide an all-encompassing perspective of the reign of God. There is no new seed in this ecclesiology.[18] Compared to EN and to Puebla, Santo Domingo barely mentions the reign of God, and what it says serves to emphasize the authority of the church, understood as hierarchy (5, 27, 33, 67). Universal church, universal kingdom, and Rome seem to be one and the same (204).

While Protestants may reject this worldview, at a different level we tend to establish our own little kingdoms here on earth and to equate them all too readily with the reign of God. While not as explicit as in Catholicism, *extra ecclesiam nulla salus* is an unspoken assumption among many Latin American Protestants who have very muddled ideas about the reign of God. The Quito Document (CLADE III) seeks to clarify the issue for Protestants.

> With the coming of Jesus Christ, the Kingdom of God became present among us, full of grace and truth. The kingdom stands in constant conflict with the power of darkness; the struggle occurs in heavenly places and is manifest in the entire creation on personal, collective, and structural levels. *The community of the kingdom*, however, lives sustained by the confidence that the victory has already been won and that the kingdom of God will be fully manifest at the end of the ages. With divinely delegated power and authority, *the community assumes its mission* in this conflict to become God's agent for the redemption of all creation. *The King* Jesus Christ *became incarnate* and calls *his community* to do the same in the world. To *follow him as his disciples* means to appropriate Christ's life and mission [emphasis mine].[19]

Instead of a static and elitist understanding of the kingdom, in Latin America we need a vision of the reign of God as community, incarnation, and discipleship. While a growing number of Protestants and Catholics are responding to the call of the king, the documents of Santo Domingo blew an uncertain trumpet.

"A Healthy Anthropology"

The documents reveal Rome's view of humanity at three points: (a) in the methodology that Santo Domingo uses, (b) in its understanding of social processes and of culture, (c) and in its domestication and rejection of grass-roots ecclesial manifestations—base communities and the so-called sects.

The see-judge-act methodology was first used at Medellín. To a degree, it guided the format of the Puebla document, which spent considerable space considering the reality of Latin America, both sociologically and theologically, before moving on to reflection and action. This is not the case with Santo Domingo. An anthropological core is flanked by an ecclesiocentric theology. The methodology was more traditional: theological foundation (see), challenges (judge), and pastoral guidelines and/or directions (act). The see-discern-act triad is present, but it has been distorted. The entire process is overwhelmingly vertical, instead of cruciform, because the horizontal dimension has been weakened. The Catholic faithful are told what to see and judge, and how to judge and act. There is very little room for human initiative, and thus for the work of the creator Spirit. Is this a healthy anthropology? Says a Catholic observer:

> [Santo Domingo] remains silent about the important points of the Latin American process, such as the theology of liberation (it speaks of a theology of reconciliation instead). It goes so far as to speak of victims, but never of the oppressors. . . . The missing elements speak eloquently—those of an analysis of reality and of history. . . . The Bible is . . . quoted to confirm what was said, but there is no biblical focus on *what* and *how* it is said.[20]

Beginning with the pope's address, culture is treated with considerable ambivalence. While the gospel does not identify with any particular culture and addresses all cultures (Address, 20), a special effort is required to inculturate the message of Jesus. The church encourages a dialogue between gospel and culture "in order to purify and improve those cultures from within" (*Final Document*, 22). The ultimate aim is to strengthen a "Christian culture" (Address, 21), based on the resurrection (*Final Document*, 24). Baptized Catholics are called to "strive so that faith . . . may become culture" (*Final Document*, 229). This culture was brought to the Americas five hundred years ago, even while the document finds "living traces of a centuries-old culture at whose core the gospel is present" (*Final*

Document, 21, see 17). The pope urged that particular attention be given to native American cultures within a "genuine inculturated evangelization" (Address, 22; see *Final Document*, 30).

The problem with this is that, first, there is no such thing as a Christian culture, a concept (or illusion) that harks back to the medieval Christendom view of society. Unfortunately, it is a view into which too many of my Protestant sisters and brothers have also fallen. Secondly, overpreoccupation with culture can end up being oppressive. The words of an African Catholic are right on target:

> Our concern should not be so much with culture as with love, truth, justice. You don't create a healthy culture by being preoccupied with culture. A healthy culture today, I would suggest, is a justice-conscious culture; an unhealthy culture is a culture-conscious culture. The gospel will serve a healthy culture by turning mind and heart away from a certain inward-looking characteristic of cultural preoccupations, outward to the service of justice and love. Such service will all the same not do away with culture but renew it almost unperceived.[21]

Thirdly, the Iberian culture that was imposed upon the Americas was less than Christian. Rome distances itself too easily today from the genocide of native Americans and enslavement of black Africans with self-serving statements about "sometimes unscrupulous colonizers" (*Final Document*, 18) and "this 'unknown holocaust' in which baptized people who did not live their faith were involved" (Address, 20, 246). While we must give due honor to the great missionary prophets—Fathers Bartolomé de las Casas, Pedro Claver, Pedro de Córdoba, Antonio de Montesinos, Martinho de Nantes, Antonio Valdivieso, and Antônio Vieira, and others—for their defense of the rights of native Americans and black slaves, this is recognition to the church as people of God and not to the church as hierarchy.[22] That all of the colonialist empires were engaged in the same crimes (20) signifies that Protestants also have a lot of forgiveness to ask of our Amerindian and Black sisters and brothers. But it does in no way lessen the sin of Iberian colonialism in which Rome was a willing accomplice.[23]

The weaknesses of official Roman Catholicism—which the Santo Domingo documents reflect—are dramatized in what is happening to the Christian base communities. They are faced with either domestication by Rome or alienation from their church.

"In the Puebla document the Christian base communities are mentioned a great deal, because of a desire to affirm them in view of the conflict with the so-called popular churches." While Medellín speaks of them "as the basic cell of the church," Santo Domingo refers to "the base community as a cell of the parish." This subtle change in language suggests that the base communities will be reduced to serving the parish, or even become quasi parishes.[24] This is, in fact, what is already taking place, at least in the

Brazilian northeast. Rural *comunidades* tend to be "virtual parishes," while in the urban areas more autonomous base communities are in danger of losing their ecclesial identity as they identify with social movements.[25] It is the latter that especially concerns the Vatican. "Such communities," says the Santo Domingo document, with some reason, "cease being ecclesial and may fall victim to ideological or political manipulation." Sadly, both kinds of CBCs are being used, either by the church or by political movements. Meanwhile, according to an ecumenical research center in Brazil:

> Intellectuals, ecclesiastical authorities, and pastoral agents are daily more amazed as they witness the conversion of leaders and activists of social movements and of the *pastoral popular* [CBCs] to the religious groups of autonomous [i.e., grassroots] Pentecostals. Even more surprising are the changes that take place in the lives of the converts — eroded family and neighborhood relationships are restored, violence is repudiated, and conduct develops within socially acceptable norms.[26]

SANTO DOMINGO AND MISSION IN AND FROM LATIN AMERICA

The above missiological considerations raise some obvious questions that should be asked of the authors of the Santo Domingo document.

Evangelization: Monopoly or Privilege and Responsibility?

All of us, Catholics and Protestants, have a difficult time recognizing the right of those who think differently from us to share the good news. The words of Jesus in this regard are instructive. He reveals a dynamic and creative tension between inclusive and exclusive or restrictive announcement. The man Jesus and Son of God challenges us to recognize the work of God in others, even in those with whom we may heartily disagree. He warned against a too hasty sectarian consignment of human actions to the forces of evil. "Do not stop him!" Jesus said of the man who was driving out demons, though not in his name. "No one who does a miracle in my name can in the next moment say something bad about me, for whoever is not against us is for us" (Mk. 9:39). He asks us to broaden our vision of his work in the world.

Using the opposite argument in Luke 11:23, Jesus roundly rejects any attempt to attribute his prophetic ministry to Satan, whose destructive and divisive work is the very antithesis of the communitarian or gathering orientation of the kingdom of God: "He who is not with me is against me, and he who does not gather with me scatters." We are told to discover where and when God is at work in human actions and social movements, and to be wary of attributing to Satan what may be of God, and vice versa.[27]

I have the suspicion that Roman Catholicism prefers to recognize as "separated brethren" only those churches that lack a fundamental component of New Testament Christianity – missionary outreach – and to reject those that are making this their central thrust. These are written off as "sects!"

Christian Conversion: For Whom?

Quite simply, anyone who has not experienced the regenerating and transforming work of the Holy Spirit. This includes Catholics, Protestants, and everybody. Many Catholics, as the Santo Domingo document recognizes, are in need of conversion; nor has every Protestant been truly converted. People are leaving the Catholic and mainline Protestant churches in fairly large numbers. They are searching for novel or more satisfying alternatives. In the 1970s, after Medellín, many Catholics may have left their church to discover in protestantism the doctrinal and ideological absolutes, which they felt their old religion was losing. But others remained (in the charismatic renewal and the Christian base communities) and spread their wings in an environment of greater freedom of choice and expression, as well as opportunities for leadership. More recently, Catholics are turning to Pentecostal options as their church curtails their freedom. Before blaming others, churches should always look within themselves to discover the reasons why they are losing membership.

Prophetic Denouncement: By Whom?

From Medellín until recently, the Catholic church seemed to have a monopoly on denouncing injustices in Latin America. Martyrs such as Archbishop Romero and many others, lesser known, have given their lives for the cause of the poor and of the kingdom. Meanwhile the mass of Protestants, held back by doctrinal strictures and lacking the institutional clout of Roman Catholicism, have often remained silent before injustice. Nonetheless, it is legitimate to ask how the Vatican – opulent and authoritarian – can be critical of quietistic, and often poor, Protestants. We are beginning to discover that grassroots Pentecostals may ultimately be more prophetic than high-profile Protestant or Catholic activists – because they are a movement of the poor. Stoll goes so far as to suggest that grassroots Protestantism may be going through the same process of conscientization as did the Catholic base communities in the 1950s.[28]

Brazilian Marxist sociologist Carlos Rodrigues-Brandão, in 1980, referred to the latent revolutionary potential in "small sect" Pentecostalism. He suggested that this movement of "the poor of the earth" was perhaps more uniquely prepared than even the Catholic base communities to confront the evils of society – because Pentecostals see themselves as engaged in a holy war, and are buoyed by a hope of "a final struggle that will re-create a social order."[29]

SANTO DOMINGO AND THE CRITIQUE OF THE "SECTS"

Surprisingly, the Santo Domingo *Final Document* is more equitable and responsible in its criticism of the Protestant presence (particularly grass-roots Pentecostalism) than various churchmen have been, including the pope (Address, 12). After years of confusion, Santo Domingo has finally made the distinction between Protestant "sects" and "socio-religious enter-prises" like the Moonies (147), as well as "semi-Christian" groups such as the Mormons and Jehovah's Witnesses (148). While the document is critical of "appeals of a fundamentalist interpretation" (38), it follows this with a recognition of Catholic weaknesses – doctrinal ignorance at a popular level, too "little preaching about the Spirit," and insufficient kerygmatic procla-mation (39–41). Santo Domingo is very critical of the "electric churches" (sic), which "emphasize immediate conversion and healing" (147, 280). Right after a recognition of "deficient religious formation" the bishops lament "proselytizing fundamentalism by sectarian Christian groups who hinder the sound ecumenical path" (133). These signs of relative moder-ation probably show the hand of the more pastoral bishops.

The hand of the "Roman bishops" can perhaps be seen in the statements on ecumenism. The Santo Domingo *Final Document* echoed the pope's affirmation of ecumenism as a "priority for the church's pastoral activity in our age" (135). Yet this was not practiced at Santo Domingo. If the Vatican deplores the scandal of divisions among Christians (132), why, ecumenical Protestants wonder, were neither the World Council of Churches nor the Latin American Council of Churches (not to mention Pentecostals with whom there has been top-level dialogue for years) invited to participate as observers?[30] While the document recommends that ecumenism be sought after "in truth, justice, and charity," it limits relations to "those churches who pray the creed of Nicea" (135). Does this exclude Pentecostals and other nonliturgical churches who are unaccustomed to praying the creeds?

While the pope used stronger language – "ravening wolves" who "prey" upon "poor and simple folk" (Address, 12) – there was only a veiled ref-erence in the conference document to the North American "conspiracy theory" of Protestant growth in Latin America (147). But not all Catholics agree with this assessment.

According to Samuel Escobar, a Protestant missiologist from Peru, "the most articulate criticism of the [conspiracy] theory has come from the ranks of modern Catholic missiologists." Fr. Franz Damen[31] and Bishop Roger Aubry,[32] who serve in Bolivia, and José Luis Idígoras,[33] working in Peru, have done their own evaluation of Protestant growth in Latin America.[34] The expression "the avalanche of the sects" used by Mgr. Antonio Quar-racino, the former president of CELAM, says Fr. Damen, suggests the worldview of a church grown "accustomed since the conquest to the ex-ercise of a hegemony in the religious field." For centuries the Catholic hierarchy "enjoyed widely the benefits that in more recent years some governments give to the sects." The word *avalanche* is suggestive of a gigantic, violent, and uncontrollable force, which has imposed itself upon an innocent and unarmed population. The opposite is true, says Damen; the sects enjoy "a relatively good reception on the part of the people." The fastest growing grassroots Protestant groups, Damen adds, are either indigenous to Latin America or have originated in North America. They have rapidly become "latinoamericanized" in both leadership and finance. He concludes that "it is yet impossible to prove that a strategic connection exists between the expansionist North American policy towards Latin America and the proliferation of religious sects in the continent."[35] Mgr. Aubry concurs that popular Protestantism is growing among the most marginalized and culturally alienated sectors of Latin American society.[36]

This seems to be the heart of the problem: that grassroots Pentecostal churches are speaking to the felt needs of the masses of poor in Latin America in ways that other churches have not been able to do. Fr. José Comblin,[37] a missiologist and CBC pastoralist, points out that the Pentecostal churches in northeastern Brazil, while innately conservative, "are poor and of the poor. A large part of the poor are already there." This startling situation seems to prevail as well in the sprawling urban areas of southern Brazil. A recent article in a leading daily states:

> The decline of the so-called historical churches—both Catholic and Reformed—and the growth of the Pentecostal sects can be seen as the consequence of the disillusionment of urban Brazilians who do not find in them where and how to compensate spiritually for the bitterness of their daily lives. Disillusionment largely explains why five churches from "new denominations" appear in Rio de Janeiro every week. This is a religious phenomenon of great consequences, if one pays attention to the recently converted mother who remarked: "We grab whatever religion is closest to us." . . . The more dehumanizing that life becomes in urban spaces it would seem that the less space there is for acceptance of historical religions. The poorer the population of Rio becomes, the less Catholic it is.[38]

Comblin insists that the reason for the ascendancy of popular Pentecostalism even over the Catholic CBCs is because "we do not have enough pastors and we lack the missionary drive of the *crentes* ('believers,' a popular Brazilian term for Protestants)."[39]

Protestantism: Alien or Latin American?

Although the document, to its credit, does not follow through with this, the pope did allude to "a certain strategy whose objectives weaken the ties that unite the Latin American countries and undermine the forces of unity"

(Address, 12). Along with the aforementioned epithet about "ravening wolves," the above papal statement smacks of an attempt to cast Protestants in the role of foreign aggressors who by their presence are breaking the peace. But this is not the case. Despite the treaty of Tordecillas, God divided the Americas between the various European empires. Rightly or wrongly, for evil or for good, the Europeans did arrive, and they did so all over the Americas — north Europeans and Spanish in North America, Spanish and some north Europeans in the Caribbean *and* in South America.

Protestants arrived very early on the South American scene, in fact, three-quarters of a century before the Jamestown colony was established (1607) and only eighty years after Columbus's first landfall. During the reign of Charles V, a party of Germans was allowed to settle in a corner of Venezuela (1529–1546). They founded the port city of Maracaibo. French Huguenots briefly established a colony (1555–1567) near present-day Rio de Janeiro. The first Protestants to evangelize the native inhabitants (even while they carried on a thriving African slave trade) were Dutch settlers who wrested a portion of northeastern Brazil from Portugal (1624–1654). In all three cases, the colonies were absorbed, destroyed, or pushed out by the Spanish and Portuguese. It took two centuries for Protestant immigrants from northern Europe (and Waldensians from Italy) to be allowed into the newly independent nations of Latin America, and that mainly out of economic necessity. But everywhere stringent restrictions were placed on public manifestations of Protestantism.[40] One cannot help but wonder what would have happened if early Protestants had been able to remain unopposed and allowed to worship freely, as was the case with the Catholic settlers who founded what is today the state of Maryland in the U.S.A.

In the nineteenth century, some of the earliest Protestant missionaries held to a reformist method of evangelization. Great "colporteurs" or Bible men — like James Thompson (Spanish South America)[41] and Methodist Daniel P. Kidder (Brazil)[42] — believed that the Bibles they sold and the schools they founded might revitalize the Catholic church. Nurtured by the same hope, Fr. José Manoel da Conceição maintained his Catholic identity for several years after his positive acceptance of the Protestant message that he received from the first Presbyterian missionaries to Brazil. He was mindful that Reformist ideas were still abroad in Brazilian Catholicism. Almost a century earlier, Jansenism and Gallicanism — radically Augustinian and independist French movements — had strongly influenced Catholic seminaries during the decade (1760–1770) that the Portuguese church remained separate from Rome.[43]

CONCLUSION

I am not trying to counterpose prior rights to the evangelization of Latin America. I am merely arguing that whatever rights we have derive from God and depend upon our own faithfulness in responding to his mission.

I am pleading for a return to our historical memory, which is about grass-roots movements, Catholic and Protestant, and not about imperial church strategies, whether Catholic or Protestant. Fr. Edouard Hoornaert contrasts the historical memory of the Christian people — as a persecuted and oppressed small ecclesial movement — and the imperial church that is ortho-dox, territorial, triumphant, and the protector of the faith against heresy. Many of the early Protestant groups were socially compassionate base com-munities. Many of them have since become fat, self-satisfied, and even irrelevant.[44] He cautions the church history that does not take into account the question of power. But that power, Hoornaert reminds us, belongs to no one. It is granted only by God.[45]

I have written elsewhere of my prayer that the Catholic CBCs not leave their church.[46] At the time I believed that they offered the hope of trans-forming Catholicism into a more biblical and Christlike movement, partic-ularly if they were willing to learn from Pentecostal Christians that sinful social structures must ultimately be confronted as demonic — the "princi-palities and powers" of which St. Paul wrote in many of his letters.[47] I still have not given up hope, although I see the CBCs as less of a possibility, given the insecure attitude of Rome toward any kind of renewal that it cannot control. As a result, many base community Catholics seem to be moving into grassroots Pentecostal churches. I could not have foreseen that the major beneficiaries of the base community vision of social transfor-mation may turn out to be grassroots Protestant churches and perhaps a new breed of ecumenical base communities! The transformation of our churches will be accomplished both from above and from below. *From above,* as we allow the Holy Spirit to blow freely where it wills (the prayer of the good Pope John XXIII when he opened the windows of the Vatican!) and *from below,* to the degree in which we are able to follow in the footsteps of our redeemer and Lord, Jesus Christ.

Instead of resisting change, Catholic and Protestant church leaders must be able to recognize the new challenges and prepare for them, as we enter a new century. They must face up to the task of responsible discipleship based on the model of the suffering servant, and not for self-serving reasons. Otherwise, we — Protestants and Catholics — are in danger of repeating the tragic mistakes of the first five-hundred years of evangelization in Latin America.

NOTES

1. Mike Berg and Paul Pretiz, *The Gospel People* (Miami: Latin America Mis-sion, 1992), 153.

2. Unfortunately, because I am far from my personal library, I have not been able to track down in the U.S.A. the source of the Zwinglio Dias statement. It appeared in a special publication on Protestant fundamentalism of CEDI (Depar-tamento Ecumênico de Investigaçao, Rio/São Paulo, Brazil), in the early 1980s.

3. I use the term "reformational" advisedly. I am speaking neither in an ecclesiastical nor a confessional sense, but of "a reformational, transformational, conversionist worldview." It is a perspective "that calls for the renewal of peoples and the reformation of society in keeping with biblical principles for our life together in God's world," a vision which many Christians of both Protestant and Catholic traditions share. See Gordon Spykman, ed., *Let My People Live: Faith and Struggle in Central America* (Grand Rapids: Eerdmans, 1988), xiii and xiv.

4. Robert McAfee Brown, "The Significance of Puebla for the Protestant Churches in North America," in *Puebla and Beyond* (Maryknoll, N.Y.: Orbis, 1979).

5. Ibid., 331.

6. One observer went so far as to entitle his report on Santo Domingo, "CELAM & the Vatican: Preferential Option for Dickering," in *Commonweal*, Nov. 20, 1992, 5, 6. CELAM is the Conferencia Episcopal Latinoamericana.

7. José Marins, Teo Trevissan, and Carolee Chanona, "The Ecclesial Process of Latin America: The Assembly and the Document of Santo Domingo." Unpublished paper, 1993, 5.

8. *Commonweal*, 6.

9. Marins, "Ecclesial Process," 6.

10. Ibid., 4.

11. Ibid., 7.

12. Thomas S. Giles, "Forty Million and Counting" and Guillermo Cook, "Growing Pains" in *Why is Latin America Turning Protestant?* in *Christianity Today*, vol. 36, no. 4 (April 6, 1992), 32, 36. See also Berg and Pretiz, *The Gospel People*, 129.

13. "Quito Document: The Whole Gospel from Latin America for All Peoples," in *New Face of the Church in Latin America — Between Tradition and Change*, Guillermo Cook, ed. Upcoming Orbis publication. Appendix.

14. In 1988, a group of conservative Latin American Protestants met in Medellín, Colombia, to denounce liberation theology. Nonetheless, the final document, while critical of this theology at certain points, was unique in that it confessed the sin of indifference by evangelicals and expressed its gratefulness to liberation theology for making them aware of their social responsibility ("The Medellín Declaration on Liberation Theology," *Latin American Pastoral Issues*, vol. xvi, no.2, July 1989, 133–57).

15. Ibid.

16. With these three words, the pope, of course, is harking back to his opening address at Puebla, where he spoke on "the truth about Jesus Christ . . . about the Church's mission . . . about human beings" (*Puebla*, 1.2–1.9).

17. Marins, "Ecclesial Process," 7.

18. Ibid.

19. Cook, *New Face*, Appendix.

20. Marins, "Ecclesial Process," 8.

21. A. Hastings, *African Catholicism* (London: SCM Press, 1989), 35.

22. Justo González, "Voices of Compassion," in *Missiology: An International Review*, vol. xx, no. 2 (April 1992), 163–239.

23. The complicity of the medieval Catholic Church in the genocide of the original inhabitants of the Americas is accepted by Catholic, Protestant, and secular writers. See Pablo Richard, "1492: The Violence of God and the Future of Christianity," in *Concilium*, no. 6 (Nov. 1990), pp. 59–67. Cf. Luis N. Rivera, *A Violent Evangelism: The Political and Religious Conquest of the Americas* (Louisville: West-

minster/John Knox, 1992); Justo González, "The Christ of Colonialism," in *Church and Society* (Jan.-Feb. 1992), 5–36. See also Ronald Wright, *Stolen Continents: The Indian Story* (London: John Murray, 1992). See also Mario A. Rodríguez León, "Invasion and Evangelization," in *The Church in Latin America (1492–1992)*, Enrique Dussel, ed. (Maryknoll: Orbis, 1992), 43–54. Unfortunately, the pope, in his addresses to Indigenous Peoples and Afroamericans, showed very little official contrition.

24. Marins, "Ecclesial Process," 9.

25. See José Comblin, "Algumas Questões a partir da Prática das Comunidades Eclesiais de Base no Nordeste," in *Revista Eclesiástica Brasileira*, vol. 50, no. 198 (June 1990), 335–81. An abridged version of this article will appear in "Base Ecclesial Communities in Northeastern Brazil: Lessons and Concerns," *New Face of the Church in Latin America: Between Tradition and Change* (Maryknoll, N.Y.: Orbis, 1993).

26. "Pentecostalismo autônomo," in *Pentecostalismo Autônomo, uma inversão sedutora?* Suplemento Especial no. 548 (São Paulo/Rio: CEDI, 1990), 5.

27. Guillermo Cook, *The Expectation of the Poor: Latin American Base Ecclesial Communities in Protestant Perspective* (Maryknoll, N.Y.: Orbis, 1985), 148.

28. David Stoll, *Is Latin America Turning Protestant: The Politics of Evangelical Growth* (Berkeley: University of California Press, 1990), 175–78.

29. I discuss Brandão's book, *Os deuses do povo* [The gods of the people] in Cook, *Expectation*, 54–58, 251. See my review-essay of Brandão's book in *Missiology*, April 1982, 245–56.

30. "El ecumenismo ausente," in *Pastoral popular*, vol. 43, no. 224–25 (Nov.-Dec. 1992), 13.

31. Franz Damen is a Passionist priest and a Belgian missionary who has specialized in the study of sects. He serves as executive secretary of the Department of Ecumenism of the Conference of Bishops in Bolivia.

32. Mgr. Roger Aubry, a Swiss Redemptorist priest, was president of the Department of Missions of CELAM from 1974 to 1979, and has been a missionary in the jungles of Bolivia since 1970.

33. José Luis Idígoras, a Jesuit theologian who has taught in several Catholic theological schools in Peru, is presently president and professor of a seminary in the jungles of Peru.

34. Samuel Escobar, "The Significance of Popular Protestantism in Latin America: Conflict of Interpretations," in Cook, ed., *New Face of the Church*.

35. Franz Damen, "Las sectas ¿avalancha o desafío?" *Cuarto Intermedio*, no. 3, Cochabamba (May 1987), 47, 52–55, 58.

36. Roger Aubry, *La misión siguiendo a Jesús por los caminos de América Latina* (Buenos Aires: Ed. Guadalupe, 1990), 106.

37. José Comblin is a Belgian priest who has worked for many years in Chile and in northeastern Brazil. He is the author of *The Meaning of Mission: Jesus, Christians, and the Wayfaring Church* (Maryknoll, N.Y.: Orbis, 1977).

38. "A 'religião que passa,' " in *O Estado de São Paulo* (Feb. 21, 1993). Cf. "Fé em desencanto," in *Veja* (Dec. 25, 1991), 32–38.

39. José Comblin, "Base Ecclesial Communities in Northwestern Brazil: Lessons and Concerns," in Cook, ed., *New Face of the Church*.

40. Pablo Alberto Deiros, *Historia del cristianismo en América Latina* (Buenos Aires: Fraternidad Teológica Latinoamericana, 1992), 588–608, 617–38.

41. I. Vergara, *El Protestantismo en Chile* (Pacífico Editora, 1962), 9–13.

42. Emile G. Léonard, *O Protestantismo Brasileiro* (São Paulo; ASTE, 1963), 28–45.

43. Ibid., 71, 89–90, 99. Cook, *Expectation*, 34–35. Thomas C. Bruneau, *The Political Transformation of the Brazilian Catholic Church* (London: Cambridge University Press, 1974), 19–22.

44. See Cook, "Grassroots Communities and the Protestant Predicament," in *Expectation*, 200–29.

45. Eduard Hoornaert, *The Memory of the Christian People* (Maryknoll, N.Y.: Orbis, 1988), 12, 20, 21, observes that history is not merely to recall the past pure and simple. It requires "the recovery of memory. . . . Our memory is conditioned by social influences of which we are unaware."

46. Cook, *Expectation*, 251.

47. Ibid., 148–54.

Evangelization in the Americas

Santo Domingo from the Perspective of U.S. Hispanics

Virgilio Elizondo

For us as Latinos in the U.S.A., the Santo Domingo conclusions offer more of an affirmation of the pastoral work we have been developing in the last twenty years than something new. It is no Medellín or Puebla, but there are some very good insights in the final conclusions. I will not attempt to comment on the entire document, since this is not my task, but merely to explore it from the perspective of the pastoral work we as Latinos have been developing in the U.S.A.

THE FIRST EVANGELIZATION

Its Successes

To begin with, I do not believe we should be so negative or apologetic about the first evangelization of the Americas. There were mistakes and abuses, but there were equally new, creative, imaginative, and heroic ways of bringing the gospel to the Americas. The profound faith of the poor, oppressed, marginated, and crucified peoples of the Americas has kept them alive in spite of the ongoing crucifixion they have been subjected to for the last five hundred years—just witness the massive Good Friday manifestations throughout the world of Latin Americans. It is the crucified Lord who sustains us in our daily struggles to survive within the dominant cultures of death.

If we measure the result of the evangelizing efforts by the profound and childlike ("unless you become like little children . . .") Christian faith of the peoples who received the gospel into their lives, we have to conclude that it was not just marvelous but miraculous. Never since the initial moments of the Christian movement were there such massive and profound conversions. The Guadalupe event is certainly basic to understanding the birth of the new Christianity of the Americas.

The gospel caught on like wildfire with the natives of the Americas—of course, receiving it in their own way and through their own cosmovision, thus producing a new tradition of Christianity quite different from the old ones of the East and the West. In every sense of the word, a new tradition of Christianity was born in the Americas, which is best expressed through the popular religious expressions of the people. It cannot be known or appreciated if you come to it through the cultural/religious categories of the great traditions of the East and the West. We have elements of both, but equally we have elements of our fascinating ancestral religions! We are truly Christian, but in our own American way. Unfortunately, these traditions of the old world have often viewed and labeled the emerging tradition of Latin America as syncretistic and false, and have even sought to destroy it under the pretext of purifying it or forcing it to conform to the Western tradition.

Its Failures

The problem was not with the evangelization of the natives, the Africans, and their mestizo and mulatto descendants. Their aboriginal cultural values were much more in conformity with the values of the gospel than those of the European culture of that time. Santo Domingo speaks (no. 17) about the positive traits—"seeds of the word"—present in the pre-Columbian cultures, but it fails to make any critique of the very negative, superstitious, and even antievangelical traits of the European culture of that period of history.

The great failure was the total lack of evangelization of the multitudes of baptized nonevangelized Europeans and their descendants who were more keen in pursuing the gods of gold than in the following of Jesus. To this date, the descendants of these peoples have practiced the Catholic customs in many ways, but by their values do not appear to be followers of Jesus. The great challenge of the contemporary church is the evangelization of the dominant culture with its increasing power over all the peoples of the continent. As long as the people of this dominant culture of death are not evangelized vigorously—not just offered pious practices and easy conversion within the culture—the evangelization of cultures will not be achieved.

Had the Europeans been evangelized with as much vigor as the American Indians were, things might have turned out differently than they have. Unfortunately evangelization took place in the Americas and not in Europe where it was needed even more. The European invaders succeed in establishing the hegemony of avarice, which is today the basis of the dominant cultures of the Americas.

THE NEW EVANGELIZATION

Where Is the Church Failing Today?

It is not surprising that the Santo Domingo *Final Document* speaks with great honesty about some of the failures of the church (nos. 41-43). It rightly brings out that many of the laity and clergy have been ignorant of the truth of Jesus Christ (25, 39, 44). In the past the church has stressed conformity to church practices but not confidence in the action of the spirit. The catechesis of the church has reached only a few and even those it has reached it has failed to touch because its catechesis has been superficial, incomplete, purely intellectual, and without motivating force of any kind. The liturgies have often been empty, because they have continued with old clericalisms and ritualisms, and have not adequately been inculturated. All these failures of the past have led to a lack of coherence between faith and life. How to remedy this situation of emptiness and superficiality? We must turn vigorously to a new evangelization of all the peoples of the Americas! Who will evangelize today?

The Evangelized: The Poor in Their Popular Religious Practices

Today it is the baptized, evangelized, and converted among the poor of the Americas — God's beloved children — who are uttering the call and inviting all to the radical conformity to Jesus of Nazareth, which they have been living since the beginning of Christianity in the Americas. This is precisely the mission of the poor Hispanic Christians in the U.S.A. who in their simple but profound practices of the faith have known, lived, and followed Jesus on his way, and especially his way of the cross. They have been ridiculed and despised by the churchgoers of the dominant U.S. culture, but in effect have maintained a purity of faith that today is capable of bringing new life to the entire church, especially the disincarnated ecclesiastics and academicians. But will the wise and intelligent of this world order — of the dominant and controlling culture — have the humility to welcome it? Can they welcome the word from those who according to the world have nothing to offer? Can those "primitive peoples" whom the West has presumed to civilize now evangelize the so-called civilized? Can the church with all its sophisticated theological baggage see the face of Jesus and hear his voice as he lives in the disfigured and struggling bodies of today's poor?

Core of the Challenge: Present Jesus Christ in a Dynamic Way

The new catechism of the Catholic church makes it clear that Jesus must be the centrality of all our preaching and activity (Catechism nos. 74, 124, 127, 139). It is evident that this has not been so in the past. We have been much more concerned with the centrality of the church, with its dogmas and rituals, than with the personal encounter with Jesus of Nazareth. Yet with our Hispanic poor, Jesus and Mary have always been the dynamic core of faith existence and life pilgrimage. We do not know all the dogmas, in fact we usually do not know any of them, but we do know Jesus quite well. From the dynamic enthusiasm of the expressions of faith of the traditions of the poor, the entire church can learn today how to evangelize effectively in our modern and postmodern world. Newness can be discovered in the very traditions of the poor, which have been ignored and underestimated by the leadership of the church—clerical and lay, ecclesiastical and academic.

New in Its Fervor: Hope for the Terminally Ill. One of the great problems of today is that many people see "being a Christian" as something nice and polite, but not as a dynamic force calling persons and society into a radical conversion and transformation. Others see it as a force to maintain and legitimize the old order of things in church and society. Still others see it as irrelevant in an age of science and technology. The historical role of religions often put religion itself into question. The gospel ceases to be effective when people see it as an obstacle to human development or simply as an ornament of society rather than a transformative force. As long as we are satisfied with ourselves and our society, we will not seek conversion—as long as we feel and appear healthy, we will not seek a physician. If Christian faith does not appear to be the answer to humanity's ills, people will seek remedies elsewhere. We must look at the contemporary illnesses of persons and society, and correlate them to the gospel as the way of salvation.

All of us in the Western world must come to the realization that we are sailing on the sea of life on the Titanic. We have constructed a way of life that we are convinced is unsinkable and that it is the only ship that can lead us to our ultimate joy and happiness! We confess belief in God, but put our trust more in our Western securities than in the gospel. We are worried about rearranging the furniture and changing the music, but do not want to admit, or for anyone to tell us, that our ship is sinking and we are all going to drown together. If we are to be saved, we must help people to become aware of the imminent crisis. This "cultural crisis of unsuspected dimensions . . . presents the church an enormous challenge . . . of undertaking a new evangelization" (no. 230).

Without the realization of the crisis and imminent death, we easily give in to pettiness, superficiality, conformity, routine, bureaucracy, institutional struggles, theories and ideologies, multiplication of law, directives and regulations. The crisis allows us to recenter and to remobilize. It is God's way of bringing us back to that which ultimately counts and makes a difference. Only to the degree that we become aware of the ultimately insufficient basis of Western consumer and individual pleasure culture will we begin to be excited and enthusiastic about seeking a true solution: in order to survive as humanity, we need to convert: salvation. This does not mean that we have to deny and reject the many life-giving aspects of our Western culture and say that the totality of culture is diabolic and perverted, but we do have to become acutely aware of what is false and excessive.

We need to clarify and expose the innermost hidden questions and fears of today's world if Jesus Christ is to appear as the salvation that we seek.

As we push the questions, we will unmask our contemporary idols — exaggerated imagery of physical beauty, upward mobility without limits, pleasure at will, individual power are but a few of today's idols. People seek to become fully human by pursuing their idols, only to find themselves destroying themselves as quickly as they destroy others in the process. In this death-bearing culture, Jesus appears as a nice friend and companion, and church-going absolves us from our need for inner conversion — conversion of mind and heart, of values and priorities, of persons and social structures.

But just as we need to have a very honest appreciation of our cultural reality, we equally need to rediscover the reality of the entire way of Jesus of Nazareth. We need to know how Jesus lived, functioned, and responded to the struggles of his own culture and religion. We need to know how he related to people, institutions, religion, and God. We cannot take for granted that we know him well. Why did the good and religious people of his own biblical religion consider him diabolically possessed and blasphemous? Why was he such a scandal to the authorities of the biblical religion of his day and time? Why did those in control consider him so seductive of the people? Those that knew the Bible well condemned him to crucifixion. Might we do the same today? One of the most urgent tasks of the entire church — clergy, religious, and laity alike — is to rediscover again and again the reality of the Jesus Christ of the Gospels. Only then will we be able to discover why it is that "no one can say: 'Jesus is Lord,' except in the Holy Spirit" (1 Cor. 12:3).

New in Its Method: A Mestizo Methodology. The Santo Domingo *Final Document* goes on to state that the new evangelization must be new in its method. It rightly brings out: "new situations demand new ways" (29). In proposing the new way, the *Final Document*, without actually saying it, suggests what I would call "a *mestizaje*" (a mixture) between the best of the fundamentalists and the best of the Catholic tradition. Taking from the fundamentalists (who in effect get it from the earliest apostolic Christianity), it emphasizes the need for witness and personal encounter while insisting on confidence in the saving message of Jesus and the activity of the Holy Spirit. These are the two foundations of the fundamentalists. Using these two sources of divine power, I personally have witnessed miracles in the rehabilitation of drug users in San Antonio by such groups as the Victory Outreach program of Pastors Freddie and Ninfa Garcia. As Catholics, we have placed more emphasis on the church with its doctrines, ministers, and sacraments than on the priority of the personal witness of each Christian proclaiming to others what the Lord has accomplished in us.

In learning from fundamentalists, the *Final Document* does not just take on their ways. In fact it enriches them by adding that which has been distinctively essential to the Catholic tradition: the insistence on "the presence of the Christian in everything that is human." The responsibility of the Christian to the world is an unquestioned and expanding element of our Catholic tradition. This aspect of our tradition has been strongly proclaimed by the popes, beginning with Leo XIII and becoming stronger with each pope. In the Bishops Synod, it was said that "action on behalf of justice is an integral element of the gospel."

As Christians we are not taken out of the world, but kept in the world to initiate new human alternatives, which will be more compassionate and just. Our apostolate in the countryside, towns, and cities is nothing less than collective charity and justice. Thus questions about the environment, migrants, minorities, health care, education, wages, land, and many others are the terrain where Christians must live out the values of the Sermon on the Mount.

As Hispanic Catholics in the southwest of the U.S.A., we are certainly learning through movements such as UFW (United Farm Workers) and COPS (Communities Organized for Public Service) the need for us to work together for the common good. Working for the integral betterment of our communities and our society is simply living out the mandate of love in a social and collective way. Without becoming politicians, we must address the moral dimensions of social, economic, political, and cultural issues; without seeking to dominate, we must be a powerful voice in the public debate on behalf of the poor and the voiceless. Movements such as the UFW and COPS are not just speaking for the voiceless but giving a powerful podium so that the poor speak for themselves. It is amazing how in these grassroots movements, it is the oppressed and previously silenced women who are today becoming the fearless spokespersons. The late Cesar Chavez of the United Farm Workers and Fathers Albert Benavides and Luis Olivares have become living legends in their own times of this type of apostolic action on behalf of the oppressed.

New in Its Expression: The Local Flavor. The final aspect of the new evangelization is that it must be new in its expression (no. 30). Taking the very example of the Jesus of the Gospels who used the imagery and situations of his place and time, we must today do cultural translations of the gospel message. Thus while the gospel message remains the same, its newness and implications for the here and now will be immediately obvious. This is the great challenge of every local church and of every sociocultural region of the world. We urgently need an image and story hermeneutics between the image-stories of Jesus and the image-stories of today's society. This demands both a profound knowledge of the reality of Jesus and of the reality we are working in. The universality of the message will not be its uniformity, but in the universal implications which come out of each particular rendition of the gospel. This is the great mystery of the gospel that when properly inculturated, it is both local and universal at the same time.

It is most interesting to note that to bring this about, the *Final Document* calls for "the pastoral conversion of the church." This will be most demanding on the local churches, for this task cannot be carried out universally at some centralized location, but must be brought about through the patient and constant dialogue—even across generations—between the message of salvation and the local culture. Inculturation does not mean a simple linguistic translation of the basic texts of salvation or even of just adding some local art and music to the Western tradition of the church. Inculturation, as the *Final Document* points out (no. 243) is a long and arduous process, which gradually penetrates into the deepest recesses of each culture through the respective language, imagery, and symbolism of each people. This is the only way in which the gospel will become firmly rooted in local soil and begin the evangelization of the culture itself.

THE ONE EVANGELIZATION FOR ALL

The *Final Document* is very explicit in stating "the new evangelization will continue in the way of the incarnation of the word"—the eternal and invisible word made human image in the flesh and blood of Jesus of Nazareth. God becomes enfleshed and thus visible and touchable in Jesus. Jesus begins the human pilgrimage to God as the source of love and unity by first becoming truly human: a very particular, well-defined, and socially-sexually situated man. He was not just some sort of asexual human universal speaking with authority to all others (as the European church has often thought of itself), but an ethnic minority within one of the many oppressed peoples of the world. By the very birth of Jesus, he enters into solidarity with the despised ethnic groups of the world. He becomes an untouchable in the flesh so that through him, people might touch God. This is the gospel's indispensable beginning—and the beginning of every authentic missionary activity anywhere and at any time. God, our loving parent, begins where every loving parent would begin: with the broken, bleeding, hurting, and disabled child. From this beginning, the gospel comes not to add hurt to hurt by destroying what is already in pain, but to heal, rehabilitate, ennoble, and enrich.

From this very real and fleshy beginning, the gospel itself gives us the universal and unchanging fundamental principles of evangelization for all ages and all places. This is clearly elaborated in nos. 230 to 248. In going to every culture in the same way (the universal way), the reception of the gospel will by its very inner nature produce the rich diversity of cultural faith expressions and local Christian traditions that are so essential and characteristic of the true catholicity of the church.

Precisely because the way of evangelization is universal, it will result in diversity and will transform the meaning and function of diversity itself. In the power of the Spirit, the curse of the divisiveness due to diversity will be converted into the enriching and enjoyable blessing of the harmonious unity in diversity—truly the ultimate glory of the God who created the one human race unique and diverse from the very beginning—all the nations, clans, and languages (Genesis 10). It is precisely in our sinfulness that we rebel and try to crush out God's diversity (Genesis 11). The source of our unity will not be our uniformity, but the love, respect, and appreciation we develop for each other, which reaches beyond the limits of loving only my own: flesh and blood, culture, nationality, and race.

The *Final Document* is very good in pinpointing the three basic stages of the process of inculturating the gospel. This process will never be carried out by one person or even over a brief period of time. In fact, it will be an ongoing process involving everyone that will expand across generations — some will seed, others will nourish, others will trim; some will articulate, others will sing, others will paint, others will dramatize, while still others will ritualize. Across generations, the culture will be christianized and even when it has been christianized, there will be the ongoing need of constantly listening to the word of God so that we will not fall under the spell of the new idols, which we all tend to create for ourselves (EN no. 15).

The three states of inculturation are simply: Christmas (inculturation), cross-resurrection (cultural confrontation unto new life), and Pentecost (the intercultural community) (no. 330). The *Final Document* uses the three core images of the entire life of Jesus to mark the three essential moments of all evangelization. They do not mark three chronological moments, but they do indicate three basic ingredients of the process.

First Stage: Inculturation — Becoming the Despised Other

Christmas is the image of the incarnation — the word made flesh and born unto us as every child is born: of a woman. God took on our human ways so that through the human the divine might be made manifest and accessible to everyone — even the "least" of human society: the shepherds. This marks the essential beginning of all evangelization. The missioner takes unto his or her own flesh the culture of the people being evangelized. Jesus did not cease being divine in becoming fully Galilean; the missioner does not cease being who he or she is in becoming the other being evangelized, but in assuming the ways of the other, missioners truly become something new. In the very newness of the two (or more) in one, they are the visible and touchable sign of the new creation: unity in diversity, newness in tradition, and openness from within rootedness. By his or her bilingual-bicultural existence, the true missioner begins the inculturation process, while at the same time being a sign of the Pentecostal unity of the human family.

The first stage of inculturation is the very positive recognition of everything that is good and beautiful in the culture — not necessarily in relation to our own norms and standards of the good and the beautiful. It is likewise the time of breaking down social barriers that marginate people and rob them of their dignity, just as Jesus did in affirming the basic goodness and beauty of the Galilean Jewish culture by becoming totally one of the people. But he likewise started from his very birth to bring out the beauty, dignity, and fundamental worth of the "ugly" outcasts of his society.

Today, inculturation begins by dialoguing the simple stories and imagery of the gospel with the stories and imagery of the local people, especially those of the marginated and hurting. Through the patient dialogue, gradually a new understanding of the people's lives and of the gospel itself will emerge. In this process, a new local church will be born. Gradually, it will develop its art forms, songs, rituals, and its own theological understanding of its living Christian faith. This takes time and much trust is needed on the part of the parent churches so as not to crush, destroy, and abort the new church in the process of being formed in the womb of its own historical time and geographical space.

Second Stage: Cultural Confrontation — Prophetic Witness

The most incredible but ordinary paradox: the people demanded that the representative of Caesar, the author of death, crucify the author and giver of life. They preferred the *Pax Romana* — the pseudo peace of this world of weapons and wars — based on conquest and military control to the *Pax Christi* based on acceptance, love, and forgiveness, which alone can bring real and authentic peace. Why?

It is true that within our culture, we feel very free but what we do not often realize is how enslaved and nearsighted we are within our own culture. Culture frees as well as it enslaves, it enlightens as well as it blinds. Culture needs to be confronted from within not to be destroyed, but to be freed of its enslaving and blinding elements.

Jesus stirred problems among his own, because he dared to question and challenge from within the culture of his own people. The sacrifice of the cross does not begin with Calvary — it actually started from the very conception and birth of Jesus. From the very beginning, Jesus revealed the glory of God in totally unsuspected, unimaginable, and undesirable ways. From the very first moment of his conception, he challenged sinful humanity by breaking all the stereotypes of the good, the pure, the credible, and the sacred. From the very first beginning, he dares to unmask the many false values even of his own biblical religion and culture. The rejection of his people, especially the leadership, started mounting from the arrival of the Magi in Jerusalem until it reached its peak in the final and absolute rejection before Pilate's tribunal.

The gospel truth about God and about human beings is not easy for sinful, culturally conditioned men and women to see, hear, and accept without feeling uncomfortable and deeply threatened. Because we place our trust on passing securities, we are afraid of ultimate security. The truth of God in Jesus and his followers will always startle the confusion of sinful humanity. As the gospel takes root in the minds and hearts of the people, they themselves begin to discover what is destructive and life-taking — both within their own culture and within the culture of the missioner who brought them the gospel. Thus they challenge their own and the church in the name of the very gospel they have received!

Third Stage: The Intercultural Community — Pentecost

At Pentecost, peoples from all the nations of the world came together, but they did not dissolve their differences away so that they could all become the same — one culture, one language, one religious expression. In their diversity as nations they each heard the word of God in their own language and were able to respond accordingly.

Incarnation affirms the culture, the cross and resurrection destroy the ghettoishness of the culture, and in pentecost people are able to open up so as to live beyond the limited blindness of their own culture. This is the beginning of the universal Christian existence, which will always be the hyphenated existence: Jewish-Christians, Samaritan-Christians, Ethopian-Christians . . . Mexican-Christians, Irish-Christians, Japanese-Christians. Conversion to Christ does not destroy one's cultural identity, but it does destroy the ghettoish tendencies of the culture. The universal of the Christian way is the universal openness to the otherness of the other!

Today, this can well be the special contribution of the minorities of the U.S.A. and the oppressed and marginated masses of Latin America. Because we have had no choice but to live the hyphenated existence within our own dominant cultures, we know from our own experience that this dual existence does not have to be a split existence but rather an enriching one. It hurts because the dominant culture, which is a monoculture and usually monolingual, does not understand or appreciate us and often puts us down. Yet we Mexican Americans, Afro Americans, Native Americans are appreciating our uniqueness more and finding ways of sharing our cultural wealth with those who have the misfortune of being locked in the prisons of their own monoculture.

From our own culture experience of hyphenation, we can better understand the Christian experience, which calls us to affirm who we are, no matter what the social world says about us, while opening up to the otherness of the others. This is what allows one to truly become a universal person without losing one's own cultural identity and uniqueness. The Christian universal is not the absolute uniformity that some have dreamt of, but unity in diversity of all men and women, of all cultures and of all nations and races. This will truly be the glory of God in heaven and on earth.

Building upon the very solid roots of the first evangelization, the new evangelization, if carried out according to the way of the incarnation and through the active ministry of the poor, can truly bring about the new humanity of the Americas. This new world could well be something humanity has never experienced before: a true fellowship in love and justice of all the peoples of the world living together in the one family of the Americas.

Santo Domingo through the Eyes of Women

María Pilar Aquino

Only when we dared to think about ourselves, when we confronted our insecurities and needs, when we recognized our unresolved contradictions and aspirations, did we realize that we had been dressing up the old ways in new clothes. It was a painful discovery. We were rejecting the old ways, but we did not know what should take their place. We also realized that, for the time being, we were alone.
— Virginia Vargas Varela, Peruvian feminist

The conceptual framework for interpreting the view of the Santo Domingo document on Latin American women must be the struggle against oppression and violence that women are carrying out personally and collectively in our everyday life. I want to emphasize this interpretive criterion, in order to identify the liberating dimensions in this document, which are in harmony with women's activities and expectations regarding the achievement of our human integrity. The same criterion helps to identify the aspects that oppose or impede that achievement, and which must be overcome.

I will not interpret Santo Domingo in terms of "continuity" or "regression" from what has been said about women in earlier episcopal conferences. That interpretation can and should be done soon, but it is not the purpose of this work. More importantly, I will not follow the "interdocumental" dialogue here, because that would mean taking the formal position of the episcopacy as the point of reference for women's progress, rather than our own experience as women. It would mean subordinating our view of ourselves to the "progress" or "regression" of the Roman Catholic bishops themselves. On the contrary, the official positions of the ecclesiastical hierarchy should be evaluated in terms of our present experience.

Although the earlier documents of Medellín (1968) and Puebla (1979) clearly express the church's commitment to the integral liberation of our peoples, they also contain a good dose of sexism in both language and theological content. As I have said elsewhere,[1] we cannot draw from these documents alone the guidelines to support and lead a liberating process consistent with our own vision of justice and the full participation of women in the church and in society. The guidelines must come "from our own wells." Rather I want to present some of the antecedents that made possible the contributions of women to the Santo Domingo document, the characteristics of the Working Commission on Women, and the great affirmations of Santo Domingo on the women of Latin America.

1. ENCOUNTERS AND DOCUMENTS LEADING UP TO SANTO DOMINGO

The perspective of the Santo Domingo document on women is the result of a complex process, in which women participated in order to affirm their own voice as the majority in our church. Of the seven internal documents that prepared the way for the final version of the Santo Domingo *Final Document*, only three stand out for their openness and sensitivity to the ecclesial practices of our communities. They are: the Preparatory Document, "Elements for a Pastoral Reflection" (February 1990); the Synthesis of Contributions to the Consultative Document, *Secunda Relatio* (February 1992); and the *Working Document*, "New Evangelization, Human Development, Christian Culture" (April 1992). Only the last two of these include elements on the situation of women in the church and in society. But for women, the most important document directly influencing the final conclusions of Santo Domingo is the document of Santafé de Bogotá, "Women in the Latin American Church and Culture" (July 1992). The following are some of the key points in these four documents, in the order listed above.

Preparatory Document, "Elements for a Pastoral Reflection"

This document, which came before the final text of the consultative document (1991), is understood as a pastoral tool to illuminate our social and ecclesial reality and open the way to the pastoral responses needed for the evangelization of Latin America.[2] The structure of this document is consistent with the vision that identifies our church in Medellín and Puebla, and thus presents four clearly developed sections: Part One: Historical View of Five Hundred Years of Evangelization in Latin America (nn. 1–142); Part Two: The Latin American Reality (nn. 143–494); Part Three: Pastoral Vision of Reality, Ecclesial Aspect (nn. 495–827); Part Four: Theological Illumination, Evangelizers in a Very New Civilization (nn. 828–974). This structure emphasizes the analysis of present reality with a view to the elaboration of broad pastoral responses that will contribute to the transformation of our continent.

Nevertheless, the analytical perspective offered in both the outline and contents of this document radically conceals the reality lived by Latin American women in their struggles against oppression and violence. Although it says at the beginning that "it is necessary to recognize the rights and hear the voice of the Indian, the black, the humble, the marginalized, the conquered" (n. 7), the critical vision of women on their own situation is nowhere to be found. The few texts that refer to women express only disconnected aspects, for example: the names of some women who have excelled in the evangelizing task (n. 7); the flourishing of women's contemplative monasteries (n. 64); the emergence of women's religious associations for the development of popular piety (n. 106); migrations from the country to the city, without mentioning their effect on women (n. 166); and finally, the presence of women in the informal economy (n. 176).

Two numbers explicitly mention men and women facing the conflict of reality (nn. 206 and 921), but they do not benefit women, because of the powerful sexist language in the document. This language, which presupposes "man" as the norm for both women and men, is clearly apparent throughout the text, but it is particularly noticeable in numbers 911 and 924.[3] The androcentric view of this document, reflected in powerful sexist language, culminates in an erroneous affirmation that "practically all our countries have moved from a patriarchal and extended family to a nuclear family" (n. 518). This not only overlooks the fact that the current nuclear family continues to reproduce the values of the patriarchate, but also that this type of family corresponds less and less to the experience of the oppressed women who bear alone the responsibility for their children.

In short, the Preparatory Document presents an inadequate and reductionist analysis of our social and ecclesial reality. For example, except for the numbers mentioned above, women are absent from the historical view at every stage. In part two the existence of a patriarchal and sexist culture is not recognized (nn. 402–94), so that violence against women is not even mentioned in the discussion of human rights and other types of violence (nn. 289–326). Part three noticeably ignores the activities of women in the evangelizing task (nn. 495–500), in the base ecclesial communities, and in the parishes (nn. 520–37); and their participation as agents of evangelization (nn. 604–14), in the means of evangelization (nn. 663–75), as receivers of evangelization (nn. 706–56), and as actors of the presence of the church in the world (nn. 787–95). The theological illumination in part four is consistent with the sexist view of the whole document.

With this outlook, the document shows its great inability to give an adequate reading to the reality of the Latin American church and society. Thus it is far from achieving the criteria that the document itself proposes: "The characteristics of the methodology to be used here are as follows. We seek a view of reality accompanied by four fundamental notes: objectivity, globality, analysis, and the pastoral element" (n. 501). The most positive thing about this document, in my opinion, is that it made clear the need to hear the women's own voice.

SYNTHESIS OF CONTRIBUTIONS TO THE CONSULTATIVE DOCUMENT, *SECUNDA RELATIO,* AND THE WORKING DOCUMENT

The *Working Document* represents a decisive step in the positive affirmation of the pastoral identity of the church in Latin America, and it is closely related to the *Secunda Relatio*. Therefore I shall present the two together. Immediately after the Preparatory Document, in April 1991 the Consultative Document[4] was proposed to the episcopal conferences for study and discussion. Around July 1991, the Pastoral Theological Institute of CELAM held a seminar in preparation for the Fourth Conference, in which all ecclesial sectors participated. At this event it was recognized that the Consultative Document had not incorporated the contributions of the local churches, and this led to the drafting of the *Secunda Relatio* Synthesis of Contributions to the Consultative Document.[5] This synthesis coherently articulates the liberating thought of the Latin American church and provided a key principle for the drafting of the *Working Document*.

Unlike the earlier documents, the *Working Document* offers a vision that clearly affirms the church's commitment to women's achievement of human integrity and their full participation in the life of the church and society.

More importantly, for the first time in the history of the Latin American church, this official document of the Latin American episcopal council shows a serious effort to incorporate women as subjects of its reflection, and their vision as a hermeneutical perspective. The *Working Document* is a significant correction of the sexist cargo carried by the earlier documents, although it sometimes mixes in androcentric symbols and language, especially in the transcription of biblical texts and magisterial documents (e.g., nn. 310, 318, 320, 340). Nevertheless, at many points it sets aside the concept of "man" as the normative category identifying humanity. The term is replaced by inclusive concepts such as "person," "human person," "human being," "humanity," "women and men," "man and woman." This procedure runs through the whole document, and it has never been seen before in an official document of the church in Latin America, nor in most of the current writings of Latin American theologians.

The fundamental documents that express the liberating voice of our people are, without doubt, the *Secunda Relatio* and the *Working Document*. Both appropriate the methodology and contents inherent in the theological reflection characteristic of the continent and the Caribbean, expressed as theologies of liberation.[6] In this sense, although the *Working Document* is more descriptive than analytical, its structure is clear and consistent with liberating thought as it articulates the analytical, hermeneutical, and pastoral practice dimensions. This is seen in part one: A Pastoral View on Latin American Reality (nn. 1–309); part two: Theological-Pastoral Illumination, Jesus Christ Yesterday, Today, and Forever (nn. 310–566); and part three: Pastoral Proposals (nn. 567–690).

Part one includes the faces of humiliated women as faces of the suffering Christ raising profound questions for the church (n. 163), and demanding of the church a preferential and solidary option so that these women may recover their voice, their place, their rights (nn. 622–24), and their full human integrity (nn. 633–34). It also recognizes the silence of the prevailing historical view with respect to women, and the persistence of a discriminatory mentality against them in society and in the ecclesial communities (nn. 85, 86, 276). It points out that although the machista culture pervades practically all our peoples (n. 168), women are now struggling against it in the awareness of their own dignity and their own rights as women (nn. 272–75).

Part two determines the christological nature of this document. Of its three chapters,[7] only the first and the third are positive toward women; the second often fails to transcend an unequal and hierarchical view of the church, although it seeks to present the church as a participatory community. Also, the end of the second chapter includes a reflection on Mary (nn. 410–24), but the general tone of the texts shows a strong androcentric nature. In part two, Jesus Christ is presented in direct relationship with the reign of God (nn. 311, 313); his egalitarian attitude causes (nn. 335–36) him to include women fully in the experience of discipleship (nn. 345, 378), to prepare them for transformative solidarity (nn. 349, 359, 363) in the power of the Spirit; and to include them in the radical equality of all believers within the church (nn. 385 and 390). This perspective is the basis of the pastoral challenge that part three of the *Working Document* expresses with respect to women: "For everyone there is an imperative to strive by word and deed for the full appreciation and recognition of women in the church and in society. It is therefore necessary to change the mentality and attitudes toward them, even if this means a profound cultural change, because equity and justice are at issue as principles of Christian life" (n. 599, cf. 652).

Thus, in general, the *Working Document* is positive toward the liberating concerns of women who struggle against structural oppression. It is not surprising that this document was rejected and replaced by another prepared in Rome.[8] Even so, we must make note of some important weaknesses. Among them are the absence of critical analysis on the patriarchal and sexist Latin American culture; the lack of awareness of the causes that keep women in a subordinate position; insensitivity to public and private violence against women; the silence of most of the church with respect to this violence; nonrecognition of the many feminist, popular, and ecumenical movements in our midst, and of the qualitative and quantitative participation of women in the base communities and in all the pastoral work of the church.

Document of Santafé de Bogotá: "Women in the Latin American Church and Culture"

In preparation for the IV General Conference of the Episcopacy, the Department of Laity of CELAM organized a seminar on "Women in the Latin American Church and Culture," with participation by representatives of organizations and movements of Catholic women from fourteen countries in Latin America and the Caribbean. The seminar was held in Santafé de Bogotá, Colombia, April 24–26, 1992.

A first document was drafted at this seminar and later sent to the national commissions of the Department of Laity for study, discussion, and correction. At the end of July a commission of four women met in Bogotá to compile these contributions and work them into the final document on Latin American Women.[9] This document, also entitled "Women in the Latin American Church and Culture,"[10] was sent to all the bishops participating in Santo Domingo. The document was subsequently studied at the Latin American Women's Congress,[11] held in Mexico City August 5–9, 1992, on the occasion of the Quincentenary of Evangelization in Latin America, and in preparation for the Santo Domingo event.[12]

The Santafé document, although its analysis is timid and sometimes merely descriptive, takes as its point of departure the reality lived by women. It goes on to illuminate that reality theologically, and proposes pastoral lines of action to change that reality. Its five sections are: Introductory Framework (nn. 1–7), Women in the Latin American Culture (nn. 8–41), Women in the Church (nn. 42–55), Doctrinal Illumination (nn. 56–80), and Lines of Action (nn. 82–113). In general the document shows great sensitivity to the diverse ecclesial practices of women committed to a process of change, and contains sufficient elements to identify the structural causes that lead to the oppression of women as women. These elements are scattered throughout the document, but they offer a hopeful point of departure for a more critical reflection, consistent with a liberating feminist vision. Even more, the document emphasizes the need to continue in collective reflection, in order to open ways toward women's achievement of human integrity and their authentic liberation (nn. 82–86). It is an open document, sensitive to the problems of oppressed women, aware of the multiplicity of asymmetrical relationships, and concerned with promoting efforts to eradicate injustice against women (n. 5).

I shall emphasize some of the central affirmations of the Santafé Document, which contribute to an interpretation of our own experiences as women in a liberating key. The introductory framework points out the urgency of better understanding the diverse feminist movements in our midst in order to strengthen their positive aspects (nn. 6, 16), while keeping a critical attitude toward them (nn. 22, 86). Part two takes note of the multiplicity of social practices that women use to achieve their rights (nn. 9–20). It presents women's struggles as transformative initiatives in the face of an oppressive global situation generated, in combination, by a machista culture that breaks up the oneness and otherness of men and women (nn. 21–32); by the prevailing neoliberal capitalist system that accumulates the labor of women through the sexual division of social labor (nn. 33–39); and by colonialism, which promotes racist and sexist attitudes, especially against peasant, indigenous, Afro-Latina, and marginalized urban women (n. 35).

Part three, dedicated to the situation of women in the church, presents a rigorous and realistic critique that is well summarized in n. 51: "There are great and persistent inconsistencies between what the ecclesial documents teach about the dignity of women, and the practice of the whole church: women continue to suffer double discrimination, as women in a men's world and as lay people in a clerical world." This situation is all the more serious because women represent "the most numerous and active sector in the people of God" (n. 42). It denounces the paternalistic and authoritarian attitude of many priests, who teach values that undermine the human integrity of women, such as abnegation, self-sacrifice, and resignation (n. 55).

Part four interprets this reality along four lines that affirm the radical equality of women and their liberating expectations. The first line draws on anthropology to emphasize the equality of men and women as sexually differentiated persons called to build a common history (nn. 56–57). The second draws on the liberating traditions of scripture to proclaim the fundamental equality of men and women in their identical dignity (especially Genesis 1:26 and Galatians 3:28–29); the egalitarian practice of Jesus toward women in relation to his criticism of patriarchal culture (nn. 62–63); and the activities of women in the early Christian movement (n. 64). The third line presents Mary as a woman who expresses "a new way of being a person and a woman" (n. 66), but this whole section lacks biblical references and is more abstract and doctrinal (nn. 65–69). Finally, the more positive ecclesiological line affirms the identity of the church as a baptismal community, expressed in the ministries and charisms inspired by the diverse activity of the Spirit (nn. 70–72, 76–78). This positive part is disrupted by the inappropriate addition of the arguments in favor of putting religious power in the hands of men (nn. 74–75). Apart from these numbers and the androcentric mariology, the theological reflection in the Santafé document offers several alternatives for a critical interpretation of our experience as women, and for a creative reformulation of the Christian categories that are alien to our own consciousness.

The lines of action presented in part five are extensive, but they are all intended to bring together efforts for the full recognition and effective participation of women, in the words of the document, "in all the areas where society is being built, as valid and unique interlocutors" (nn. 82 and 87–100). It points out the need and urgency for the church to listen to the voice of women, and to face "the challenge of making a qualitative leap, inside and outside the church: to promote the dignity of women decisively and actively. To be faithful to its origins, the church must also become a true sign of communion and participation among men and women, joyfully accepting the charisms that each has received from the one Spirit" (nn. 83 and 103–13).

Finally, the Santafé document proposes changes in the language, symbols and images that transmit sexist contents and promote hierarchical values against women (nn. 91–93, 97, 108). Although this is a document "of hope" in the present hour of the Latin American church, I want to mention here some of the things I find missing. Above all, it seems to me that the document continues abstracting its subjects, by not making explicit the social location where its reflection begins. "Oppression against women," as described in the document, is not described in terms of the factors that influence our struggles for emancipation, such as the race, social position, or intellectual tradition by which women are identified. The preferential option for the poor and oppressed sectors as subjects of social and ecclesial change, which is embedded in Medellín, is entirely omitted in this document. Thus the epistemological location does not help to interpret, accompany, and activate the day-to-day struggles of poor and oppressed women for justice and human integrity, for themselves and those who depend on them. Two things partly account for the absence of a hermeneutical perspective consistent with the struggles of these women. The first seems to be that the document is primarily concerned with the crisis caused for the church by emancipation movements, including the feminist movement, which are based on principles of modernity. The second, consistent with the first, is the lack of active participation by women from the popular sectors and from the basic ecclesial communities in the whole process that led to the drafting of this document.

The document also contains a mixture of languages that, in reality, reflect the ambiguous meanings that are used to identify our own identity as women. The concepts of "feminine identity," "feminine voice," "feminine image," are often repeated, but the meaning of "feminine" is never explained. I suspect that for many Latin American women, this concept is still rooted in the androcentric mentality and reflects very well what the clerical sector of the church is promoting for women. Until women begin to reformulate our own identity, it will be necessary to question the concepts and meanings that we have inherited from the patriarchal culture. Meanwhile it would be better to use concepts like "women's identity," "women's voice," "women's image," and so forth.

All told, the document is not a closed text or the culmination of a completed process. On the contrary, it seeks to strengthen the liberating tendencies that already exist in reality, and thus encourages an unprejudiced dialogue among the diverse feminist movements, women's organizations and movements, and between them and the best traditions of the Christian faith. The content of the document was a decisive influence on the *Final Document* of Santo Domingo.

THE WORKING COMMISSION ON WOMEN AT SANTO DOMINGO

With some exceptions to be noted later, the view on women presented in the Santo Domingo document is generally positive, considering the substantial changes made in the final document from the earlier direction that characterized the Latin American magisterium. The results we see in the numbers referring specifically to women partly reflect the makeup of the Working Commission on Women. This commission brought together eleven people, including four bishops (two Mexicans, a Salvadoran, and a Brazilian), four religious sisters, two lay women, and a Presbyterian bishop as observer.

Since it was an exclusive meeting of bishops—that is, of male, celibate clergy representing a patriarchal structure—it is surprising that six women were brought in, who are automatically excluded from the leadership of the church merely because they are women, regardless of their religious status. This does not mean that they all represented our interests as women; only that some of them made an effort to ensure the effective recognition at Santo Domingo of women's struggles against marginalization and violence.[13] Within the commission itself there were tendencies against the spirit of solidarity that inspired the preliminary work reflected in the Santafé document. Considering the contradictory circumstances surrounding the conference, the results offered in the final document with respect to women can be considered a key moment in an open process toward the new tasks that lie ahead.

THE GREAT AFFIRMATIONS ON WOMEN IN SANTO DOMINGO

The objective of the Working Commission on Women was to draft seven numbers for inclusion in the *Final Document*. These numbers appear in the first chapter of part two, nn. 104–10. However, other commissions also refer to situations that involve women in different ways, although they are not directly related to this specific commission. This procedure accounts for the unevenness and ambivalence of the document's affirmations on women.

Three fundamental blocks help to understand the view on women offered in Santo Domingo. The first suggests the key assumption of the church in interpreting the reality that women live, the second makes explicit what this experience is and what should be done about it, and the third expounds the model of the patriarchal nuclear family, which the church holds up as normative for heterosexual human relationships. Apart from these blocks, there are other scattered numbers in a descriptive tone. Here I shall discuss the central aspects of these blocks without describing the general structure of the document, because I understand other essays in this volume will do that.

First Block: The Fundamental Interpretive Principle

In part two of the Santo Domingo *Final Document*, a good part of the second chapter, entitled "Human Development," constitutes the central reference point for understanding the church's identity and mission in the

Latin American reality. This section contains the point of departure for interpreting the reality that women live, and to which the church must respond. Above all it is a reality that, against God's will, massively violates human rights (n. 164) — in the words of the document, "not only by terrorism, repression, and murder, but also by the existence of conditions of extreme poverty and unjust economic structures that give rise to vast inequalities. . . . Violence against the rights of children, women, and the poorest groups in society . . . are worthy of special condemnation" (n. 167). In this reality, the church is called to discover "the face of the Lord in the suffering faces of the poor . . . [in the] suffering faces of women who are humiliated and disregarded," who challenge the people of God "to a deep personal and ecclesial conversion" (n. 178).

The church's response to this reality, consistent with the life and mission of Jesus Christ, is to share in depth the "daily struggle to live" of these sectors (n. 179). Therefore the church in Latin America commits itself, firmly and irrevocably, "to a gospel-based and preferential option for the poor" (nn. 178, 180), to promote an alternative order "in keeping with the dignity of each and every person, fostering justice and solidarity, and opening horizons of eternity for all of them" (n. 296). This clear option for the poor and oppressed, for the broad sectors of women who struggle for their own human integrity against violence and oppression, is the fundamental principle for a critical interpretation of the reality we live, and for knowing what to do about it in the direction of justice. With this affirmation, the Santo Domingo *Final Document* substantially corrects the abstractness of the Santafé document and improves on it. But both documents challenge us to broaden and deepen this option into an option for ourselves as women.

Second Block: The Situation of Women and Lines of Action

Numbers 104 to 110 express the direct contribution of the Working Commission on Women, and constitute the most positive part of the Santo Domingo *Final Document.* This whole section is built on a summary of many aspects pointed out in the Santafé document.[14] Although some central aspects of Santafé are left out of the conclusions of Santo Domingo, and although the section on "Women" was given a penultimate place in the pyramidal structure of the church contemplated in Santo Domingo, the working commission achieved at least three things. First, the section was not absorbed, overshadowed, or inhibited by the generic section on the faithful laity. Second, it was not incorporated in or reduced to the section on the family. Third, the text of the conclusions shows at least some sensitivity to the problem of sexist language. The last of these was only partly reflected in the conference; while some texts speak of "women and men," or "human person," others strongly maintain the sexist cargo (numbers 13, 27, 34, 159, 165, 183, 231, and many others). Unfortunately, the English translation does not reflect these key aspects, because the translators eliminate all the sexist language for North American society; that does not resolve the problem of Latin American women.[15]

The Santo Domingo conference describes the growing awareness of the equal dignity and equivalent rights of women and men in society and the church (n. 105) as a "new sign of the times" (nn. 164, 167). The dignity and rights of women are based on the radical equality — since the creation — which all persons acquire on Christ (n. 104). It often draws on recognition of the power of women in building the world and the ecclesial communities, as actors in their own right (nn. 104–6). But it also observes: "Such acknowledgment clashes scandalously with the fact that women are frequently excluded, their dignity is imperiled, and they are often subject to violence" (n. 106). Therefore, the document affirms, the church must confront this situation with renewed force: "The new evangelization should firmly and actively promote the enhancement of women's dignity. Hence we must delve more deeply into women's role in the church and in society" (n. 105).

The pastoral lines of action offered in the document all come, some in weakened form, from the Santafé document. In my opinion they should not be discounted but critically deepened and broadened, by both men's and by women's communities, movements, and organizations. Among the many lines suggested in the document, I will point out some that can serve as a basis for the others. It emphasizes the need to develop an attitude of critical analysis toward the messages, stereotypes, values, languages, symbols, and images that are transmitted about women in society and in the church (nn. 108–9); to denounce abuses against Latin American and Caribbean women, especially those that violate their life and their own dignity as women (nn. 107, 110); to create effective space for the inclusion of women in decision-making processes in all areas of human activity (nn. 107, 109); to promote comprehensive formation of the clergy and the whole community for the effective recognition of the common rights and dignity of women and men (nn. 107–9); to develop pastoral methods that do not reduce the role of women in education, in the reading of scripture, in the leadership of evangelization, and in political activity (nn. 107–9); to recognize and enable the leadership of women in the movements that struggle for women, as well as in organizing and leading the new evangelization (nn. 108–9).

Third Block: The Patriarchal Family and the Vocation of Women

I shall address the theme of the family in the Santo Domingo *Final Document* only with reference to a paragraph that appears in n. 105b of the section on women. Here, with respect to the current "reductionistic claims about women's nature and mission," it quotes the Puebla Document (n. 846) in affirming the church's desire "to set forth the gospel teaching on woman's dignity and calling, emphasizing her role 'as mother, defender of life, and educator of the home.' " This text is itself reductive of women's vocation, since it emphasizes the role that the patriarchal culture has imposed on them because of their mere biological capacity for motherhood. This reductive view follows the same clearly patriarchal logic as that of the whole section on the family (nn. 210–21). And what is more serious, it ignores the rigorous criticism by the Santafé document of a culture that promotes marriage, motherhood, and domestic tasks as the normative means for the authentic fulfillment of women (cf. Santafé nn. 24–25, 29, 31, 33, 80–81).[16]

CONCLUSION: TENTATIVE ANALYSIS OF PROGRESS AND SILENCES

To close, I shall add some other elements that support the liberating vision that accompanies women's struggles, and which must be strengthened in our present and future reality. In addition to what I have described as a positive contribution of the Santo Domingo *Final Document* with respect to women, we must observe that the section titled "Women," in contrast to the overall logic of the document, does not begin from doctrinal principles but from a concrete situation that demands a response. The affirmations made in this section are based, to varying degrees, on the diverse social practices of women and on the expectations that arise out of the diverse contexts of reality in Latin America and the Caribbean. I believe Latin American women can see ourselves in most of the texts brought together in this section, especially in its spirit of solidarity and its attitude of explicit commitment to the liberating struggles of peasant, indigenous, Afro-American, and urban working women. That is especially true of those who live in difficult situations, such as separation, divorce, homosexuality, single motherhood, and prostitution.

The greatest weakness of the section on women relates directly to the confusion that affects the document in general, because it was shaped in isolation from the liberating tradition of the Latin American communities. Consequently this section runs the risk of dissociation from other areas radically related to a true women's liberation: for example, the new international economic order, human promotion, ecology and the earth, labor, culture and inculturation, the church and its ministries, and others. All these areas should be examined from a viewpoint that coherently expresses the concerns of women and men, or that at least suggests how these areas affect women, which the document does not do. Apparently the clerical sector at Santo Domingo, like many Latin American liberation theologians, still fails to recognize the patriarchal nature of the Latin American and Caribbean culture, church, and society. Therefore they reduce the process of women's liberation to a "gender issue" of concern only to women, without seeing that a position in favor of women is itself a hermeneutical perspective related to the option for the poor and oppressed, just as racial and ecological perspectives are.

The Santafé document makes several suggestions that are worth pursuing more rigorously, since they were eliminated from the Santo Domingo conclusions. These include the need for a creative and unprejudiced dialogue with Latin American feminist movements; for participation of women in decision-making spheres *in the church* and in society; for criticism and reformulation of the "feminine model" of women; for the promotion of women in professional biblical and theological studies; for criticism of the authoritarian and sexist attitude of the clergy; for self-criticism by women as transmitters of patriarchal culture; Jesus' criticism of the patriarchal system together with formal criticism of sexism in the church. All these dimensions can become transformative insofar as they involve the voices and the smiles of women, whose day-to-day labor already anticipates the fullness of the church in the Basic Ecclesial Communities.

Translated by Margaret D. Wilde

NOTES

1. See my paper "La Presencia de la Mujer en América: Perspectivas Eclesiológicas," in MEMORIA, *Congreso Femenino Latinoamericano* (Mexico: UFCM, 1992), 65–102. Indo-American Press in Bogotá, Colombia, will publish an extended version of that paper.

2. Two documents preceded the preparatory document: the collection of reports (1988), and the First Draft of the Consultative Document (1989).

3. "For the church that seeks to evangelize incarnationally, it is an unavoidable pastoral theological concern . . . to evangelize every man and all men in their global context" (n. 911). "Who is the new man, the model of man, and the horizon of all humanization?" (n. 924).

4. The title of this document is "New Evangelization, Human Promotion, Christian Culture. Jesus Christ Yesterday, Today, and Forever."

5. The *Prima Relatio* (1991) is the synthesis of responses to the preparatory instrument. See the presentation of the *Working Document* published by the Latin American Episcopal Council (CELAM), June 1992, pp. xxiii-xxiv. Also see José Alvarez Icaza, *Crónica de Santo Domingo* I, II and III: Centro Nacional de Comunicación Social (1992), Mexico City.

6. See the *Working Document,* nn. 203–5 and 499.

7. Chapter 1: The Salvific Act; chapter 2: The Proclamation of the Salvific Act; chapter 3: The Fulfillment of the Salvific Act.

8. In Santo Domingo the *Working Document* was relegated to the position of a text for consultation. Of the eight people who drafted this document, only one was accepted in Santo Domingo, although the secretary general of CELAM nominated all eight. The experts who drafted the Santo Domingo *Final Document* came from Rome.

9. The commission was accompanied by Msgr. Gregorio Rosa Chávez, bishop of San Salvador and president of the Department of Laity of CELAM.

10. Published by the Department of Laity in the CELAM Bulletin, no. 249 (1992), 1–15.

11. The congress was organized by the Unión Femenina Católica Mexicana. I was invited to participate by the national president, María Eugenia Díaz de Pfennich, one of the two lay women who participated in the Commission on Women in Santo Domingo.

12. Five hundred twelve women participated in the congress from fourteen countries—twelve in Latin America, plus the United States and Spain—all representing a variety of movements and organizations of Catholic women.

13. In fact the Working Commission on Women underwent serious internal tensions due to the opposing views within it, including those of the women themselves. One of the two lay women regularly blocked the commission's work because of her ultraconservative views. The most positive section in the Santo Domingo *Final Document* on women is largely due to the work of María Eugenia Díaz de Pfennich and Bishop G. Rosa Chávez, who also participated in the process leading up to the Santafé document.

14. The numbers in the Santo Domingo text correspond to those listed in parentheses from the Santafé document: n. 104 (58, 62–64); n. 105 (10, 29, 30, 83); n. 106 (9, 17, 48); n. 107 (82, 84, 88–89, 106); n. 108 (86b, 97, 102, 105); n. 109 (91–94, 96, 112); n. 110 (88, 98, 111).

15. This procedure is also followed by those who translate into English the books of the (male) Latin American theologians of liberation, such as Juan Luis Segundo, Jon Sobrino, Pablo Richard, Leonardo Boff, Segundo Galilea, and others. While the translation makes these authors more attractive to North American readers, it does nothing to help Latin American women, because it does not change the patriarchal mentality of these authors. I would rather see the works translated as they appear in the original language, so as not to inflate false balloons.

16. It is worth noting that on this point, while the Santafé document quotes n. 841 of the Puebla Document, which affirms equal tasks for women and men with respect to the transmission of life, the Santo Domingo *Final Document* uses n. 846, which limits these tasks to women in the domestic arena.

From Lamentation to Project

The Emergence of an Indigenous Theological Movement in Latin America

Stephen P. Judd, M.M.

PROTAGONISTS OF MEMORY, HOPE AND RESISTANCE: THE INDIGENOUS PRESENCE AT SANTO DOMINGO

Perhaps one of the most significant events that coincided with the Fourth Conference of Latin American Bishops (CELAM IV) assembled in Santo Domingo was an event that occurred thousands of miles away in Europe. That was the announcement of the awarding of the Nobel Peace Prize to the Guatemalan Indian woman and social activist, Rigoberta Menchú. She, more than anyone else, symbolizes the anguish and hope of the struggle of indigenous people throughout Latin America over the course of the past thirty years. Her personal story is one with which millions of indigenous people identify. By granting her this award their plight was again brought to the attention of millions more around the globe.

Similarly, this award highlighted both the conflicts and contradictions as well as the opportunity present within the bishops' conference. Against the backdrop of the Quincentennial Commemoration the bishop delegates found themselves wrestling with the symbolic connection between the conference itself and the Columbus Quincentenary celebrations. Many were uncomfortable with the October 12 opening date for the conference and the memories of conquest and the exploitation of America's indigenous peoples that continues today. Church leaders of all stripes were confronted with a memory that they have thus far been unable to resolve, namely the extent to which the church was a conscious or unwitting accomplice and partner to Spanish and Portuguese colonial expansion. Rigoberta Menchú is a vivid reminder of that past and present some would like to forget or explain away. It is important to point out that the official indigenous presence at Santo Domingo was limited to two lay delegates, one from Ecuador and one from Guatemala.

These contradictions emerged in a number of ways and threatened to eclipse the purpose and theological issues within the conference. For one thing, it was impossible to ignore the mammoth Columbus Lighthouse which dominates Santo Domingo's harbor and serves as a reminder of the present-day realities of Latin America, what some critics term "the Conquest continued." Thousands of slum dwellers were removed from the site where the government of Joaquin Balaguer invested an estimated 120 million dollars in the construction of the monument to glorify the achievements of Spanish colonial conquest and expansion.

When Pope John Paul II arrived a few days before the opening of the conference, observers and the nearly one thousand press people speculated on how he could possibly finesse these contradictions. How would he not manage to convey a triumphalistic air in the face of such dubious and explosive symbols as the lighthouse? That was a near impossible feat given the fact that one of the major public events on his schedule was an October 11 Mass at the outer edges of the lighthouse. The closing words of his sermon illustrate well the predicament. While he drew attention to the present-day plight of Latin America's indigenous and Afro-American people, in the next breath he acknowledged Columbus' role in making possible the glories of the first evangelization.[1] The fact that the Holy Father consented to canonize the nineteenth-century Spanish-born Augustinian friar and bishop, Ezequiel Moreno—the first such canonization ceremony on American soil—further demonstrated the church's inability to deal adequately with the indigenous reality, past and present, at Santo Domingo.

Pope John Paul's opening address to the conference on the afternoon of October 12 was a similar exercise in navigating through a morass of inevitably mixed messages. Here he partially succeeded in communicating a much more coherent message. Calling the first evangelization in the sixteenth century a kind "of tribunal for human rights" he related the atrocities of the Conquest to the present-day situation of indigenous people.[2] Notably absent from his discourse, however, was any trace of a conviction in the potential of the Christian witness of indigenous people and their religious worldview within the scope or criteria of his much heralded call for a "new evangelization." They were again reduced to the objects of the church's pity and noblesse oblige and not viewed as the protagonists of memory, hope, and resistance.

The presence of indigenous people could not escape the deliberations of the conference itself. All throughout the two weeks, both inside and outside the walls, a debate waged on over whether the conference should sponsor a public pardon ceremony in the downtown cathedral. Clearly, this put Santo Domingo's cardinal archbishop, Nicolás de Jesús López, in an awkward position. He adamantly refused to grant permission for the public ceremony. Finally, a smaller, less dramatic ceremony was held inside the conference, but this concession did not lessen the heated debate that continues long after the conclusion of CELAM IV.

Over on the other side of Santo Domingo's harbor lies a less imposing but no less powerful monument to another, lesser-known representative of Spanish colonization and evangelization. Juxtaposed to the Columbus lighthouse is a statue erected by the Mexican people and government to the memory of the Dominican friar, Antonio Montesinos. At the nearby cathderal on the Fourth Sunday of Advent in 1511 Montesinos preached his fiery sermon against the monstrous atrocities committed against Native Americans. Those immortal words from the sermon, "are not these natives people?" have resounded through the centuries. There in the congregation that day was no other than Bartolomé de Las Casas who picked up Montesinos's challenge and initiated a prophetic current that has its adherents today in those who, like the liberation theologian Gustavo Gutiérrez, espouse the cause of indigenous people.[3] Then as now the humanity of indigenous peoples is still questioned, if we judge by the recent, sad history of extermination campaigns in places like Guatemala.

Below we will examine how the emergence of this prophetic current has contributed to raising a new awareness of the indigenous worldview and potential for articulating a new theological perspective. In order to interpret the significance of the Santo Domingo Conference and Final Document for the cause of Latin America's indigenous peoples and, subsequently, the emerging model for evangelization among them one must first examine the development of this theological perspective that has its origins within developing social and cultural movements throughout the indigenous world of Latin America. Rigoberta Menchú is but one of the outstanding leaders of that movement that incorporates claims for cultural identity and autonomy along with concerns for political and human rights. It has only just begun to surface within the last several years, roughly from the period of the Puebla Conference in 1979 to the present through a number of parallel and complementary developments, each of which has made a contribution to articulating a new current of original and creative theological reflection and spirituality.

FROM PUEBLA TO SANTO DOMINGO: FACTORS IN THE DEVELOPMENT OF AN INDIGENOUS SOCIO-CULTURAL MOVEMENT AND THEOLOGICAL PERSPECTIVE

During the past several years there has been a remarkable growth of historical awareness of indigenous identity in spite of the vast processes of modernization in Latin America. This socio-cultural phenomenon occurs within the larger movement of the "irruption of the poor" as Gutiérrez has so accurately described it.[4] Vast social transformations across Latin America coupled with rapid urbanization have not spelled the demise of indigenous cultures, but rather fostered a new expression for them. Numerically, there are 40 million indigenous people whom writers like the Brazilian Darcy Ribeiro call, "pueblos testigos" (witness peoples), insofar as they give witness to other values than those of the modern world in the survival of ancient and often clandestine cultures. In their capacity to regroup in the face of modernizing influences and trends they are becoming a growing force of the rural and urban landscapes of Latin America. Within this growing movement is a tacit acceptance of modernity balanced by a recovery of peoples' historical memory in shaping a new identity.[5]

A prime factor and occasion that has helped to focus the contribution by indigenous people has been the attention given to the 500 Years Commemoration. Beyond the highly publicized protests surrounding attempts to celebrate the Columbus Quincentenary is a much more profound emergence of a social movement for pressing the claims of indigenous peoples. Underneath phrases like "from lamentation to a project, from protest to proposal," lies a vast potential for creating alternative visions of society.[6] Contrary to some interpretations, this movement does not represent a rejection of modernity, but rather its redefinition from the foundation of this newly recovered sense of identity. No longer must people seek a sense of identity in a clandestine existence.

A striking feature of this resurgent movement has been the profound theological awakening that has its sources in a combination of factors. The social and political upheaval in Latin America manifested in the so-called crisis of institutions, the newfound awareness of indigenous identity and the influence of intellectual movements sympathetic to the indigenous cause converge to raise awareness of this emerging movement. International awareness of environmental concerns has played a major role as well. To no small degree this movement has been promoted by a new style of evangelization that has quietly contributed to fostering the indigenous religious worldview and spirituality.

Sometimes this perspective has developed within an ecclesial environment with the explicit or implicit approbation of the church. Prophetic bishops like the late Leonidas Proaño in Ecuador actively promoted it. Thus, at times, it takes place within an informal world of religious practice and rituals on the margins of officially sanctioned church activities. This development supersedes the discussions on popular religiosity to embrace an original theological reflection and poses a challenge to the church to introduce a "pastoral indigena" rather than an indigenista patronage or advocacy role vis-à-vis indigenous peoples on the part of church elites. Moreover, it calls for interreligious dialogue within the church and even presses legitimate claims for different indigenous rites.

An important parallel development comes about as the result of the promotion of the indigenous perspective by church-related groups and pastoral institutes that were formed in the aftermath of Vatican II and Medellín in the late 1960s. Outstanding examples are CENAMI in southern Mexico and the Instituto de Pastoral Andina (IPA) in Peru. Recently, the Ecumenical Association of Third World Theologians (EATWOT) has sponsored a number of reflection groups and international meetings to focus attention on the indigenous theological perspective. Theologians like Leonardo Boff, Javier Albo, Paulo Suess, Diego Irarrazaval, though not indigenous themselves, have taken up the question.[7] Unlike previous *indigenista* intellectual movements they do not pretend to speak for the indigenous peoples but attempt to chronicle and document the fruit of the indigenous religious practice, reflection, and perspective. Increasingly, these groups frame the question of the indigenous contribution in terms of an evangelization that has its starting point in the historical life experience and worldview of indigenous peoples. Similarly, missionary groups like Maryknoll in Latin America have been instrumental in promoting the values of indigenous theology.

This perspective has taken root in the thinking of official church documents and in such national episcopal conferences as those of Bolivia and Guatemala, but it is reflected in the thought and practice of individual bishops as well. What defines this movement is a characteristic discovery of the perspective of "the other" as the chief paradigm for doing theology. According to the Mexican theologian and Zapotec Indian, Eleazar López, this movement received a new thrust in 1985 when the CELAM Department of Missions (DEMIS) called for an indigenous pastoral perspective and praxis rather than a stance based solely on the defense of indigenous peoples.[8]

For the most part, official church pronouncements demonstrate a fundamental weakness in that they are still framed in the language of an "evangelization of cultures," following the guidelines of the Puebla Conference as well as official understandings of inculturation expressed in papal discourses. Phrases like "seeds of the word" dominate the theological discussion but fall short of incorporating the rich potential of the indigenous ritual world or reverence for the earth. The slight but significant opening introduced at Puebla originates in the use of the phrase, "the people who evangelize."[9] This represented a shift away from regarding the people as simply the objects of evangelization to seeing them as protagonists. While limited in its scope, this shift paved the way for the discussions of today.

Adherents of a restorationist Catholic culture ("a Catholic substratum") or a Neo-Christendom model of church view this resurgent movement and indigenous popular religiosity in an instrumental way. As evidenced in many of the preliminary drafts of documents for Santo Domingo, they regard it as a weapon to oppose the perceived threats of modernity and secularization and the phenomenal growth of Protestantism in Latin America.[10] Indigenous theology and spirituality understands itself as much more than a functional response to the institutional church's crisis of credibility and would resist efforts to define it in such a limited way.

Over the course of this papacy meetings between John Paul II and indigenous peoples, and his pronouncements on those occasions, have served to encourage this resistance. In some instances the pope's oral and symbolic discourse has gone beyond the perfunctory nod or paternalistic gesture to indigenous peoples that often gives the impression of a folkloric display with little or no substance behind it. More than any one contribution of this papacy to the indigenous cause has been the pope's efforts to raise a greater awareness of the need for an authentic inculturation of the gospel. Implicit in this encounter, after a history of many missed encounters, is an opening to a greater dialogue between proponents of indigenous theology and church leaders.

THE ROLE OF INDIGENOUS THEOLOGY IN THE SANTO DOMINGO PROCESS

Briefly, I would like to trace the development of indigenous theology with respect to the process leading up to and during the Santo Domingo Conference in 1992. In the pre-Santo Domingo process the Bolivian and Guatemalan bishops took the initiative in presenting the indigenous perspective in their critique of the Consultative Document. They noted that under the category of "Christian Culture" these documents attributed a key role to the Catholic "substratum" as a chief factor in shaping Latin American identity. This provoked a polemical debate. References to Christian culture or the Catholic "substratum" equates, in the view of many, a homogenous, uniform expression of the Christian message. Critics were quick to point out the absence of any appreciation for the pluralism of Latin American religion and culture, and its potential contribution to Catholic identity and theology. One's Catholic identity, they affirmed, owes as much to an encounter between the gospel and the Maya, Quechua or Aymara culture and religious worldview as it does to an evangelization from a European-centered worldview. The Guatemalan and the Bolivian responses to the Consultative Document best captured the spirit of this poignant critique, which resulted in a reformulation of key sections of the preliminary documents.[11]

Claims for an indigenous perspective also found their way into the surprisingly critical and incisive document entitled "Secunda Relatio," which compiled the objections of many to the biases of the preliminary documents. Thus indigenous theology was raised to a new level in the Santo Domingo process. Similarly, the "Documento de Trabajo" or Working Document published immediately prior to the conference opening attempted to incorporate those objections together with the indigenous perspective, although it did so with less emphasis than the previous incisive critiques.[12]

To discover an explicit statement of the indigenous perspective, shaped and refined in a series of conferences and theological meetings throughout indigenous areas of Latin America, we focus in on Eleazar López's letter to the Apostolic Delegate in Mexico, Bishop Girolamo Prigione, prior to Santo Domingo.[13] This letter, a kind of quasi-manifesto, attempted to address criticism from the Vatican Sacred Congregation for the Faith and Doctrine. In so doing it provided a good synthesis of the content and claims of this new theological movement.

For López and others indigenous theology is a composite of religious practices and popular theological wisdom that isn't necessarily the product of an ecclesiatical influence. In this sense it shouldn't be confused with efforts to label it as popular religiosity. Thus, it predates the encounter with the first evangelization in the sixteenth century and cannot be labeled as merely a hybrid product of indigenous practices and Christianity. Similarly, it has survived the early campaigns to extirpate "idols" and indigenous sacred spaces and more contemporary attempts to categorize these as superstitious or diabolical. Its practitioners are varied and range from native healers to members of religious confraternities who fashion the wisdom, the ritual cycle, and cosmovision of indigenous peoples into a coherent religious worldview and ethical system.

What is so strikingly characteristic about this theological perspective lies in the claims it makes for a Catholic Christian identity. According to López, it wishes to stand under the judgment of the gospel. Moreover, it makes claims for a space within the church and thus, it understands itself as ecclesially bound and accountable. However, it emphasizes the need for a dialogue with the universal church and with other particular churches. By no means does it see itself in isolation from other expressions of the Christian tradition. For the dialogue to take place it will be necessary to utilize both the traditional theological discourse as well as to incorporate the mythical-symbolic language that is such a distinguishing feature of indigenous theology.

Indigenous theology acknowledges the openings that stem from Vatican II and the process of renewal in the Latin American Church since Medellín that favor such a dialogue. At the same time this movement asserts its connection to the growing awareness of indigenous peoples and the emergence of movements throughout Amerindia that press for autonomy and respect for human rights. A figure like Rigoberta Menchú epitomizes this movement and she herself traces her commitment to a religious formation that stressed respect for the human rights of indigenous peoples and respect for their culture.

Given this combination of factors, there were many promising signs that this perspective would get a positive hearing at Santo Domingo. In the first place, those on the Commission for Indigenous and Afro-American peoples formed a composite picture of bishops with a long history of advocacy in espousing the indigenous cause. By and large bishops of the stature and trajectory of Julio Cabrera and Gerardo Flores of Guatemala, Edmundo Abastoflor of Bolivia, José Dammert of Peru, and Erwin Krautler of Brazil lay claim to a history of heroic support for the development of indigenous theology. They arrived at Santo Domingo prepared to articulate that perspective. Prior to and during the conference they worked in close collaboration with theologians like López and Irarrazaval. It seemed at first like a propitious moment.

Judging by the content of the Final Document one would have hoped for more. Certainly, in quantitative terms, there is more attention paid to the indigenous world than in Medellín and Puebla combined (see nos. 243-251 and respectively).[14] Whether significant breakthroughs were made in the depth of the theological and pastoral reflection is the subject of endless debate. In our view, great strides were made. Moreover, the stage was set for further developments over the next few years.

For example, the Final Document succeeds in dispelling the previously held notion that indigenous, Afro-American, and mestizo cultures are peripheral to the Western European cultural legacy. The implicit bias that Christianity is coterminus with Western civilization has been laid to rest. It is safe to say that there is at least a tacit recognition of what Johannes Metz calls a "polycentric Church."[15]

Evangelization is no longer couched in language that speaks of an "evangelization of cultures." Rather, there arises a new understanding that evangelization takes place "within" cultures. The prepositional change is not without its far-reaching implications. The perspective that underpins this section of the Final Document bears a close similarity to Leonardo Boff's often cited call for an evangelization that has as its starting point the culture of the oppressed and marginalized.[16] In other words, one cannot dismiss the factors of oppression and domination that have stunted the development of cultures. Cultures, indigenous or Afro-American, are not static fixtures but are in a state of flux and continue to redefine themselves in a constantly shifting socio-political context.

The section on pastoral lines (no. 248) calls for a number of obvious responses that have been a feature of different church documents for a number of years. Yet this is the first time that a document on a Latin American level has given such a pronounced emphasis to the claim for an interreligious dialogue within Latin America. A corollary of this breakthrough is the challenge to "accompany the theological reflection" of indigenous peoples and groups, recognizing that their formulations may shed new light on Christian faith and hope.[17]

The much applauded section of the Final Document that treats of "human promotion" provides more specificity in terms of the indigenous question. Here there is a recognition and affirmation of the right to land, claims for autonomy and the right for organizations that press cultural claims (no. 249).[18]

We still may speculate whether, indeed, the Santo Domingo Final Document reflects the depth of the indigenous experience and movement and its theological contribution. Are these sections mere concessions given in the context of 1992 or do they carry with them the force of conviction together with the will to forward the cause of an indigenous Catholic theology? Read side by side with the key points of López's letter, they lack the urgency of his claims, but manage to include them, while most importantly, leaving room for the dialogue everyone so fervently desires.

CONCLUSION: THE EMERGENCE OF A NEW
THEOLOGICAL CENTER

Clearly, one of the chief results of the Santo Domingo Conference was not a polished Final Document intended to stir the imagination in the fashion of Medellín and Puebla. As many have already pointed out, the mere fact that there was any document at all represented no small achievement, given the configuration of outside forces present within the conference. What emerged from Santo Domingo, however, was the rebirth of a spirit to search for the originality of the Latin American experience. Many of the new generation of bishops and church leaders who participated in the conference came away renewed and recommitted to discover in the historical experience of Latin America and its rich diversity of peoples and cultures a unique dimension of the Christian message. Santo Domingo represents a watershed development in raising awareness that Latin America offers humankind something that transcends a mere imitation of the Western European socio-cultural and religious legacy.

The resurgent indigenous social movement with its accompanying theological developments represents a search for this originality. Embodied in that movement is the challenge of "otherness" that so many intellectuals have echoed over the past several years. The arrival of a fledgling theological project from the indigenous themselves is, indeed, welcome news. Just as liberation theology burst onto the scene at the time of Medellín, the indigenous theological movement may become Latin America's next important contribution to the Christian world. Perhaps, the recognition and momentum achieved at Santo Domingo may propel it onto the global stage as a force to be reckoned with.[19]

Bishop Gerardo Flores of Coban, Guatemala, commented during the Santo Domingo Conference that this meeting marked a new stage in the church's awareness of the indigenous presence. "If Puebla saw the face of Christ in the Indian," he remarked, "then Santo Domingo will usher in a period when people can think beyond the disfigured face to embrace a fully rounded and robust new actor with a great contribution to make to all humankind."

NOTES

1. Pope John Paul II, Homily at the Canonization of Ezequiel Moreno, Santo Domingo, October 11, 1992.

2. Pope John Paul II, "Opening Address to the Fourth General Conference of the Latin American Episcopate," English text published in *Origins* Vol. 22: No. 19, October 22, 1992, paragraph 1, #5.

3. Gustavo Gutiérrez, *Las Casas: In Search of the Poor of Jesus Christ* (Maryknoll, N.Y.: Orbis Books, 1993). From the outset, the life and work of Las Casas

has been a constant source of inspiration for Gutiérrez in his own theological development.

4. Gutiérrez, *The Power of the Poor in History* (Maryknoll, NY: Orbis, 1983).

5. Anibal Quijano, "Recovering Utopia," NACLA, Vol. XXIV, No. 5, February, 1991.

6. Phrases like "from lamentation to project" have frequently appeared in the presentations and debates at a series of conferences held in indigenous areas of Latin America over the past several years. Some have been co-sponsored by the Ecumenical Association of Third World Theologians (EATWOT) and local pastoral institutes. The First Conference/Workshop held in Mexico in September 1990 has been widely acclaimed as a defining moment for the indigenous theology movement.

7. Several outstanding titles have appeared that reflect this particular genre including Paulo Suess, *La nueva evangelización: desafíos históricos y pautas culturales* (Quito, Ecuador: Abya-Yala, 1991) and Leonardo Boff, *New Evangelization* (Maryknoll, NY: Orbis, 1992). Diego Irarrazaval has published extensively in a number of Latin American and Peruvian journals. The soon-to-be published Orbis title, *The Indian Faces of God* (ed. Manuel Marzal) includes an important essay by the Bolivian Jesuit, Xavier Albo.

8. Eleazar López Hernández, "Carta a Mons. Girolamo Prigione," Mexico City, June 25, 1992.

9. III CELAM Final Document in *Puebla and Beyond*, eds. John Eagleson and Philip Scharper (Maryknoll, NY: Orbis, 1979), paragraph #1147.

10. IV CELAM *Documento de Consulta*, April, 1991 (see section entitled "Cultura cristiana").

11. Conferencia Episcopal de Guatemala (CNG), Carta pastoral colectiva de los obispos de Guatemala, "500 años sembrando el Evangelio," August 15, 1992. Conferencia Episcopal de Bolivia (CNB), *Aporte de la Conferencia Episcopal de Bolivia a la IV Conferencia del Episcopado Latinoamericano, Santo Domingo, 1992.*

12. Consejo Episcopal Latinoamericano (CELAM), *IV Conferencia General del Episcopado Latinoamericano 'Secunda Relatio': síntesis de aportes al Documento de Consulta*, Bogota, Colombia, February 1992.

13. Eleazar López, "Carta a Mons. Girolamo Prigione"; see especially paragraphs 7-23.

14. Consejo Episcopal Lationamericano (CELAM), *Conclusiones IV Conferencia*, "Nueva Evangelización, promoción humana y cultura cristiana: Jesucristo ayer, hoy y siempre," Santo Domingo, October 12-28, 1992.

15. Johannes Baptiste Metz, "Hacia una Iglesia universal, culturalmente policéntrica," *Christus*, No. 625, May, 1989.

16. Boff, *New Evangelization* (see especially Part I, Chapter 8).

17. CELAM IV, *Santo Domingo Conclusiones*, paragraph 248.

18. *Conclusiones*, paragraph 249.

19. Pablo Richard, "La teología de la liberación en la nueva coyuntura: temas y deafíos nuevos para la década de los noventa," *Pasos* (DEI), No. 34, March-April, 1991, p. 8.

Contributors

María Pilar Aquino teaches theology at the University of San Diego. A native of Mexico, she received her doctorate in theology at the University of Salamanca. Currently she is president of the Association of Catholic Hispanic Theologians in the U.S. (ACHTUS). She is the author of *Our Cry for Life: Feminist Theology from Latin America.*

Edward L. Cleary is a Dominican priest whose first assignment in Latin America was in 1958. Since then he has taught Latin American studies at a number of schools and universities, including Columbia and Notre Dame. He currently teaches at Providence College in Rhode Island. His books include *Crisis and Change: The Church in Latin America Today,* and (as editor) *Path from Puebla: Significant Documents of the Latin American Bishops since 1979.*

Guillermo Cook is associated with the Latin America Mission, an independent Protestant non-denominational mission society. A citizen of Argentina, he has served as Director of the Centro Evangélico Latinoamericano de Estudios Pastorales, General Coordinator of the Third Latin American Congress on Evangelization, and Associate General Secretary of the Latin American Theological Fraternity. His books include *The Expectation of the Poor: Latin American Basic Ecclesial Communities in Protestant Perspective,* and the forthcoming *New Face of the Church in Latin America: Between Tradition and Change.*

Virgilio Elizondo is rector of San Fernando Cathedral in San Antonio, founder of the Mexican-American Cultural Center, and the author of numerous books, including Galilean Journey: The Mexican-American Promise, and (as editor) *Way of the Cross: The Passion of Christ in the Americas.* An editor of the international journal *Concilium,* he is also an active member of the Ecumenical Association of Third World Theologians.

Alfred T. Hennelly is a Jesuit priest and professor of theology at Fordham University. He has written a number of books on Latin American liberation theology, including *Theologies in Conflict* and *Theology for a Liberating Church.* Most recently he edited *Liberation Theology: A Documentary History.*

Stephen Judd is a Maryknoll missioner with fifteen years of pastoral experience in southern Peru among the Aymara and Quechua peoples. He served as executive director of the Instituto de Pastoral Andina in Sicuani near Cusco. He received a doctorate in the sociology of religion from the Graduate Theological Union in Berkeley with a dissertation entitled "The Emergent Andean Church: Inculturation and Liberation in Southern Peru, 1968–1986." Currently he serves on the General Council of the Catholic Foreign Mission Society of America (Maryknoll).

Jon Sobrino is a Spanish-born Jesuit priest and theologian who has worked since the 1960s in El Salvador. The author of such books as *Christology at the Crossroads*, *Jesus in Latin America*, *Spirituality and Liberation*, and *Archbishop Romero: Memories and Reflections*, he teaches at the Universidad Centroamericana José Siméon Cañas in San Salvador. His most recent books are *Jesus the Liberator* and, as editor (with Ignacio Ellacuría), *Mysterium Liberationis: Fundamental Concepts of Liberation Theology*.

Index